Harry Pearson lives in Northumberland in a lovingly restored Victorian post office, which he shares with his partner, the aniseed-ball heiress Catherine Barraclough, their daughter Maisie and two smoke-blue Persian cats, Chekhov and Dai. The household rejects the dubious benefits of the modern broadcast media, preferring to spend their evenings singing Schubert *lieder* while gathered round the spinet.

Pearson's first book, *The Far Corner*, was a runner-up for the 1995 William Hill Sports Book of the Year Award. His second, *Racing Pigs and Giant Marrows*, was shortlisted for the 1997 Thomas Cook/*Daily Telegraph* Travel Book of the Year. His work appears regularly in the *Guardian*, *When Saturday Comes* and a number of those glossy magazines which smell of after-shave and have women in bras on the cover.

'Not a book for those who forbear to laugh or cry out loud . . . The gags come thick and fast as Pearson uses his travels in the North-east of England during the 1993–94 football season to regale us with legend, anecdote, fact and history. As an acutely observant iconoclast, nothing, not even North-east leek-growing, is allowed to remain sacred . . . The book is driven by the ebullience of Pearson's own indefatigable sense of humour . . . A refreshing amalgam of scholarship and scurrility, it plugs into the mind-set of the true football fan'   Frances Edmonds, *Guardian*

'One of the finest in a vast library of sports books published this year'   *Sunday Times* Sports Books of the Year

'Pearson is as tall as he is funny and, believe me, he is very tall'   *The Face*

'One of the best books ever written about football. Whether it's league or non-league, Pearson's northern wit and gritty approach to the game make this a riotous read'   *Hyper*

THE FAR CORNER

A MAZY DRIBBLE THROUGH
NORTH-EAST FOOTBALL

Harry Pearson

ABACUS

First published in Great Britain in 1994
by Little, Brown and Company
Published in 1995 by Warner Books
This paperback edition published in 1997 by Abacus
Reprinted 2000, 2002, 2003, 2004, 2005, 2007, 2009, 2010 (three times),
2011 (twice)

A CIP catalogue record for this book
is available from the British Library.

ISBN 978-0-349-10837-7

Typeset by Hewer Text Composition Services, Edinburgh
Printed and bound in Great Britain by
Clays Ltd, St Ives plc

Papers used by Abacus are from well-managed forests
and other responsible sources.

MIX
Paper from
responsible sources
FSC® C104740

Abacus
An imprint of
Little, Brown Book Group
100 Victoria Embankment
London EC4Y 0DY

An Hachette UK Company
www.hachette.co.uk

www.littlebrown.co.uk

For my grandfather, Harry Fixter, who lifted me over the turnstile

Acknowledgements

Thanks are due to the following for anecdotes, opinions, lifts, jokes and midget gems: Catherine Barraclough, Bill Brewster, Peter Doddman, John Ferguson, Andy Lyons, Steve Leach, Steve Marshall, William Pym, Andy Smith, Pete Smith and Ken Twigg.

It would be a good deal more difficult to write anything about non-league football in the North-East were it not for *Northern Goalfields*, Brian Hunt's meticulously researched history of the Northern League, and *The Amateur Game*, W. Reid's earlier and more personal book on the same subject. My copies of both are dog-eared with use.

Contents

Preface

After I left school I worked as a barman in a Cleveland hotel. The place had pretensions to being more than a mere pub. There were nuts and olives in saucers on the bar top, veal *cordon bleu* on the menu and we had a cocktail list. One day a man came to the bar and ordered a pint and a pousse-café, adding 'for our lass' in case I thought he was a ballet dancer or something. Pousse-café is a generic term for a cocktail in which a variety of liqueurs of differing densities are floated one on top of the other. The type we served was made with crème de menthe, yellow chartreuse and cherry brandy. It was called a Traffic Light because the colours lined up red, amber and green. It takes patience and a steady hand to make such a cocktail and when you have done so successfully there is a feeling of quiet satisfaction. I carried the finished drink carefully to the bar and set it gently down in front of the man, a faint air of smugness flickering about my callow cheeks. The man eyed my handiwork suspiciously for a moment, then stuck his little finger in and swirled it round. So much for serving drinks from the *Savoy Cocktail Book* on Teesside.

My view of North-East football owes something to the pousse-café. It is equal parts cynicism, sentimentality and sarkiness. I'm not sure which floats to the top most readily, though the laws of physics dictate that it must be the one with the highest sugar content. In writing this book I have, like the man at the bar, endeavoured to stir the ingredients into a whole. If at times the mixture has separated rather too obviously into its component parts then I can only blame surface tension.

The Far Corner is an account of my travels around the region's football grounds during the 1993–94 season. My criterion for choosing which games to attend was a complex equation based on historic importance, cultural significance and how much money I had for bus fares. From the outset my plan was to be as random and haphazard as possible, and it must be said that, save for one minor lapse when I wrote the Whickham v. Bamber Bridge FA Vase tie down in my diary three weeks in advance, I stuck to this slap-happy strategy with bulldog tenacity. The idiotic opinions espoused in these pages are entirely my own (except, of course, when they are quotations from club chairmen and FA officials) and though there may be times when I wander well away from the facts about football in the North-East, I hope I have never strayed too far from its spirit.

Introduction

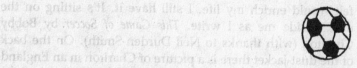

I support Middlesbrough. When people ask me why, I say: because I'm a glory-seeker.

That isn't the real reason. The real reason is that I was born a few miles outside the town, in a village called Great Ayton. Captain James Cook, the explorer, went to school in Great Ayton. When we were told that by our primary teacher we were very impressed. We went, 'Ah brilliant, Miss. Was the man with the pointy ears with him an' all?'

We didn't really. We had all known about Captain James Cook (1728–1779) since the day we were born. Before, practically. He was the greatest man in the history of Cleveland. He visited Hawaii, landed at Botany Bay and made the first map of New Zealand. It's quite poignant, when you think about it, that the most important figure in my home town's history should be famous for getting as far away from it as was humanly possible.

At primary school we spent a lot of time learning about famous people from the North-East. There were four of them: Captain James Cook (navigator), George Stephenson (railway engineer), Bobby Shafto (went to sea, silver buckles on his knee) and Bobby Charlton (footballer). Of these by far the best was Bobby Charlton, because he was still alive and had a bald head like Mr Barlow who taught 2A in the temporary classroom and because he scored goals for Manchester United and England (the world champions). In fact so impressed was I by Bobby Charlton that I asked my mum for a book about him. This was a new departure for me. You didn't ask for books. Like shoes and jumpers, books were given to you *whether you wanted them or not.* Usually instead of something useful like a Hot Wheels Track.

I saw the Bobby Charlton book advertised in an issue of *Charles Buchan's Football Monthly.* It was the first book I ever felt would enrich my life. I still have it. It's sitting on the desk beside me as I write. *This Game of Soccer* by Bobby Charlton (with thanks to Neil Durden-Smith). On the back of the dust-jacket there is a picture of Charlton in an England shirt, cheeks puffed out, shooting with his left foot. Above it, in pencil, in the wobbly disjointed writing of a small boy I have added the helpful caption 'Bo bby Ch arlt on'. In those days I was always writing captions on pictures in football books. Perhaps this was some early indication that I wanted to be an editor. Or a vandal. Which pretty much amounts to the same thing.

Only joking.

In the main, though, my freelance caption-writing was a desperate bid to boost the status of Middlesbrough FC. In those days the Boro languished in a numbing pool of mediocrity just below the top clubs in Division Two. They never featured in any of the football annuals I was given at Christmas. To rectify this situation I would find a likely black and white picture, one of, say, Peter Thompson of Liverpool giving the ball a 'Did you spill my pint?' stare as he dived forward to nod it goalwards, under the headline: 'The eyes have it! Peter Thompson of Liverpool has his sights fixed as he connects with a spectacular header.' Then I'd take a black felt-tip, colour in the white collar and cuffs of Thompson's Liverpool shirt so that it more closely, at least to my eyes, resembled Boro's solid red top, cross out the words 'Peter Thompson' and 'Liverpool' and write in above them with my felt-tip, 'Arthur Horsfield' and 'Middlesbrough'. It fooled practically nobody. Nevertheless, as a reward for my ceaseless efforts Boro won the Second Division championship five years later, though Jack Charlton rather churlishly took the credit.

On the second page of *This Game of Soccer* there is a picture of the house in Beatrice Terrace, Ashington where Jack Charlton and brother Bobby were born. I had no idea where Ashington was, but I was determined to see Bobby Charlton's house. I asked my mum, 'Where's Ashington?'

'Near Newcastle,' she said. Her lack of precision was a dreadful error. From that moment on whenever our Riley 1.5 crossed the Tees, heading north into County Durham and the general direction of Tyneside, I began scanning the area for anything that resembled the famous building. The Charltons' house was a Victorian mid-terraced brick miner's cottage. There were a lot of Victorian mid-terraced brick miners' cottages in the North-East, and over a period of about eighteen months I must have pointed at all of them.

'There it is!'

'What?'

'Bobby Charlton's house.'

'No it isn't.'

'It looks like it.'

'His house is in Ashington.'

'Isn't this Ashington?'

'No.'

'Where's this?'

'Stockton.'

And so it went on. I spotted lookalike dwellings in Bearpark and Fatfield and Billy Row and Pity Me. Off the A1, the A19, the A68 and from the train to Seaton Carew.

'There it is!'

'Oh, for Christ's sake . . .'

Only the recently begun urban renewal programme prevented my mum and dad from going mental. Had it not been for the respite provided by the concrete and design concepts of new towns such as Peterlee and Washington, my ceaseless cries of excitement would have driven them mad. Sixties town planning saved my parents' sanity. Sadly, it had the reverse effect on everybody else's.

Then, after a particularly lengthy and fruitless spell of Bobby-Charlton's-house-spotting, I was packed off to my grand-parents while my mum and dad recuperated. Undeterred by my failure, and sticking to my task with all the doggedness of

Barry Davies pursuing a metaphor, I asked my grandfather, 'Where's Ashington?'

'Northumberland,' he said, and, pulling a pre-war road atlas of Great Britain off the shelf, he sat down in his chair by the fire. I went and perched on the arm, looking over his shoulder, my eyes watering from the astringent mist of Brylcreem, lanolin and Yardley's that seemed to hover permanently around him; the miasma of manhood.

We often did this. My grandfather didn't own many books, but those he did have were large, well used and full of pictures. He'd turn the pages, point things out and tell stories. Sometimes these tales were relevant to the substance of the picture, often they had only the loosest connection to it. A painting of *HMS Discovery* in a book about Captain Cook might warrant a detailed summary of rigging techniques, or a brief dissertation on the strength of the tea served up on Tees tugboats (you could float a spanner on it); a drawing by Frederick Remington of outlaws crossing the Rio Grande could prompt the tale of Wild Bill Hickock (shot in the back while gambling), or cousin Gilbert (swam in the Tees with his bowler hat on). My grandfather's anecdotes were tinged with small town egalitarianism, an equality of emphasis. He made no more or less of a drama out of the Battle of Quebec than he did of a right hook that decked an Eston plater in a pub on Redcar seafront.

My grandfather took a pencil from a cup on the mantelpiece which propped up his pools coupon. He opened the road atlas deliberately, flicked through it, pausing for some reason over a street map of Bristol. Eventually he found the North-East. Pressing the book open and using the pencil as a pointer he showed me Ashington. He did not stop there. Soon the pencil was tapping other towns and villages. Every one of them had some footballing significance, a history, a tale attached: Crook (once beat Barcelona), Gateshead (Hughie Gallacher committed suicide there), West Auckland (won the first World Cup), Esh Winning (birthplace of Raich Carter), Cockfield (the wonder village), Durham (sold George Camsell to the Boro), Bishop Auckland (the best amateur team in history),

Hazlerigg Colliery (where Len Shackleton worked), South Bank (little Wilfie Mannion).

My grandfather's hand circled the map, stirring up soccer wherever it went.

Catherine and I had been talking about moving out of London. We'd been talking about it for years, but we were gripped by metropolitan inertia. Though the city was hell the world outside its walls seemed even more intimidating: a wild and lonely place, where darkness fell early and everybody bathed once a week, on Sunday evening when *Songs of Praise* was on the telly. Then, finally, something happened that pushed us into action. The people next door began waking us up at 3 a.m. with a combination of loud music and orgiastic sex. This was by no means as pleasant as it sounds. Our neighbours were in their mid-forties and smoked so much their front door frame had nicotine stains. Their coughing could have tarmacked a five-a-side pitch. During the coal strike miners picketed our next-door neighbours' mouths. They were hard-bitten Cockneys and about as appealing as a pair of scabby iguanas with halitosis. The music was Spandau Ballet. Whenever I see Gary Kemp I still come over all queasy. You probably know the feeling.

We decided to move to Northumberland. This may seem a bit drastic, but you had never heard our neighbours in the throes of passion. We had, and we weren't taking any chances. Even now, in the quiet hours before dawn, when the wind blows from the south . . .

We went up and stayed with my parents and drove all over the North-East looking for a house to rent. Catherine is from Herefordshire, so as we meandered across the region I pointed out local sites of historical interest: Tow Law (Chris Waddle played there), Langley Park (home village of Bobby Robson), Blyth (made it to the fifth round of the FA Cup), Billingham (where Gary Pallister got started) . . . Often after five or six hours of this Catherine was so overcome with emotion she would burst into tears, or scream joyously and beat me about the head with a rolled-up copy of *Loot*. North-East football affects people that way – ask anybody.

The strip of land we criss-crossed that spring was the same one whose place names had provoked my grandfather's stories. It stretched from Ashington in the north to the southernmost edge of Teesside, from the sea towards the foothills of the Pennines. It was less than fifty miles long and twenty miles across at the widest point. In area it was not much larger than that part of the South-East encompassed by the M25, but it was populated by a fifth of the people. The assumption in the rest of Britain is that all the region's citizens are Geordies. This is not the case. Once, coming away from Filbert Street after watching Boro play Leicester, one of our group was set upon by a local moron who yelled 'Geordie maggot' at him before head-butting him in the face. Later, sitting in a BR snack bar with a can of cold Fanta pressed to the bruising round his eye, he said, 'I don't mind the beating so much, but I fucking object to being called a Geordie.' People from Teesside, you see, are rather unimaginatively known as Teessiders; people from Tyneside are Geordies (after a type of safety lamp used by miners), while those from County Durham are Mackems. The Mackem epithet comes from the difference in pronunciation of the words 'make' and 'take'. Geordies say myek and tyek; Mackems mak and tak. Teessiders, for those of you who are still awake, mairk and tairk. Calling a Teessider or a Mackem a Geordie is in regional terms a *faux pas* of the order of going into a pub in the East End of Glasgow and proclaiming Jock Stein to be the greatest football manager England ever produced. In his excellent book *The Soccer Syndrome*, John Moynihan refers to the Spurs centre-forward Bobby Smith as 'a Geordie blacksmith'. I find this profoundly irritating because Big Bobby was from Lingdale, an ironstone mining village in East Cleveland. Calling him a Geordie was about as accurate as calling someone from Cambridge a Cockney. And that really got up my nose. You see, when you come from an area, as I do, whose only major contribution to civilisation is the invention of the friction match (John Walker,

Stockton-on-Tees, 1827), you tend to try to hang on to all the shreds of self-esteem that are available to you. Obviously, I can see that all this is pathetic, provincial and small-minded when looked at objectively. But then again, Bobby Smith is not a bloody Geordie whichever way you look at it.

There is a view, often voiced in fiction, that when you return to a place after many years away you notice how much it has changed. Moving from London back to the North-East, however, I only noticed how much it was the same. True, real heavy industry had been superseded by Industrial Heritage Centres in which you could go down a lead mine, ride on a tram, operate a threshing machine, catch consumption and die a premature death; redevelopers had sprinkled shopping centres and multiplexes and superstores and leisure centres all over, as if they were hundreds and thousands and the area was a particularly unsaleable birthday cake; and gourmet snacks and silicon chips now had greater importance than pits and ships. But there were still twenty-four flavours (all of them ersatz and buzzing with E numbers) of soft drinks racked in the grocer's; every village still had at least one shop selling nothing but sweets and cigarettes, as if to deliver a V-sign to the Health Minister; you could still walk for miles on Saturday mornings without the smell of frying batter ever leaving your nostrils; and in streets, and playing fields and unidentified patches of grass there were still little kids running with footballs at their feet while all their mates yelled, 'Away man and pass it, you greedy get.'

These things hadn't altered. Nor had the effect the area had on me. Because I had only to sit down at my word processor and type in the words 'North-East' and 'Football' and something strange happened. Like anger to the Incredible Hulk, this magical formula brought about a strange and dramatic transformation. A normal, reasonably rational human being, I found myself changing into a strange and primitive beast, his head a-swirl with a mantra of half-remembered facts and phrases, his mind numb, his cognitive powers addled, his scepticism permanently locked in reverse gear. My fingers, as if possessed by some mad demon, would fly across the keyboard, and I would gaze with mounting horror at the awful words that began to flick up before me: 'Lenny White. Little Len the Lion. White by name, Black and White by nature! A liquorice humbug of a lad. A real live-wire. As slippery as dripping and as hard to keep down as a bellyful of tripe on the North Shields ferry during the storm that preceded the Magpies' 1952 Cup run. And Charlie Buchan, baggy-shorted, bandy-legged, big-hearted. The wee shimmying sorcerer of Sunderland. His feet like magic wands. Abracadabra alacazam! Another opposition defence was sawn in half. And George Hardwick. A tackle as stiff as his moustache, skills as sleek as his hair. Boro's thinking full-back. As cool as a cucumber and as brilliant as a beetroot. Red through and through! Aye, great names, great names. For in them days a poor footballer was as welcome in the North-East as was a workshy shirker in the shipyards during the boom years, when the chimneys of the terraced houses that ran down to the river belched out smoke from the coal-fired ranges on which ruby-cheeked mams were baking the home-made stotties that me and a thousand other scabby-kneed bairns from all across the region would stick beneath our flat caps to keep our heads warm during the endless games of "netty-door" football we played in the cobbled alleys that ran between the rows of back-to-backs in the place we knew simply as home. In short, no place at all!'

Eventually, sweat-soaked and reeling, I would collapse in a stupor and dream strange dreams of a far-off mythical place where the people were called 'folk', the beer was called 'ale', the men were called 'lads', and the lads were called 'Jackie'.

And, weirdest of all, when I came round and read what I'd written, from the title 'Football Fervour!' to the shaky signature at the bottom, 'George Clarts (Our Football Correspondent)', I found that against all expectation these clichés, worn to a shine by perpetual use, reflected a kind of truth. Gustave Flaubert, or some other Gallic fancy-dan in a silk cravat and blanco-ed spats, said that a full heart sometimes overflows in the emptiest phrases. He was writing of physical passion (well, you know the French), but the same holds true of other passions too.

When I moved back to the North-East the one thing that really surprised me was the people's love of football. A decade away had led me to believe that it was all a myth. From my vantage point in the South I had regarded it all with detached amusement, snickering up my sleeve when I heard the phrase 'a hot bed of soccer', and chortling like a chipmunk when some chucklehead advanced the view that the 'Geordie' fans were second to none. But after a week back I realised I was wrong.

I found a copy of *Newcastle United – A Complete Record* in the Royal Family section of the local W. H. Smith's.

I went to get a haircut and the barber said: 'I don't get to football as much these days. I go to most of Newcastle's home matches, some of the reserve games, a few of the youth team's and if Carlisle are playing midweek I pop along there. Mind you, I used to be a right fanatic.'

A cab driver during the course of a fifteen-minute journey started twenty-two stories about great players he had seen and never got beyond the third sentence of any of them before a new one intercepted and ran off with it. Eventually he stopped his flow and said, 'Whereabouts is it along here, lad?' And I said: 'About three-quarters of a mile back, halfway between Albert Stubbins and Billy Hindmarsh.'

A retired farmer I met on the riverbank said: 'It was just after the war, versus Sunderland, there was over sixty thousand in and I made the mistake of getting up against one of them barriers. And every time Newcastle attacked the crowd come forward and down I went, bent double over this barrier. I never saw the ball but twice, and then only when it were fifty foot in the air. And when we got off the bus in Consett I had to walk three miles back home in the pitch black and a foot of snow.' He grinned, shaking his head, 'And I said to myself "Way, y'bugger."'

A middle-aged woman with white hair and severe glasses was out walking a dachshund named Duke. She asked me who'd won the Cup final replay and when I told her Arsenal, she scowled and looked up at the sky. 'No wonder it's bloody raining,' she said.

However, it was not the things I heard that convinced me I'd been wrong about the importance of football in the North-East, but something I didn't hear. Not once since the day I moved back until this moment two years later, not one single time, has anyone from the region responded to the news that I have been, or am just about to go to a game, by saying: 'Oh, but the supporters are so terribly violent.' Because in this area all people are fans, and some people *are* terribly violent. And that fact doesn't come as a revelation to anyone, so nobody bothers to comment on it. Which, after a decade of self-justification and aggrieved defensiveness, came to me as a blessed relief. By the time we left London, wearied by hundreds of hours of argument on the topic, I had reached the stage when my response to any comment about the intolerable behaviour of football supporters was to go red in the face, point at the interlocutor, and yell, 'Shut your fucking mouth or I'll kill you, you gutless bastard,' which, while it did bring discussions to an abrupt end, was hardly a winning intellectual gambit.

How football came to be so important in the North-East is open to question. It would be easy to suggest that its popularity owed much to the Industrial Revolution, and the subsequent spread of heavy industry throughout the region, creating the atmosphere of sooty poverty in which lungs collapse and football thrives. It seems to me, though, that the game was in the region long before the steam hammers and the smelters arrived; that it was a natural resource of the area, like coal, iron and fluorspar. The Victorians simply came along and extracted it.

If anyone brought football to the North-East it was the Roman legions. In its heyday the area around Hadrian's Wall was the most militarised part of the Empire. That the legionaries played a particularly nasty form of soccer is well known. As a result the citizens of South Shields, Corbridge and the other garrison towns along the wall were treated to live Italian football some 2,000 years before Channel 4 brought it to the rest of the country. Roman soccer was much like the *Calcio Storico* played out annually in Florence to this day (an event preceded by the arrival of a large metallic object which sends out showers of sparks and aerial explosives in a manner that suggests it is the prototype of a Fiat 127 Catherine and I once owned). The highlight of the *Calcio Storico* is the presentation of the trophy to the winning team. This is not a cup or some other such silvered gewgaw, but an ox. The sight of the players doing their lap of honour while attempting to balance it on their heads is most amusing.

After the departure of the Romans the North-East suffered a series of traumatic invasions from land and sea. Each of the invaders made their own contribution to the footballing culture of the region. The Vikings brought a version of the popular long-ball game, or longship-ball game as they knew it. They also came up with the names for Wednesday, Thursday and Friday. Unfortunately they couldn't think of one for Saturday, so all games were played midweek. The Saxons introduced Teutonic discipline to local defences; the Angles taught goalkeepers the value of geometry, and the Pictish players got drunk and had a bundle in a nightclub.

A new period of stability followed the Norman Conquest. Interestingly enough, the Normans are the only Dark Age invaders to become a Christian name popular with the region's most uncompromising defenders. Which is probably just as well. Jute 'Bites Yer Legs' Hunter doesn't seem quite so intimidating somehow.

Medieval times saw the annual Shrove Tuesday football matches, such as those still played in Alnwick and Sedgefield, become an integral part of the area's festivities. These games were characterised by their brutality. In the midst of the rough-housing the significance of the ball seemed to escape most of the players, a tradition which continues in Hartlepool to this day.

The first golden era of North-East football came in the late sixteenth century. At this time the border region between England and Scotland was a demilitarised buffer zone populated by families of marauding hoodlums, or reivers, so violent they make the Kray Twins seem like the Righteous Brothers (if you're from the East End you can reverse this analogy). Among these reiver families were the Armstrongs, Grahams, Bells and Fenwicks. Most notorious of all, though, were the clans of the North Tyne: the Robsons, Milburns and Charltons. The reivers' everyday life was one of cattle theft, arson and murder, so naturally when a Holy Day came around they needed to unwind. They did this by playing football, or ba', as it was known, against one another. The games lasted from dawn to dusk and were characterised by punching, kicking and gouging. Indeed, the only way a reiver's football match differed from an ordinary afternoon at the office was that no weapons were allowed.

The first international football match is commonly supposed to be that played between England and Scotland in Glasgow in 1872, but in actual fact the Scottish and English border reivers were arranging international fixtures way back in the 1580s. Of course, the teams of that time were totally unrepresentative and selected according to regional and personal prejudice. So no change there. One of the most famous of such games was played out at the Redeswire in north Northumberland. It was notable for being the first Anglo-Scots clash to be interrupted by a pitch invasion. The hooligan element on this occasion was, according to a contemporary ballad, 'five hundred Fenwicks in a flock'. Unlike their latterday counterparts, this mindless minority did not content themselves with smashing the goals, stealing the turf and pissing on the penalty spot, but instead began loosing off arrows at the two teams. Thankfully for the players, the Elizabethan Fenwicks' bowmanship proved about as effective as their twentieth-century descendant Terry's tackling, so everyone escaped unharmed.

This, then, was the seam of raw footballing ore the Victorians discovered. It was not long before they had begun to refine it into something more recognisable to the contemporary eye. At vast offal-eating extravaganzas in hostelries such as the Three Tuns in Durham and the County Hotel, Darlington, mutton-chop whiskered philanthropists, their mouths full of tripe and committeeman jargon, addressed points of order through the chair and generally articulated the strictures that were to define North-East football in the modern era.

The first of the region's teams entered the FA Challenge Cup in 1884, when Middlesbrough were overwhelmed by Old Etonians. Sunderland became the first North-East team to win a national competition when they took the League title in 1892. They repeated the feat the following year and again in 1895, when Middlesbrough made it a regional double by opening the Northern League's account in the Amateur Cup, getting the better of Old Carthusians in the final. When the Great War began the North-East had three teams, Middlesbrough, Newcastle United and Sunderland, in the First Division of the Football League and one, South Shields, who were about to enter the Second Division. The region's teams had won eight League titles, appeared in six FA Cup finals, winning one, taken the Amateur Cup eleven times and been beaten finalists on another nine occasions. For an area with a population a third of that of London it was a pretty good record.

As I sat on the arm of my grandfather's chair that day in 1967, the North-East still held on to its reputation as one of the great centres of soccer, but the grip of its professional clubs on such a claim was at best tenuous. It had been thirty years since any of them won the League, twelve since the last FA Cup triumph. Newcastle and Sunderland struggled to stay in the First Division and Middlesbrough had just been relegated to the Third for the first time in their history. Darlington's promotion from the Fourth was the only bright spot, although the fact that Hartlepools United (still a plural in those days) had not had to apply for re-election was another minor triumph. Even the Northern League, the second-oldest football league in the world, and the source of the amateur game's strength in the area, was entering a period of slow decline. Only two things had remained constant: the region's passion for the game and its ability to produce top-class players. That season there were sixty-two footballers from the North-East playing in the First Division. Of these many played for Newcastle or Sunderland, but those who didn't included Howard Kendall, Jimmy Husband, Tommy Baldwin, Norman Hunter, George Armstrong, Ralph Coates, David Thomas, Mick McNeil, Colin Bell and, of course, Bobby Charlton.

Twenty-five years later, as I stood on the brow of a grassed-over slagheap and watched, far below, Sunderland Under-19s hoofing the ball into Feyenoord Under-19s' penalty area, nothing much had changed. The love of the game was still here, the quality players were still here (or rather they were in Marseilles, Rome, Liverpool, Glasgow, Southampton and practically anywhere else you'd care to name, and some places you wouldn't), and the local sides were still struggling: Newcastle were massively in debt, Middlesbrough had embarked on a course of relegations and promotions so rapid rumour had it that the lion on the club badge was about to be replaced by a yoyo, Sunderland were rudderless, Darlington had just emerged from a spell in the GM Vauxhall Conference and the now singular Hartlepool were – well, just Hartlepool really. The last triumph any of the region's clubs had tasted in a national competition had been Whickham's victory in the 1981 FA Vase.

The local papers, embittered by this downturn, had sought physic in nostalgia and filled their columns with a kind of backs-to-the-wall historical boosterism that was eerily reminiscent of the outpourings on leaflets handed out by the tourist offices of tinpot dictatorships: 'Per capita sugarbeet harvest in the pre-war years was the greatest on earth', 'In Championship terms Sunderland are the most successful team outside the top flight', 'This recently discovered wonder proves conclusively that the Republic has the oldest plumbing tradition in the Americas', 'The magic of the Cup has always brought out the best in the Magpies . . .'

In the pubs and clubs of the region the fans too had taken up an entrenched position – a kind of fizzy-lager mentality. Everywhere you went you were bearded by angry men eager to compare attendance figures: 'Did you see that?' they spluttered. 'They're top of the First and they only got twenty-two thousand one hundred and thirty-four! We're sixth from bottom of the Second and we got four thousand more!' They'd pause for a moment, their cheeks flushing, 'See what I mean? See what I'm saying?' And I did. What they were saying was that more people in the North-East were prepared to pay to watch failure than would pay to watch success elsewhere. It was a boast peculiar to football, a strange mix of warped logic and ferocious constancy, like bragging that you had continued eating at the same café every day for twenty-five years even though the food was shite. Because to football fans loyalty is *the* most important thing. The fact that there were so many devotees in the region was a source of pride. It was manly stuff, the braggadocio of faithfulness. Football is the only subject that can induce a bloke to swank about his fidelity.

North-East football had the past, it had the crowds; unfortunately, when it came to the present, it was strictly Christmas Day in the workhouse.

When we lived in London I used to go to a barber near Waterloo Station. He was a good barber, but you had to be careful to avoid the subject of religion. One mention of the Almighty or His mysterious movements and you'd be stuck fast in that chair for what seemed like an eternity while the barber flicked his scissors round the exposed flesh of your ears saying '1995. Yes, that's when it's going to happen. It's forescribed in the ancient scrolls, you see. Armageddon. June the Fifteenth 1995.'

'Better remember to cancel the milk, then,' I'd say breezily, and the barber would give me a maniacal look and begin stropping his razor.

The man who ran the corner shop was a bit like the evangelical barber. Except that in his case the topic to avoid was Len Shackleton. With the barber I'd nip in for a quick trim and come out two hours later with a white-walled US Marine crew-cut and an annotated pamphlet on the Book of Deuteronomy. With the shopkeeper I'd pop across for a box of matches to get the fire lit before breakfast and come back at teatime with a tin of marrowfat peas and the words 'Clown Prince of Soccer' embossed on my subconscious as if with a Dymo printer.

Now, you're probably thinking that avoiding the subject of Len Shackleton during a simple transaction would be easy enough. In normal circumstances you'd be right. But the shopkeeper was not normal. He was obsessed. The shopkeeper was a large bow-fronted individual, with a Northumbrian tan – a kind of wind-blown glow which renders the cheeks so ruddy it looks as if their owner washes his face with a Brillo pad rather than a flannel – and a hooter the colour of Red Windsor cheese. For him Len Shackleton was like the core of some strange and powerful neurosis. Everything, every action and thought, came back to Shack. I'd ask for a Bounty and as he searched for it his eyes would glaze over and his mind would start to free associate: Bounty – Marathon; Marathon – Battle of; Battle – Fields; Fields – Gracie; Gracie Fields – Capri; Capri – Ford; Ford – Trevor; Trevor Ford – Ivor Broadis – Len Shackleton.

I'd know when he arrived back at this central point because he'd stop looking for the Bounty, mutter, 'What a forward line!' then stare at me as if I were some distant object he'd just brought into focus and say, 'Did I ever tell you about the time Shack was training with the international squad at the Bank of England Sports Ground?'

And I'd say, 'Yes, but I haven't listened the last ninety-nine times, so you'd better refresh my memory.'

'Well, Walter Winterbottom was manager then. And a right bull's knacker he was, too. He was outlining some complicated bloody manoeuvre on the blackboard – I think he'd been a schoolteacher – and he said, in conclusion, "Mannion passes it out to Finney on the left, Finney crosses to the centre and Shackleton scores. Any questions?"

'Shack's hand goes up.

'"Yes, Shackleton?"

'"What corner do you want me to put it in?"'

At the punchline the shopkeeper would go on a jinky little run round the bacon-slicer, chuckling drily to himself. When he'd recovered he'd say, 'You're after a pack of pan scrubs, am I right?'

And I'd just take them and run for it.

This isn't to say that Shackleton (or indeed God) wasn't a worthy subject for adoration. He was an entertainer (I'm talking about Shack here, though, heaven knows, Jehovah's had his moments too), arguably the best ball-player in British football history, and a free spirit in an era when the maximum wage and draconian contracts bound players to a club like feudal peasants to a fiefdom.

The Bradford-born Shackleton signed for Newcastle in 1946 and scored six goals on his debut against Newport. Eighteen months later, after one of the boardroom disputes which in those days used to spring up at St James's as quickly as toadstools on a dungheap, he was transferred to Sunderland for the then record fee of £20,050. He played nearly 350 games for the Wearsiders and scored a century of goals before an ankle injury ended his career at the age of thirty-seven.

In every posed picture of Shackleton you see, he's wearing the same lopsided, gap-toothed, knowing grin. It's as if he's spotted that the photographer's flies are undone and is working out how to use the information to cause maximum embarrassment. Creating embarrassment was one of Shackleton's fortes. It's said that when the Welsh international centre-forward Trevor Ford was signed by Sunderland, Shack was peeved by the attention the new man received and exacted revenge by passing the ball to him with so much spin on it that it was impossible to control. As the burly battering-ram scuffed yet another chance wide of the goal, Shackleton would turn to the crowd with a quizzical shrug, as if to say, 'You can't seriously prefer that idiot to me, can you?'

'Ah, the stories I could tell you,' the shopkeeper would say. Then he'd proceed to do so. After a while I discovered that there was one way you could stop him. The shopkeeper was a Sunderland fan. He'd been born in West Wylam, thirty yards or so south of the Tyne. 'I'm from County Durham,' he'd say, 'and all Durham lads are Sunderland supporters.' This wasn't strictly true. Bobby Robson was born in Sacriston and he supported Newcastle; Bryan Robson, from Witton Gilbert, did likewise. The division between the two constituencies had less to do with a river boundary than it did with familial ties, or the destinations of your town or village bus route.

One day, during the tale of Shackleton and the autobiography (he had a chapter headed 'What the Average Director Knows About Football' and the next three pages were blank) the shopkeeper said, 'The thing with Shack was that he was a perfectionist. He had skill, but he worked on it too. He honed it.'

'Like Kevin Keegan,' I said.

His mouth dropped shut. He was a Sunderland man. Kevin Keegan was to him what the Pope is to Ian Paisley. The spell Keegan had spent at St James's was an evil memory. In those two seasons as club captain he'd led Newcastle back into the First Division, then been whisked away by helicopter after his final match in a scene eerily reminiscent of the opening minutes of *La Dolce Vita*. To the shopkeeper it was like the Counter-Reformation. Taking advantage of his momentary state of paralysis I plonked down the money for the Vick's Vapour Rub and escaped. I walked home, savouring my new-found knowledge and wondering how best to go about persuading Catherine that my purchase represented a tasty alternative to Marmite.

We had been living in Northumberland for about a year. One day, I was walking past the shop and the shopkeeper came running out brandishing a copy of the *Evening Chronicle* in much the way people do in films when the President has been assassinated, or war declared. Only he was smiling. Kevin Keegan was coming back as Newcastle manager. 'Six million in debt and on the verge of relegation and the saviour's returned,' he said. 'They'll sink like a stone and take that clown with them.'

In the town, which was staunchly Magpie, the reaction to the news of Keegan's return was, if anything, even more over the top. Shopkeepers who knew I was a Middlesbrough fan came racing out of doorways, lunatic grins on their faces, and jabbered at me in an ecstatic yet curiously vengeful manner, as if they suspected that all along I'd been laughing at them behind their backs (and how right they were!). The atmosphere was much as it must have been on Mafeking night. It would be an exaggeration to say there was dancing in the streets, but the bearded busker who played MOR tunes in the market place had certainly upped the tempo on his midi-organ and was now crooning out a jaunty version of 'For the Good Times'. Or, as his smoochy social club vocal styling rendered it, 'Bawdy Boob Dimes'.

The response to the news in the local press was less measured, though marginally more tuneful. The following morning's papers showered Kevin Keegan with the kind of accolades that would have made God blush: 'Saint Kevin to the Rescue – Pages 10–11', 'The Second Coming', 'Messiah in the Dugout'.

The shopkeeper was delighted with it all. 'Look at this, just look at it,' he said, jabbing his finger into a cartoon that portrayed Kevin Keegan in a suit of armour preparing to do battle with a dragon labelled 'Third Division'. 'What a laugh. Third from bottom and sixteen games to go. They're knackered.'

'You don't think he'll make a difference, then?' I asked perceptively.

'Not a chance. *Not a chance*. It'll be like McMenemy all over again. Only this time it'll be us that's laughing.' He paused for a moment, sucking on a tooth: laughter – clown; clown – prince. 'When Shack came out of his final medical after that injury at Arsenal, you know what he did?'

'Yes,' I said, without much hope.

'He said, "That's it, lads. It's over. The doc says I'll never play again." And he took out a coin, tossed it in the air, caught it on the instep of his foot, then flipped it up into the breast pocket of his jacket. There'll never be another like Shack. Never.' He shook his head, lips pursed. 'Now,' he said, a moment later, 'Is it Hamlets you have, or Slim Panatellas?' I suppose I can always give them to someone for Christmas.

The shopkeeper's comparison between the return of Kevin Keegan to Newcastle in February 1992 and Lawrie McMenemy's appointment as manager of Sunderland in the summer of 1985 was a fair one. When he took the job at Roker Park, McMenemy was arguably the most famous football manager in the country. An avuncular TV pundit, his easy manner had earned him a following from far beyond the confined world of soccer. He appeared in television adverts, was the subject of an episode of *This Is Your Life*, and shared the British Hairdressing Federation's Best Groomed Hair Award with actress, Felicity Kendal. Supermarket magazines ran lifestyle features on him, old ladies from Fife invited him round for tea. Kevin Keegan was famously described by Duncan McKenzie as the Julie Andrews of football. Lawrie McMenemy was just a couple of cakes short of being the game's Jane Asher.

Born in Saltwell Park, McMenemy had played as an amateur for Gateshead in the old Third Division North before becoming a clerk in the education office of the local council. After a spell as manager of Bishop Auckland, which saw them win the Northern League and Cup double, he was appointed as coach at Sheffield Wednesday. His boss at Hillsborough was Alan Brown, the man who had presided over the first relegation in Sunderland's history. Maybe it was an omen. Spells at Doncaster and Grimsby followed, then in 1973 McMenemy moved on to Southampton. During his twelve years at the Dell, Saints won the FA Cup and consistently finished in the top six of the First Division. In 1980 McMenemy pulled off one of the transfer coups of the decade when he brought a former European Player of the Year to the south coast club in a £420,000 deal. That player was Kevin Keegan.

McMenemy turned down many lucrative offers to leave Southampton, even rejecting the Manchester United job in 1981, but he had always wanted to return to the North-East. The deal that took him to Sunderland not only satisfied this desire, it also made him one of the richest and most powerful managers in British football. His salary was reputedly worth £500,000 over three years ('Lawrie is a handsome man who

does a handsome job and he deserves a handsome salary,'
Sunderland chairman Tom Cowie told reporters), and he was
also given a seat on the board which, according to McMenemy
himself, made him 'almost unsackable'.

'At Roker Park,' McMenemy said of the task at hand, 'the
potential is virtually unlimited. The fanatical support and the
facilities are there. All the manager has to do is guide the team
on the right lines.'

Two years later he was gone, and Sunderland were in the
Third Division. McMenemy, so the joke went, was like the
Titanic. He should never have left Southampton.

On the day he had arrived at Roker Park, the former
guardsman had been mobbed by thousands of fans and
saluted by the local papers. By the time he left there was
a bitterness towards him that bordered on psychosis. At
Seaham, shortly after England had been knocked out of
the World Cup, I heard an old man of seventy or so say
of Graham Taylor's failure: 'Well, he had that McMenemy as
his assistant. After what he did at Roker they should never
have allowed him near a football pitch again. The FA should
have put a sniper at every ground in the country and ordered
them to shoot to kill if the bugger came too close.'

In accepting the Newcastle job, this was kind of vicious turn-
around Kevin Keegan was risking. 'The people of Newcastle
will always be my friends,' he had said after his final game
at St James's in 1984. 'I hope I'll always be theirs.' Now he
was about to find out. Tightrope walking across a cheese-wire
without his trousers on might have been a safer option.

The price of failure would have been a high one, but Keegan
didn't fail. In an acrimonious final game of the season at
Leicester, Newcastle avoided the drop. On the same day
Middlesbrough secured promotion to the Premier League,
their fans noting bitterly which of the two events drew the
bigger headline.

A few days later when I went to pick up the paper, I noticed
a story on the front page. 'Somebody's named their baby after
Keegan,' I said.

'What, Little Get?' the shopkeeper replied sourly.

He was doubly pissed off. Not only had the Magpies shattered his dream, Sunderland had lost to Liverpool in the FA Cup final. That they had got there at all was largely down to one man, John Byrne. A Mancunian whose louche skills at their best conjured up images of Stan Bowles, Byrne was one of that well-travelled breed of strikers who invariably appeared in sixties football annuals under the title, 'Have Boots, Will Travel', wearing a Stetson and clutching a six-gun. He had arrived at Roker Park from York via Le Havre and Brighton, a circuitous route which suggests a successful career as a mini-cab driver might await him when he retires. Byrne had netted in every round of the Cup. In the final, with the scores still level, a deflection fell to him about eight yards out. He couldn't have miskicked more completely if his shoes had been soldered together and the ball filled with helium.

The Merseysiders went on to win in a manner which brought back unpleasant memories of the last time a team from the North-East had appeared in the final – 1974, when Newcastle, Supermac and all, had taken on Shankly's Liverpool team and been comprehensively demolished. The third goal, scored by Kevin Keegan, was greeted by David Coleman's infamous gurgling cry: 'And Newcastle were undressed.' Sunderland had been similarly stripped.

Things got worse for the shopkeeper the following season. Newcastle took the Second Division Championship at a canter. Special K, as the local press insisted on calling him, seemed unstoppable, despite being named after a breakfast cereal.

Meanwhile, at Roker Park, Sunderland were struggling against relegation. Malcolm Crosby, a pleasant, undemonstrative man with a nose so large he seemed in permanent danger of swallowing it, attempted to inspire the team by insisting that the media referred to him as All Bran. The ploy failed and Crosby was sacked. His replacement, Terry 'Pop Tart' Butcher, was already playing for the club. As an England player Butcher had always been committed, though, sadly, never to a secure institution. He brought a similar red-blooded approach to his job as player-manager, performing a bizarre jump-clap-jump routine in front of the Fulwell End which was frankly embarrassing for a man in his thirties. And if it made me squirm, imagine how his wife must have felt.

'Have you heard the news?' the shopkeeper said. 'Keegan's been killed in a freak accident. He was walking across the Tyne and the Shields ferry hit him.' He guffawed loudly at his joke. It was laughter from the edge of the abyss.

Sunderland avoided relegation on the last day of the season. Unfortunately, Middlesbrough didn't. It was the Teessiders' third relegation in eight years, the second time they had failed to stay up in the top division for more than one term and the ninth time in a row their fate had been determined in the final game of the season. You could tell which Boro fans bit their nails – the sleeves of their jumpers were empty. Hartlepool, meanwhile, had stayed up in the Second Division, something that was without parallel in the club's history, and Darlington had struggled in the Third, something which wasn't.

Non-league football in the North-East was by this stage heavily embroiled in a squabble of such bewildering complexity that whenever I started reading about it I was reminded of Lord Palmerston's remark on the Schleswig-Holstein question: 'Only three men ever understood it fully, and one of them has since gone mad.'

Basically, the trouble had begun in the early eighties when the crusty old buffers at FA headquarters in Lancaster Gate, acting with a swiftness that would have left even Tony Adams trailing in their wake, decided to establish a formal framework for non-league football. They decided to call this new structure the pyramid, partly as that was its nominal shape, but mainly because it was the most modern building of which any of them had heard. The apex of the pyramid was the Conference, the champions of which were to be promoted directly into the Football League, and below that it broadened out in a series of increasingly regionalised feeder leagues. The idea was to provide the opportunity for straightforward promotion through the system, so that any club could fulfil its dreams by moving up level by level from park football to the glittering portals of the First Division. And Arsenal could fulfil my dreams by doing the same thing in reverse.

Naturally enough, the Northern League was invited to become part of the new system. The offer was rejected. The decision owed much to realism about economic and geographical circumstances, but the Northern League management committee, who at times seemed to combine the press relations aptitude of Paul Gascoigne with the communication skills of a Trappist monk, presented their arguments in such a ham-fisted manner that they were dismissed by the FA as arrogant, insular and out of touch, a state of mind with which the men from Lancaster Gate were all too familiar.

The national press took a similar attitude. When I mentioned the Northern League to a London-based journalist, he said, 'It's all right, apart from the people who run it.' When asked to elucidate he explained: 'A well-balanced bunch of men. Chips on both shoulders.'

The stereotype of the Northerner with an inferiority complex is so pervasive in English society that a whole book could be written refuting it without budging it an inch from the national psyche. When it comes to the Northern League and its perceived defensiveness, however, certain facts are worth bearing in mind. To list the number of times the league and its servants, both players and administrators, had been shabbily treated by the Football Association is to risk sounding like a cross between the Four Yorkshiremen and Dave Spart, so I'll make do with just one. And a half. The 1939 Amateur Cup final was contested by two Northern League sides, Bishop Auckland and Willington. Not one of the twenty-two players in that final were selected to play for that season's English Amateur international side. Furthermore, none was even invited to take part in the trial match. And that was between the North and South! The fact that, routinely, seven of the eight international selectors were southern-based was a point not lost on the Northern League. If there was mistrust of things emanating from the South, then it was based on more than ingrained prejudice.

Whatever the rights and wrongs of the decision, while

the rest of non-league football slotted into the pyramid, the Northern League went it alone. In 1985 the league's chairman, Arthur Clark, wrote that '[The] Northern League clubs have no intention of becoming part of the new structure'.

By 1989, though, things had changed. Bishop Auckland, North Shields and Whitley Bay (who, ironically, were Clark's old club) had all left the Northern League for the prospect of advancement offered by the pyramid. Spennymoor United were soon to follow them. Arthur Clark's 'no intention' quickly became 'investigating the possibility' and in 1991 the Northern League joined the pyramid, as a feeder for the Northern Premier League. In 1992 the Northern League champions, Gretna, were promoted into the NPL. And that, you might think, was the end of the story.

Alas not. Old feuds from the first days of the pyramid's inception quickly surfaced and more trouble between the FA, the Northern Premier League and the Northern League management committee became inevitable. The respective sides pouted like sulky adolescents and whinged on about hurt pride, insults and overdue apologies. Sadly, there was no one around to knock their heads together, with the result that Whitby Town, Northern League champions in 1992–93, had to wait until four days before the start of the new season to find out what league they would be playing in. The Northern League having refused them permission to leave, they remained where they were.

Was the Northern League still part of the pyramid? Who knew. And, you might well be thinking by this stage, who gave a monkey's.

And so it was, with the usual mixture of hope, trepidation, confusion and hangovers, that the 1993–94 football season began.

Newcastle United v. Tottenham Hotspur, FA Carling Premiership
Saturday 14 August 1993

In the window of the print shop at the foot of Dog Leap Stairs there was a photo of the Tyne Bridge under construction. I stopped and looked at it whenever I'd been to the Crown Posada. The first steel spars are just edging out across the river; down below, parked practically next to the Guild Hall, you can see a submarine. I was looking at the two erectors standing nonchalantly on one of the outstretched girders, chatting as if they'd just met on a pavement somewhere in town, while six inches to either side of them there was nothing but fresh air and a hundred-foot drop into the river. And in those days you wouldn't have wanted to drop into the Tyne from any height. Now it's clean enough to rank as one of the finest salmon rivers in England; then it was an open sewer. Originally it was said that a Geordie was someone who'd been born within smell of the Tyne. By the early sixties that included an area from Dumfries to Filey. My father remembers coming up to Newcastle from Middlesbrough for a meeting at some offices down on the quayside. 'How do I get to the river?' he asked a porter at Central Station.

'Go in the Gents', flush yourself down the toilet and you'll be there in thirty seconds,' the porter replied helpfully.

I walked up Northumberland Street. By the time I got to the statue of 'Wor Jackie' the Centurion Bitter and pre-match nerves had started to nudge me into George Clarts mode: 'Jackie Milburn,' I prattled uncontrollably, 'Wor Jackie. The

First World Wor indeed! Raven-haired, eagle-eyed, swift, swallow, chicken-in-a-basket. The magpie who popped up like a jackdaw-in-a-box to head home the winner that set the Black and Whites on the road to Wembley once more. Robledo, he was another star! Not a Geordie, but a Jorge. He came from Chile. And, my word, it was chilly on the afternoon he made himself part of United's great Cup-fighting tradition. And why were they always fighting cups, you might well ask. I'll tell you. Because this was in the days before television. People had to make their own entertainment. Cup-fighting, rug-wrestling and pummelling plates were but three of the pastimes that found popularity among the tough-as-teak, cobble-close families that eked out an existence in the sooty streets of the Toon.'

In St James's the mood was even more hysterical. It was the kind of wild and wanton hilarity which at a children's party would have all the mothers shaking their heads and saying, 'There'll be tears before bedtime.'

'Whack your lass with a Christmas tree. Ay-oh, ay-oh,' the fans chanted. 'Keegan. Keegan. Keegan. Gets the ball, scores a goal. Andy, Andy Cole. Toon Army. Toon Army.' Shredded paper fluttered through the air, black and white flags were unfurled, arms waved, a brass band played. 'Oh me lads you should've seen us gannin' . . .'

A crop-headed youth of such vast proportions that any Norwegians present must have been tempted to harpoon him and take him home for supper came into the Gallowgate eating a pie. It was one of those special football pies with asbestos-grey pastry that cracks to release the odour of a 1,000-year-old tomb. They're called football pies because they're made out of old casies. They even use the laces. 'Who ate all the pies?' the crowd howled. 'Who ate all the pies? You fat bastard. You fat bastard. You ate all the pies.'

The blubbery boy responded to this by shoving half the pie in his gob and then laughing. I rather wished he'd done things the other way round. I was picking gristle out of my ears for weeks afterwards. 'He's fat. He's round. He sprays his pie around. Big fat bastard. Big fat bastard,' the crowd celebrated.

The Gallowgate was the last standing area left at St James's. Opposite was the newly completed Leazes Stand, built on what had once been the popular end of the ground. Catherine's aunt recalled going in there just after the war with her father, brother and uncle. They'd been warned to stick together, but within five minutes were tens of yards apart, bobbing about as randomly as bottles in a choppy sea, the crowd surging back and forth across the terracing. At least she didn't end up down the front. The front of the Leazes End was notorious. A combination of heavy pre-match drinking and the impossibility of reaching the lavatories through the crush meant that standing there was like being at the bottom of a waterfall, albeit one that would never feature in a Timotei commercial. Ah, the good old days, eh? Earthy Chaucerian fun and the rapid spread of contagious diseases.

I'd been looking forward to seeing Peter Beardsley play ever since he'd been transferred back to Newcastle. Of the triumvirate of great players, Waddle, Beardsley and Gascoigne, who'd risen at St James's in the 1980s, Peter Beardsley was the one I most enjoyed watching. There was a mischievous neatness about him – part Jack Russell, part Jack Buchanan. He passed sharply and decisively, and he had a way of dummying over the ball with a wiggle of his right knee that put me in mind of a club comic imitating Elvis. The thing I liked best about Beardsley, though, was that when he ran with the ball you caught a glimpse on his face of the joy of the thing; a reminder of those same moments when, as a kid, you went round a defender, or ran on to a pass, and all there seemed to be in front of you were acres of grass, and as the adrenaline kicked into your system you got that bio-chemically ignorant childhood feeling that you could go charging on with that ball at your feet for ever and ever and never run out of breath. Then some thunder-thighed numbskull would lumber up and give you a dead leg.

In Peter Beardsley's case the thunder-thighed numbskull was Neil Ruddock. In a friendly match at Anfield five days before Ruddock had fractured Beardsley's cheekbone with his elbow. The injury put Beardsley out for the first month of the season. Now he was said to be considering suing Ruddock for damages. Perhaps the supporters who'd bought tickets expecting to see him should have taken similar steps.

The game kicked off. Somehow the expectation had drained all the life out of it. The previous season Newcastle had seemed able to generate a destructive tempo of passing and movement at will, overwhelming opponents with a continuous flow of swift, jabbing attacks. Today they had all the rhythm of a one-legged tap dancer. Spurs sat back and waited for a break. Compared to the pre-match activity it was dull stuff. The William Tell Overture followed by a stylophone recital.

Not that I noticed much of it. By now my attention was focused on a little man with glasses and a ginger moustache who had come in to E Section with two friends ten minutes before kick-off. I had never seen them in E Section before. I suppose they were only there because the Twats Section was shut. For the next half an hour these three men put on such a concentrated display of idiocy I began to suspect they were being employed by the Northumbria Tourist Board as part of a *Viz* Comic Heritage Trail. The little man was the ringleader. He was in his mid-twenties. The ironed creases down the front of his jeans suggested he still lived at home with his mother. He was certainly deeply frustrated. 'Get your tits out for the lads!' He bellowed at the raffle girls, his face turning puce and the veins on his neck bulging. Nobody except his mates joined in. 'What's the matter with these miserable cunts?' he shouted. 'They're worse than fucking Mackems. We hate Cockneys and we hate Cockneys . . .' (If any Londoners out there were thinking of inviting him round for dinner, I'd save the cassoulet and the tiramisu for somebody else if I were you.) When one of his friends dropped some matches and bent over to retrieve them the little man jumped on him and simulated anal intercourse. 'Soft southern rent boy,' he ranted at an injured Spurs player, 'You're just a soft southern rent boy.'

Then the little man made a mistake. 'Scotty!' he roared

at Kevin Scott, the Newcastle centre-half. 'You're a fucking poof.'

'Scotty's all right by me,' a voice behind me growled.
Everyone turned to look, including the little man. The speaker
was in his late thirties, with deep-set eyes and a head and neck
as solid as a butcher's block. His voice was a high-powered
whisper. It sounded like a steam hose. His face was pale.

'You what?' the little man yelled. He was standing on his
toes, staring up the terrace. He was about twelve feet below
the other bloke.

'I said,' the other bloke repeated in exactly the same slow
hissing tone, 'Scotty's all right by me.'

The little man's face flushed. He looked round at his mates,
but for the first time all afternoon they seemed to be taking an
interest in the game. 'He's playing like a fucking lass, man!' he
screamed, saliva spraying everywhere. He was turning purple
now, but whatever the other man was thinking he remained
if anything paler than when the row had started. It was as
if the blood was draining away from him and into the little
man, swelling and colouring him like a bruise.

'He's all right by me,' he said again. I noticed that his
lips, thin to begin with, had disappeared altogether. I always
regard this as a bad sign. My rule is: no lips, no argument.
Think of the great white shark. Would you get in a dispute
with it? I think not. The little man must have had the same
rule because he tried a more placatory bellow, 'All I'm saying
is, mate . . .'

Unhappily we never got to hear the rest because at this
point Sheringham rather rudely interrupted the discussion by
putting Spurs in front. They never looked likely to surrender
that lead. Newcastle, for all their desperate effort, seemed
incapable of worrying the Tottenham defence. Lee Clark,
outstanding the previous season, was as anonymous as
Salman Rushdie; Cole hardly had a touch, and the back
four, Kevin Scott included, looked flimsy. Only goalkeeper
Pavel Srnicek came out of the match with much credit.
Signed by Keegan's predecessor, Ossie Ardiles, Srnicek had
struggled during his first season. A wafer-thin man, he had

stopped shots well, but reacted to crosses with a vampiric panic. He seemed to have conquered that phobia, though he still hadn't ditched his ridiculous haircut. He sported the short-front-and-sides-long-back style favoured by so many Eastern Europeans. It was a throwback to the first days of the Czech pro-democracy movement, when the crowds in Wenceslas Square could clearly be heard chanting: 'We want freedom. We want democracy. We want Chris Waddle's old barber.'

For Ossie Ardiles Spurs' win represented some sort of revenge at least. The Tottenham manager had been sacked by Newcastle in a manner that followed football's usual shabby pattern. 'Ossie's job is as safe as houses,' United director Douglas Hall had told the press on the Friday. The following Monday Ardiles was fired. Just as well Douglas Hall isn't a builder, really.

As we filed out I noticed the little man in front of me. He'd been surprisingly subdued after his clash with the butcher's block bloke. Now he'd spotted a small boy with his father and was leaning over talking to him in a liddle-biddy-baby voice, saying: 'Is it your first game at Newcastle? Who's your favour-ite player? Robert Lee? Aye, he's a canny footballer . . .'

Luckily for the child the little man stopped talking at this point because I heaved up all over him. It would be all too easy to dismiss the little man's behaviour as simply the product of abysmal ignorance, woeful insensitivity, and arrested mental development. But what the hell, eh?

As I trotted down the stairs of the Gallowgate I could hear the fans in front of me comforting one another:

'Well, I hope Sunderland lost anyway.'

'Against the run of play.'

'One–nil.'

'A goal in injury time.'

'From a penalty.'

'Aye, disputed.'

The requested measure of embittering injustice didn't come. Humiliation, however, did. After 66 minutes at the Baseball Ground Sunderland were 5–0 down. Their support left by the busload. One fan made a detour via the dugout, took off his team shirt and dropped it at Terry Butcher's feet in disgust. 'I'm keeping it and hope to return it to him in better circumstances,' Butcher said.

The chief agent of Sunderland's destruction was former Roker Park favourite Marco Gabbiadini. 'He's five feet ten inches of thickly muscled, finely tuned goal scoring machine,' the shopkeeper had said to me when we'd first moved. A few months later, when Gabbiadini was sold to Crystal Palace for £1.8 million, I said to him, 'You'll be sorry he's going.'

The shopkeeper almost fell into his bacon-slicer. 'You've got to be joking,' he said. 'That useless fat swine? Good riddance to him.'

Sunderland's results didn't improve much over the next month. The local press pointed out that Butcher had gained fewer points in his first twenty-five matches in charge than Lawrie McMenemy had in his. It was a low blow. Butcher reacted to it with a kind of self-critical braggadocio; a swaggering display of I'm-a-winner shirt-rending that managed to be both painfully sincere and buffoonishly macho. 'I looked in the mirror last week,' he said, 'and I didn't like what I saw.'

Newcastle's rocky start continued too. The Wednesday following the Spurs defeat they travelled to Coventry, where Mick Quinn was waiting for them. Quinn had been the big hero at St James's prior to Keegan's return. He was one of those players fans warm to. Easygoing, with a waistline expanding faster than the hole in the ozone layer, Quinn liked a bet, enjoyed a beer and was happy to stand around chatting with anyone he met. When you mentioned him to local taxi drivers they'd say, 'Oh, he's a good lad, Micky,' then laugh. One said: 'He got in once with a chap I'd not seen before. I says, "Who's this, then?" Micky says, "Al Pacino." I says, "Oh aye, and I'm Paul Newman." And Micky says, "Well, you don't fucking drive like him." You could have a crack with Micky. He'd no side to him, that lad.'

While the rest of the players sprang on to the pitch and bounced up and down, flexing their limbs gymnastically,

Quinn rumbled out of the tunnel like a steam locomotive. The only reason he ran was to keep warm; all through the game he eyed the dugout furtively as if he was thinking of nipping round the back of it for a sly fag. In the dark, athletic reality of the modern game, Quinn was a beacon of hope for park footballers. Every goal he scored was a victory for the ordinary man. And Mick Quinn scored a lot of goals.

He didn't get on with Kevin Keegan, though. It's easy to see why. Keegan was unashamedly ambitious and dedicated. If Quinn was either of these things he masked it with happy-go-lucky facetiousness. Towards the end of the 1991–92 season, as United seemingly slipped towards relegation, the ever-loquacious Quinn made some injudicious remarks about his boss to a journalist. They got banner headlines in a Sunday paper. Quinn was fined two weeks' wages. His time at the club was effectively over.

Moving on to Highfield Road Quinn continued to find the net and also to aggravate his former manager. Another set of comments in the press had Keegan 'branding him a Judas'. It's odd how certain verbs crop up in the newspapers time after time, yet are never used in the same context in ordinary conversation: brand, lash, rap. Have you ever heard anyone say these words? 'Today my employer rapped stop-in-bed worker. Later I lashed his obsession with time-keeping, branding him "a right pain in the arse."' Anyway, as a result the match was seen as a clash between the two men. If this was the case then it finished 1–1. Newcastle lost: Quinn missed a penalty.

The Magpies' season spluttered on. A win against Everton was sandwiched between draws with Manchester United and Blackburn. On the terraces at least Newcastle went into the record books by unfurling the largest flag in Britain. At 120 feet by 80 feet it was the biggest piece of material seen on a football ground since Paul Mariner dropped his handkerchief during a match at Portman Road in 1976. Unimpressed, the team drew again, 1–1 with Ipswich.

Something drastic was needed to kick-start Newcastle's season. And things don't come much more drastic than Lee

Clark's record 'Wor Lee'. In committing himself to vinyl, the crop-headed Clark was following a well-trodden path for North-East players. Who could forget Jack Charlton's classic 'Geordie Sunday', a treacly, spoken tale of an Ashington childhood – Telly Savalas meets *When the Boat Comes In*? Or the memorable 'Willie Maddren's Reggae', surely the only occasion on which Jamaican dance music has been used to celebrate a Middlesbrough central defender? Whatever 'Wor Lee's musical merits ('He should have called it "Por Lee",' the shopkeeper said. 'It certainly makes me feel ill,') it had the desired effect. In their next game Newcastle hammered in three goals in the last fifteen minutes to beat Sheffield Wednesday 4–2. The following weekend Peter Beardsley returned.

While all this was going on Middlesbrough had got off to their best start in history. They'd won the first game 3–2 at Notts County, whacked Sunderland's tormentors Derby 3–0 at Ayresome Park, trounced Barnsley 4–1 at Oakwell, then travelled to Wolves for another 3–2 win. You might think that as a Middlesbrough fan I would have greeted this with glee. Alas not. Years of following Boro have left me with a deeply ingrained pessimism. When I die they will find the words 'I might have bloody known it' written on my heart. After the Wolves result came up on the teleprinter I started frantically searching through my *Rothmans* to see what the longest winning run at the start of a season was for a team eventually relegated. I couldn't find it. I did, however, discover that Boro once finished bottom of the old First Division with 37 points (with the current three-points-for-a-win system they'd have got 48) having scored 81 goals and conceded just seven more. It was a League record. I did a lap of honour round the winter cabbages.

The run of success owed much to the young players Lennie Lawrence had been forced to bring in because of lack of funds. Eighteen-year-old Republic of Ireland youth international Alan Moore was the star, but my personal favourite was the full-back, Richard Liburd. A nineteen-year-old who'd been bought from Eastwood Town of the Northern Premier

League, Liburd lolloped about with his shirt hanging out and a broad grin on his face looking like a cartoon schoolboy. If he got the ball on the edge of his own six-yard box, facing towards goal, Liburd's instinct was to dribble his way out of danger. And the amazing thing was he kept getting away with it.

Because of international matches Boro didn't play again for nearly two weeks after the Wolves game. Against all my better instincts a niggling feeling of expectation started itching at the edges of my subconscious. What if we won the next game, and the next, and the next? Surpassed Newcastle's victorious start to last season? How many points would make promotion a certainty? Who were our main rivals? Leicester? Charlton? Forest? I woke up in the night sweating, my mind racing through calculations and permutations of wins, defeats and draws. Hope was like malaria, it was feverish and untreatable, and no matter what you did to prevent it it kept on recurring.

Thankfully the unbearable tension of it all was ended on 10 September, when Southend beat us 1–0. From then on things got back to normal.

Whitley Bay v. Chorley,
FA Trophy First Qualifying Round
Saturday 18 September 1993

I was sitting at the station scribbling notes in my reporter's notepad. I felt self-conscious about this, partly because the only people you ever see scribbling down notes at a station are train-spotters, but mainly because the only notepad I was able to buy in the local newsagent's was one aimed at adolescent girls. It was wedged in between a mound of fluffy pencil cases and a box of those rubber monster things you stick on the end of pens and it had a photo on the front cover of a teenage Lothario sprawled on a bed of straw, sporting a come-hither look. He had so much oil on his pectorals you could have deep-fried a halibut in it. Every time I took the notepad out of my pocket I tried to flip it over quickly before anyone saw the cover. In fact, I tried to flip it over before I saw the cover, because every time I caught sight of the boy, tousled blond mane, button-fly Levi's, I was gripped with a powerful urge. Something about his raging juvenile hormones reawakened a desire I have repressed since my schooldays. Eventually, on the Metro between Benton and Palmersville, I could control myself no longer. I whipped out the notepad, jabbed my biro repeatedly into the picture, then scribbled 'Leeds Utd are poofs. True' across it. After that I felt much more relaxed. Although, strangely enough, everyone else in the carriage looked rather edgy.

Whitley Bay is the Geordie seaside resort, the Clacton of the North-East. In our desperation to escape from the Old Kent Road Catherine and I came to look at a flat here. There were vomit stains on the pavement outside and the disco pub across the road was advertising 'Wicked Willy's Naughty Knicker Night'. It all seemed sadly familiar. The woman from the building society who showed us round thought renting was a bad idea. She thought we should get our feet on the first rung of the housing ladder. She was in her mid-twenties and her hair was so stiffly lacquered she must have polished rather than combed it. She talked as if she was reading off an autocue in that vibrato nasal voice some North-Easterners affect because they think it makes them sound posh. If you'd blocked her nose she wouldn't have been able to make a sound. Unfortunately I didn't get the chance. She said: 'You're making your money work for you, not for the landlord. My husband and I bought an investment property in Seaton Delaval three years ago and sold it last month making two K on the deal. The property market's been down in the last couple of years, but it's going to take off again soon – we can feel it bubbling up below the surface. So there's never been a better moment to become a first-time buyer.' And all the time she was talking I was nodding and assenting and wondering if there actually is a moral distinction between someone who is lying and someone who is simply talking bollocks.

That day, battered by the blather of the bourgeois hopeful from the Halifax, and depressed by the leaden skies and dishwater sea, I had thought Whitley Bay rather desperate. Coming back to it on a bright autumn afternoon when the dewy grass of the Park sparkled as a many-jewelled carpet 'neath the golden rays of smiling Prometheus, I felt quite lyrical about the place.

I bought an egg mayonnaise stottie at a café and went and sat on the promenade. On the beach a father was demonstrating that the old magic was still there by dribbling repeatedly round his five-year-old son. The boy waddled after him gamely, earnestly wailing, 'Aw, away man, Dad!' every time he was nutmegged. The father, who was evidently mentally embarked upon a solo dribble that would bring the European Cup to Tyneside, was not put off by this fiendish foreign plea for sympathy. Turning once again he executed a knock-kneed shimmy that left the last Milanese defender trailing in his wake and then hammered a shot into the back of the net he plainly imagined to be hanging from the sea wall. The ball rebounded with some force, striking his pursuing son on top of the head and toppling him on to his backside. I had never thought much of fatherhood: watching this scene, though, I could see it might have its compensations. I bit into my stottie. I don't know who it was that invented egg mayonnaise sandwiches, but I suspect it was someone with a heavy investment in the dry-cleaning industry.

At Hillheads Park the programme hounds were truffling through the club shop. A Brummie in a shellsuit so garish it looked as if someone had eaten a kaleidoscope then puked over it was moaning about the admission price. 'Three-fifty! Three-fifty! Are they taking the piss or what, eh? It's two quid at Blyth. Two quid at Croft Park, innit?' He was talking to his son, a lump of a lad with maroon lips. They evidently lived in the area because the lumpy lad had a North-East accent and skin the colour of baked beans. Orange skin is *de rigueur* among the swinging singles of Tyneside. Rumour has it that bouncers at the pubs and clubs in the Bigg Market stop you at the door and say, 'Sorry, pal, you can't come in. You're not wearing a tan.' As a consequence there's a permanent run on bronzing lotions. Sunbeds sell like hot cakes. I once met a bloke who was a trades union convener and a prospective Labour councillor in Sandyford and he was bursting with joy because he'd just bought one. He said: 'Any time you want to use it, just pop round,' as if inviting someone to come to your flat and lounge about in their underpants was the the most natural thing in the world. Also I couldn't square socialism with sunbed-worship. Call me old-fashioned, but I can't imagine Manny Shinwell preparing for his historic victory over Ramsay MacDonald at Easington by spending an hour each day lying on the kitchen table wearing nothing but a G-string and a coating of coconut butter – though I'm prepared to be proved wrong by photographic evidence.

There were about 300 fans in the ground at kick-off. Two

coachloads of them had come from Lancashire. This was quite usual. Whenever Lancashire teams played in the North-East they always brought two coachloads of fans with them. In fact, it may well have been the same two coachloads every time, so homogenous were they. They were uniformly jolly and friendly and sporting; they always had among their ranks a genial granny in a lilac leisure suit and a hand-knit scarf with white hair springing from her head like kapok stuffing coming out of an elderly and well-loved cuddly toy, and a portly old chap armed with some amusing noise-making device such as a klaxon or rattle which he set off at regular intervals, following it each time with a peal of hearty laughter. Another sad victim of the care in the community scheme.

I sat in the main stand next to a man wearing a Walkman. Just before kick-off an old bloke came round collecting the extra you have to pay to sit. The man in the Walkman pretended not to hear him. Then when the old bloke tapped him on the shoulder and asked him again, he said, 'It doesn't say you have to pay extra to sit. Where's it say that?'

The old bloke replied: 'There's a sign as you come in.'

'What sign?' the man in the Walkman said. 'I didn't see any sign. Where's the sign?'

'On the side of this stand,' the old bloke told him.

'Well, I never saw it,' the man in the Walkman said grumpily, dipping into his pocket. 'You want to put it somewhere people can see it.'

It was a lot of fuss to make over 20p.

Despite their position in the Northern Premier League, Premier Division, Whitley Bay are not among the giants of North-East non-league football. They weren't admitted to the Northern League until 1958 and though they took the title in successive years in the mid-sixties they never exercised the type of domination enjoyed by the likes of Bishop Auckland, Blyth or Crook. They had never won the Amateur Cup, nor got beyond the third round of the FA Trophy. Their lofty perch, in fact, owed less to achievements on the field than it did to the politicking that went on off it.

Hillheads, though, was a smartly kept ground and it was

nice to think that this was where 'Jinky' Jim Smith, the Magpies' contribution to the seventies 'wayward genius' boom, had finished his career, keeping himself amused during dull passages of play by picking divots off the pitch and hurling them at members of the crowd whose cries had offended him.

The match kicked off and the Chorley fans started shouting (rather too loudly, I felt, given that they were the people responsible for foisting Paul Mariner on an unsuspecting world). They all sounded like Sir Rhodes Boyson. Except, of course, that you'd never hear Sir Rhodes Boyson shout, 'What's the matter, ref, d'you need to lend a fucking pencil?' He'd say 'Borrow a fucking pencil,' obviously.

The only people shouting louder than the Chorley fans were the Chorley players. The 'keeper in particular had a voice like a foghorn and kept up a constant stream of inane footballing comments. 'Hold them, hold them, hold them!' he yelled, periodically clutching his genitals as if to illustrate his point. 'Push out, push out, push out!' he bellowed. 'Tuck in, tuck in, tuck in!' Midway through the half the man to my left cracked. 'Will you shut up, goalie,' he called out. 'I'm trying to have a kip.'

It had no effect. The goalkeeper carried on with his senseless, high-volume patter. Why does anyone bother to shout 'Challenge for it!' when the ball's in the air? Do they really think the man underneath it needs telling? Perhaps they think if they didn't give him instructions, he'd sit down and make a macramé plant-holder instead. Or do a bit of origami. Whatever, the Chorley 'keeper wasn't prepared to put it to the test. 'Challenge for it, challenge for it, challenge for it!' he barked. 'Work the line, work the line, work the line!' 'Worry him, worry him, worry him!'

'Call the environmental health,' the kip man groaned.

Eventually, broken by this psychological warfare, Whitley Bay conceded an own goal. Usually when a player scores an own goal I can work out what he was trying to do. And this was no exception. Mark Outterside was clearly trying to head the ball into the top left-hand corner.

'Fuck off, Jimmy, you get,' the misanthrope in the Walkman snapped suddenly, apropos of absolutely nothing. It was the only time he spoke.

At the start of the second half it was evident the Bay men had come up with a strategy to quell Chorley's most potent threat. From the first corner they won, they floated the ball into the six-yard box, allowed the 'keeper to catch it, then the centre-half steamed in from the edge of the penalty area and clattered him in the slats with such force he remained mute for the rest of the game.

An eerie silence descended on Hillheads, punctuated only by the occasional cries of the Chorley captain, a Liverpudlian who shouted 'Wairk! Wairk!' as if he was rehearsing for a part in an Alan Bleasdale play, and the squawking of the seagulls.

With twenty minutes to go the home fans were raised from the torpor when John Kiddie equalised. The biggest cheer of the day came a few minutes later when Whitley Bay's stocky, ponytailed midfielder slid ferociously into a fifty-fifty tackle and came away carrying the ball. Football crowds always respond to good tackling. Yet the pressmen and the TV pundits never seem to mention it. Perhaps a swerving run, or a sixty-yard pass volley are more worthy of comment – they are artists' skills, tackling is merely craftsmanship. Architecture is always more valued than engineering.

The game ended 1–1. Whitley Bay lost the replay. Forty minutes after the final whistle I was on the train as it rattled out across the river. To the east the Tyne Bridge arched against the blue September sky.

The rain fell as it only can in Northumberland. It clattered about the roof like Topol on amphetamines. The reverberating thunder woke me up, sending me into a panic that Rutskoi or one of the other Soviet blockheads currently besieged in the Russian White House had pushed the red button in a pro-democracy protest. Once I realised I was not about to be incinerated in a nuclear blast, I lay awake thinking about finance. Radiation had been a happier prospect. The car had failed its MOT and the words 'corroded', 'dangerous' and 'unsatisfactory' had jumped off the test sheet and slapped my bank balance in the kidneys.

I took the dog out early that morning. In the lanes around the house the leaves of the chestnut trees had begun to turn pale yellow. The dog and I waded through the temporary lake that filled Church Lonnen with conkers bobbing around our feet like mines. It would take every penny we had to keep the car on the road. We couldn't afford another one. Money was so tight my ankles had gone numb. Still, at least I could content myself with the thought that I was better off than Hartlepool United. But then someone who was dressed in a barrel, living in a ditch and subsisting on chickweed would have been better off than Hartlepool. The club had entered yet another period of financial crisis. The Inland Revenue were sniffing round the Victoria Ground, the players were owed £18,000 in back wages, the PFA had been called in to help with payments, an inward transfer and loan embargo was being enforced and attendances weren't covering overheads. The only consolation for Pool fans was that arch-rivals Darlington had managed to get through the first two months of the season without winning a game and their manager, Billy McEwan, had resigned two days after receiving a vote of confidence from the board.

Hartlepool weren't the only North-Eastern team flirting with financial ruin. Ashington, birthplace of Jackie Milburn and the Charlton brothers, had had their clubhouse closed by the council, the manager and players had left and they'd had to field a scratch team in the opening match of the season. South Bank, founder members of the Northern League, had been forced to close down for a year because they couldn't afford to repair damage done to the ground by vandals. Whitley Bay had struggled through a troublesome close season. North Shields, another team who had quit the Northern League to join the Northern Premier, had folded completely; their ground, Appleby Park, sold off to meet their debts. The Robins had been the last Northern League team to win the Amateur Cup, beating Sutton United at Wembley in front of over 47,000 people. The following season they'd shared the European Amateur Cup-Winners' Cup with Almas of Rome. Now, as members of the Vaux Wearside League, a reformed outfit was playing in a public park against the likes of Windscale and Jarrow Roofing.

In an area where one recession seemed to merge seamlessly into the next, the football clubs had struggled on through closures and shut-outs, redundancies and strikes. It was unsurprising that some should have gone to the wall. The real surprise was that more hadn't done so.

Dunston Federation Brewery v. Billingham Synthonia,
FA Cup Second Qualifying Round
Saturday 25 September 1993

I suspect that in Conrad's *Heart of Darkness*, when Kurtz cries out 'The horror! The horror!' he is not recoiling from the black void at the centre of the human soul, but simply recalling a trip to the Gateshead Metro Centre. The Metro Centre is vast. The walk across it takes so long it's a surprise Wainwright never wrote a guide. It is hotter than the rain forest. You expect to turn a corner and come across a group of tribesmen hunting for wild pigs. Shopping in it is a nightmare of Gyles-Brandreth-is-PM proportions.

I realise I am swimming against the tide in this. The Metro Centre is jammed with people, all of whom disagree with me. After two minutes in it you realise why the Americans talk about shopping mauls. The place is chock-a-block with people who have travelled from miles around to pass a happy couple of hours spending money and having a go at one another. The trek across the place is accompanied by a soundtrack of beeping cash registers and familial discord. 'One more word out of you young lady take that look off your face I don't care what Gary's mam and dad let him do give it a rest you sound like a bloody two-year-old you've tried the damned thing on six times already I'm not enjoying this any more than you are will you stop whining . . .' As a counterpoint there is a constant drone of adenoidal sophistication coming down the microphone of a woman selling skincare products. At the intersection of several glittering precincts, midway between

The Roman Forum and The Antique Village, she is slapping gunk on the face of a volunteer and telling her audience that 'the human skin absorbs the regenerating nutrients from the soothing avocado and papaya emulsion'. I find this a fascinating concept. Why do we bother with boring old eating? If the skin can absorb nutrients shouldn't we just bathe in nourishing soup instead? And how many drunks have the courts condemned who were no more than innocent victims of a stood-in-a-puddle-of-brown-ale incident? Millions, probably.

I wasn't in the Metro Centre by choice, then. I was there because I needed to find out exactly where Dunston FB's ground, Federation Park, was. So I was going to look it up in one of the bookshops. I had to do this pretty regularly over the season. I could have avoided the hassle by simply buying a copy of the *Non-League Club Directory*, but I was unable to do so. It was a psychological thing. I had bought the *Non-League Club Directory* once a few years earlier and for the next six months everyone who came to our flat was greeted by cries of 'Broadmoor Staff Eleven turn out in the Chiltonian League. I bet there's an intimidating atmosphere at their home fixtures,' 'Lostock Gralam had a disappointing season,' and 'Lewes FC play at the Dripping Pan, you know.' Eventually, a friend who had watched a lot of Oprah Winfrey and knew all about tough love snatched the book off me one day and threw it into a concrete mixer. Deprived of Standon & Puckeridge and Spartak Downend I went through weeks of agonising cold turkey, ultimately emerging a chastened, but tougher man. And that, basically, is why I had to go to the Metro Centre.

There were about 120 people inside Federation Park. One of them was the shellsuited Brummie. He was saying: 'Dicks! Dicks! Can you believe it? Dicks!' I assumed he was talking about Liverpool's purchase of West Ham's captain, Julian Dicks, though he may just have been expressing incredulity about penises. Astonishment was clearly the Brummie's *métier*. I was to see him regularly over the next few months and he was always in a state of wide-mouthed amazement about something. The colour of tea, the texture of pies, the smell of onions, all were revelatory to him. He experienced the world with a newborn child's sense of wonderment, greeting each fresh moment with exclamations of surprise and puzzlement that I for one found deeply touching. And I told him as much just before I pulled the trigger.

I took a seat in the Paul Gascoigne Stand, which, perhaps surprisingly, didn't seem in danger of imminent collapse. The shadow of Gazza looms large over Dunston FB. It's his home territory, the clubhouse is full of memorabilia and when he's back on Tyneside he drinks down the road at the Excelsior. It had not been a good year for Gascoigne. In the blizzard of publicity surrounding his belching, his scraps, his girlfriend and his eating habits, it was sometimes hard to remember what had made him famous in the first place. Niggling injuries had hampered his first season in Italy and when able to play he had performed only fitfully. The media had pounced on his perceived demise and transformed it into the usual cautionary tale – a moral fable in which that perennial favourite the Decline in Standards of Personal Behaviour in the Modern Era got another good airing. They had turned a man into a metaphor for his age. As usual the posturing of the press was not without its ironies. One of my neighbours is a retired police officer who spent thirty years in stations around the North-East. Like all Northumbrians he is a voluble man, and a football fan. If I had written down the things he has told me about his professional encounters with some of Britain's most famous players this publisher's lawyer would now be wearing a white jacket with buckles on and have thorazine rushing through his veins instead of port. And, bizarre though it may seem, the bad behaviour does not suddenly commence, like sexual intercourse, in 1963, but in 1948 – the year my neighbour went into the force. Now, I would suggest that if my next-door neighbour knew about these shenanigans, then journalists did too. The North-East remains something of a village, and like all villages it is rife with gossip. In those days, however, the common thinking among the press was that if an English international wanted to knock off some girl who worked behind the bacon counter in Prudhoe Co-Op, then that was his business – and his wife's too, if she found out about it. And quite right, you may say.

Strangely, though, when Gazza involved himself in disreputable antics, these same players – men who had been hauled, drunk, disorderly and shag-happy from Wallsend brothels, assaulted by jealous husbands and cracked over the skull by betrayed spouses – were held up as shining examples, paragons from a more noble age, against whom the modern stars simply did not measure up. 'In this condom culture we will never see their like again,' the hacks wailed, without ever seeming to realise that the luminescent glow emanating from the giants of the past came not from any inner sanctity, but from the liberal coats of whitewash that had been applied to them over the years. The only falling moral standards Gascoigne's behaviour really highlighted were those of the pressmen themselves.

Paul Gascoigne got all this attention because he is a brilliant footballer. Once, on her birthday, I took Catherine to see him play for England B against Yugoslavia B at the Den. I know how to treat a woman. We had seats along the touchline, close to halfway. Next to us was a cheery octogenarian Millwall fan with a cap, a mac, and a nose the shape and colour of some gastronomically prized fungus. Every few minutes he turned to us and said: 'International football at the Den! I've been coming here seventy-five years. Cor, who woulda thought it?' I think he'd escaped from an Ealing comedy.

A few minutes into the game Gascoigne got the ball on the near side of the field tight in against the touchline. He was no more than twenty yards from us when he executed a high-speed shuffle and shimmied past two defenders in the space of a few paces. Catherine said: 'He's got feet like a dancer's.' And that was about right. He was a pudgy Fred Astaire in studs.

A few months later, playing for the full England team against Czechoslovakia at Wembley, Gascoigne really put on a show. In the final minutes, having already set up three goals, he scored one of his own. The TV cameras suddenly cut to Bobby Robson, up on his feet grinning like a kid. Pointing at Gascoigne, he turned to Don Howe and a whole nation could read his lips: 'That is fantastic!' It's one of my favourite football moments. Not just because of the quality of the goal, but because of the way Robson reacts to it. That wide-eyed, lolling smile on the England manager's face is a reminder of why football is such a fine thing; it has a rare ability to induce that kind of all-consuming, irrational and totally childlike happiness in an adult. Paul Gascoigne was one of the few players who could bring it about. And that, to my mind, is the thing that should always be remembered about him.

The players ran out on to the pitch against the backdrop of the Federation Brewery, a vast aircraft hangar of a place unnervingly reminiscent of an Eastern European chemical factory. In Dunston's ranks were two of the largest footballers I have ever seen: a centre-half who looked like he'd been signed from the pages of an action comic and a forward someone informed me had been bought from Tow Law – though whether from the football club or the livestock market he didn't say.

The game was being filmed for *Match of the Day*'s 'Road To Wembley' segment (at this early stage the road resembled a ten-lane highway populated entirely by the Y-reg Cortinas, Datsun Cherries and Lada Rivas of lower non-league football). The sight of the cameras sent the flock of urchins who invariably inhabit non-league football grounds into a frenzy. You could hear their voices, boosted by excitement, echoing across the pitch: 'Looker, looker, Michael, man! It's TV. It's a camera. You know what we could do, right? We could wait until it points at us, and then we could all jump up and down and pull silly faces and wave our arms above our heads and shout like mad and that. And everybody sat at home watching would go, "Hey, look at those stupid little wankers. They look like baboons with St Vitus' Dance!"'

'D'you really think so? Aw, fantastic! Champion idea, Lee, man!'

This obsession with appearing on television is quite a recent development. Certainly in my youthful days we were far too busy diligently finishing our Latin homework, or collecting milk-bottle tops for the *Blue Peter* Guide Dog Appeal, to be bothered with such trivial matters. Times change, I suppose, and, I can't help thinking, not always for the better. One has only to recall the appalling events so recently and tragically played out on Merseyside . . . I'm sorry. For one terrible moment there I was overcome by the powerful feeling that I was writing a column in a Sunday newspaper.

Billingham Synthonia have the unique distinction of being the only club in Britain named after a fertiliser (though several other possible candidates immediately spring to mind). Formed in 1923 as part of Imperial Chemical Industries' multi-tentacled Social and Sports Club, they entered the Northern League in 1945 and took the first of their three titles in 1957. As a young man working at ICI Frank Bough was on Synners' books (insert your own 'enjoyed a period of domination' joke here), but despite having a soccer Blue from Cambridge, he wasn't good enough to get a game. Billingham had made it through to the first round proper of the FA Cup on six occasions, most recently in 1989–90, when they were beaten by Lincoln City. Perhaps Synners' greatest claim to fame, though, was that it had been while playing for them at their old Belasis Lane home that Brian Clough had been spotted by Middlesbrough.

Dunston, by contrast, were new arrivals. Formed in 1975, they were promoted into the Northern League from the Vaux Wearside League in 1991 and won the Second Division title two years later. The second qualifying round was as far as they had ever got in the FA Cup. They were not destined to break that record.

The lack of Lancastrians meant the crowd was quiet compared to Hillheads. Quiet is perhaps not the right word – comatose would be nearer the mark. When Andrew Banks scored for Billingham it raised nary a ripple of applause, despite the fact that he had carried the ball from the halfway line slaloming through three defenders en route. (In the replay the skilful Banks was sent off for striking a team-mate, thus giving new meaning to the term 'a dribbling idiot'. The loudest roar of the first half, in fact, came not from the spectators but from a Synthonia player who reacted to an X-rated tackle by pointing at the stud marks on his thigh and yelling: 'How, pal! What's this shite?' at a volume that rattled windows on a nearby council estate.

Things livened up briefly in the second period when Dunston equalized through substitute Chris Redhead, but despite their pressing the home team never seemed likely to win. Synthonia played much the neater football and two of the veterans of their last Championship-winning side, forward Charlie Butler and central defender Tony Lynch, were easily the best players on the field. Lynch, a balding man with a long body and bandy legs, seemed to clear every high ball that was pumped into the Synners' half. He headed it vast distances and when the leather came in contact with his pate it made a solid splatting sound like a Greek fisherman tenderising an octopus.

Charlie Butler, blond, sunken-eyed and possessing a torso and limbs so pencil-thin he made Tommy Hutchison look like Jabba the Hutt, drifted about across the front of the Dunston back four all afternoon. He was getting on a bit, not quick, but he was purposeful and decisive and seemed to know more about the game than the men who were trying to mark him. It was Butler who created the best moment of the game when, late in the second half, he glided once again from left to right, neatly collected a pass and slid through a gap on to the edge of the penalty area. His shot rebounded off the post.

The game ended 1–1. Charlie Butler scored the winner for Billingham in the replay. I walked back to the Metro Centre station across acres of packed car parks, dodging in and out of the manic hordes as they raced their swishing, heavily laden trolleys over the tarmac. It is surely only a matter of time before shopping becomes an Olympic sport.

Sunderland v. Peterborough United, Endsleigh Insurance League Division 1
Saturday 2 October 1993

In the village they were getting ready for the Leek Show. It was a small affair with about four dozen growers presenting their corpulent cuties for inspection. Nevertheless it was still a solemn occasion. In the North-East leek-growing is a serious business. Obtaining membership of a top leek club is more difficult than joining the Garrick. Sir Kingsley Amis wouldn't get a look in; Robert Robinson would be out of the door before he could say 'Brain of Britain'. The competitions are fierce and unscrupulous. Jealous rivals slash one another's prize specimens, or shoot holes in the leaves with air rifles. Leek growing, you see, isn't just about size; it's about physical perfection too. On show day growers lift their entries, clean the flags, polish the barrels and comb the soil out of the beards. Once suitably primped, these chunky Chippendales are swaddled in damp towels and transported to the show tent to battle it out for the top prizes.

Foodies are fond of saying that these sort of massive leeks don't taste as good as normal garden ones. This is true. But then a normal garden leek won't win you a fortnight's holiday for two in Majorca, will it?

We passed the blazered leek-growers in my neighbour's son's Peugeot. My next-door neighbour and his son were in the front, I was sitting in the back like the head of the Politburo. We were driving along the A695 listening to a debate about football corruption on Radio 5. Similar programmes had been going out all week, sparked by allegations made on TV about the dealings of Terry Venables and Brian Clough. One of the people involved in the debate was the players' agent, Eric Hall. I had never seen a photo of Hall, but I'd heard enough of him to form a mental picture of an oleaginous man in a shiny suit with sovereign rings and one of those elaborately tinted, back-combed barnets that look as if they've been purchased from a Lebanese soft furnishings store rather than grown organically. On the defensive from the outset, Hall adopted the simple protective technique of talking so much no one else could get a word in. He was so unstoppably garrulous you got the impression that even if you stuffed a sofa down his throat he'd still be able to sing the National Anthem. The merest suggestion of rules or guidelines for agents produced a hyperbolic whinge invariably involving the Soviet Union, communism, Nazi Germany, democracy and Freedom. Patriotism may be the last bastion of scoundrels, but there are also plenty of them hiding in a turret marked 'Principles of the Market Economy'.

At the end of the discussion (I use the term loosely) the presenter offered the view that the FA should start an inquiry into corruption headed by somebody such as Gordon McKeag. For some reason the idea of the former Newcastle United chairman leading a corruption inquiry produced a rumble of laughter in the North-East so loud that several pigeon lofts collapsed.

At Roker Park the electric scoreboard opposite the Fulwell End flashed up its usual incessant round of messages: 'Happy Birthday Bob. Love Mandy.' 'The NEB, Caring about Sport in the North.' 'Today's guests are from Cleveland Social Services (so keep tight hold of your children).'

Meanwhile two blokes standing behind me were engaged in a competition to see who could use the most expletives in a sentence. It was touch and go for a while, both of them having mastered the fine art of sandwiching a quick fuck in between syllables. Eventually the one on the left nicked it by skilful use of the name Sean Cunnington. Some people say that repetitious use of obscenities is indicative of poor education, a lack of vocabulary and an inability to form a cohesive argument. But I say, bollocks. The real reason people stock up their word count with ruderies is that it makes the conversation last longer. If the two blokes behind me had cut out the foul language they'd have said everything they had to say before kick-off. If I'd adopted that approach I could have written this book in half the time and buggered off on holiday for a few months. Sadly, I was just too conscifuckingentious to do so. Anyway, as it was the blokes entertained themselves for the entire match, which was certainly more than Peterborough managed.

I had always had a soft spot for the Posh. I had a friend who lived there and when I went to stay with him we'd go along to London Road to watch them. It was in the days when Noel Cantwell was manager. My friend and his brother sang the praises of the Peterborough golden boy Dave Gregory. He was, so they said, coveted by all the top clubs. Offers from Man United and Leeds were imminent, they said; Arsenal were watching him avidly. Eventually Dave Gregory was indeed transferred, to Stoke. I never rated him anyway. My favourite in United's team was an ageing winger named Tommy Robson. Robson had come to Peterborough from Chelsea. He was dark-haired, industrious and specialised in shooting from outside the box. I found out later that he was born in Gateshead.

Any charitable thoughts I might have had towards Peterborough were quickly dismissed. They were so unambitious they started time-wasting during the kick-in. Once the game got underway they hoofed the ball into the stands at every opportunity, fouled, spoiled and rolled around in agony whenever they were touched. Their physio ran on and off the pitch so often he must have covered more ground than any of his players. If he'd been on piece-work he could have retired at half-time.

Sunderland, meanwhile, huffed and puffed to little effect. Terry Butcher had spent heavily during the close season and some of his purchases, most notably Derek Ferguson, were obviously good players. Somehow, though, the team, like the club itself, remained oddly directionless and lacking in charisma. Don Goodman, despite his shambling style and ample girth, was a dynamic goalscorer, and Gary Owers showed occasional flashes of skill, but them aside the team seemed short of distinctive characters. Over the previous two seasons I had been to Roker Park as often as I had to any other ground in the North-East, yet while I could easily identify most players at the region's other clubs I always struggled to distinguish those at Sunderland. For the former 'team of all talents' it was a depressing come-down.

Sunderland briefly broke from their committed but unco-ordinated style at the end of the half, and the result was a good goal for Northern Ireland international Phil Gray, from Ferguson's neat through ball.

During the half-time interval the blokes behind me talked about their hooligan exploits. One of them said: 'Newcastle Station' – I'm bowdlerising here: what he actually said was 'Fucking Newfuckingcastle fucking Stafuckingtion', but we haven't got all day – 'There's me and twelve Mackems and this big crowd of Geordies, about three hundred of them, come down the street, right? And there's just me and these four other lads, and we're like looking at these two thousand Geordies. And eventually I goes to the other bloke that was with me, I goes, "What d'you think, mate? D'you reckon me and you can have five thousand Geordies?" And he goes, "if I wasn't in this wheelchair I'd take them on meself." And then I just charged, right. And these fifteen thousand Geordies just scattered like fuck.' And then his friend said: 'You should of been at fucking Wolves . . .'

I've heard a lot of this sort of thing over the years on trains and terraces. The stories always remind me of those escalating boasts of childhood: 'My Dad bought me a trampoline and it's got a Scalextric set in the middle and when you turn it inside out it's a swimming pool with a diving board and a water slide like on *The Banana Splits* and everything.' It's impossible to know what sort of person would take this claptrap seriously. Apart, of course, from tabloid journalists and bearded academics. Eventually I got so sick of listening to them, I turned round and said, 'Pal, you're talking shite.' And they just scattered like fuck.

Peterborough came out in the second half seeking an equaliser. They didn't get one. Their only tactic was to loft the ball in the general direction of the Sunderland penalty area. This proved totally ineffective as their attack carried all the aerial threat of a dodo. Twelve minutes from the end Gary Owers got Sunderland's second when a feeble shot from twenty yards took a deflection that wrong-footed Bennett in the Peterborough goal. Normally such a deflection would be described as 'cruel', but as this one effectively killed off Posh I think 'merciful' would be more apt.

I spent the remaining minutes gazing round Roker Park. Sunderland had once been one of the best supported teams in the country. In the thirties they had packed over 65,000 into the ground for the derby with Newcastle and three people had been crushed to death as a result. During the sixties, when they were a struggling First Division outfit, their average attendances had been the fourth-highest in the country at just over 40,000. Even in the mid-seventies 30,000 had regularly turned up to watch them. Yet despite the loyalty of their support, and their location in the heart of an area that produced three times as many professional footballers per capita as any other part of the country, Sunderland had not, apart from the entertaining 1973 Cup final victory, won anything for over fifty years. It was hard to see how the club could have got into such a rut; harder still to see how they could extricate themselves from it. They had certainly made enough attempts to buy themselves out, most notably in the fifties, when a spending spree that saw the likes of Len Shackleton, Don Revie and Billy Bingham pass through the gates of Roker Park earned them the nickname 'The Bank of England club'.

In the mid-sixties in another financial splurge, they'd brought Jim Baxter to Wearside for £72,000 and an £11,000 signing-on fee. The great Baxter was peeved with Glasgow Rangers for selling him in the first place. Evidently having read somewhere that the best revenge is to live well, he set out on a retributive binge of belt-busting excess. By the time he left Roker Park 'Slim' Jim had expanded to such a size that it was an offence for him to cross a cattle grid. Nottingham Forest had paid Sunderland £100,000 for Baxter, which, pound for pound, must have looked like a good deal. It wasn't. Eighteen months later they gave him a free transfer back to Rangers.

The Bank of England era ended in 1957 with an illegal payments scandal that resulted in the suspension of two directors and the sacking of manager Bill Murray. A year later Sunderland were relegated for the first time in their history. The local paper's sports edition was printed on blue paper to mark the occasion. The biggest impression Baxter made on the pitch was when he fell over.

Even the Cup win in 1973, which might have signalled a turning-point, only turned sour. The victory came during the government pay freeze. The club was legally barred from increasing the wages of the squad, with the result that star players such as Denis Tueart and Dave Watson left. Within two seasons, the young team which might have dragged Sunderland out of the mire had completely disintegrated.

And then there was McMenemy.

After such disappointments it's easy to see how disillusion could set in among the supporters. The fact that nearly 18,000 had turned up to see two such mediocre teams certainly said something about Sunderland fans. 'Suckers', most likely.

Tommy Leishman was standing on the riverbank watching the salmon. The season was coming to an end, but the fish were still swimming upstream. They leaped clean out of the water and belly-flopped back in with a resounding smack. Nowadays wild salmon is a rich man's dish; once it was so plentiful in the Tyne there was a clause on the local apprentices' contracts of indentation that the employer would not feed them salmon more than five times a week.

Tommy Leishman was a retired shipyard worker from Wallsend. He'd been a riveter at Swan Hunter. The noise of the gun had left him deaf in one ear and the knuckles of his hands were chalky with rheumatism. He was recovering from an operation. He said: 'They've took that much out of us I'm hollow. If I eat my dinner, then jump up and down, I rattle like a pair of maracas.'

Talking to Tommy Leishman wasn't easy. His accent was as thick as a plumber's mate and you had to lean over and speak into his good ear. The main problem, though, was his dog, Earl. Earl was a nondescript terrier with hair the same colour as Billy Bremner's and the temperament to match. All the time I was talking to Tommy Earl would be leaping and fizzing, and my dog would be snarling and trying to hide behind my legs. By the time the conversation was finished his lead would be wrapped round my calves like the stem of some B-movie man-eating plant.

Thankfully, today Earl was bad, so Tommy had left him behind. He said: 'Have you seen the *Journal*? The Mackems' super-stadium's been banjaxed.' His voice was a fifty-fifty mixture of mirth and malice. It's hard to convey the bitterness of the rivalry between Newcastle and Sunderland. It goes beyond football. I once heard two Geordies on the train mocking a Wearsider because his city had inferior shopping facilities. That's how ridiculous it gets. 'Aye, it's scuppered,' Tommy said.

Sunderland's proposed new stadium was part of a £70 million complex next to the Nissan car plant in Washington. The 48,000-seater ground was to incorporate shops, restaurants, a multiplex cinema and an indoor arena. After initial objections the scope of the plan had been narrowed and the stadium capacity cut to 40,000. The objectors still weren't satisfied.

'Nissan've complained,' Tommy said. 'They say a crowd of thirty thousand'll paralyse the road system. Shows how much the Japs know about football, if they think thirty thousand'll turn up to watch them red and white buggers.'

For the time being at least he was probably right. At that moment the main danger to the North-East's road network came not from roving football supporters, but from roving football clubs. So many teams were planning to change grounds, the removal vans looked likely to cause regional gridlock.

The whole thing had started a few years before when Newcastle's chairman, Sir John Hall, had engaged in a bout of Coleridge-style dreaming and envisioned a 50,000-seater pleasure dome next to the Metro Centre with a sliding glass roof to keep out the elements. Sadly, the man from Porlock came a-knocking at this point and that was the last that was ever heard of it. Inspired by Sir John's poetic imaginings, and the more down-to-earth recommendations of the Taylor Report, the super-stadium concept really took hold. Durham City announced they were quitting Ferens Park for a new Conference-standard stadium at Belmont. Stockton started work on an £800,000 ground at Tilery. Bishop Auckland proposed a 10,000-capacity stadium on the outskirts of the town. Middlesbrough revealed plans for a £15 million, 30,000-seater ground at Riverside Park. And Darlington . . . Well, Darlington acquired a second-hand grandstand roof from Stockton Racecourse, then found they were unable to erect it because of the sewer running behind the Polam End.

Most of the old grounds were going to be demolished and the sites used for housing, but I felt sure at least one would be kept open as a Heritage Centre (heritage, after all, was the region's only growth industry) so that in a hundred years' time our ancestors could come and marvel at its open-topped urinals and the way the smell of frying onions still lingered round the floodlight pylons, and scratch their heads, make tutting noises and say, 'Ee, we don't know we're born, do we?'

Tommy Leishman said: 'They'd never even have called thirty thousand a crowd after the war. I went up to St James's one time for an FA Cup tie. There was fog that thick you could have topped a trifle with it. We waited outside for fear it would be called off. There was no refunds. We waited and waited, expecting an announcement. Then, ten minutes before kick-off, we paid up and went in. They called it off five minutes after. There was over fifty thousand in and no money back. They'd waited specially.' He sucked his teeth. 'They were bastards,' he said, then he laughed. 'I still went to the replay, mind.'

Billingham Synthonia v. Gateshead, FA Cup Third Qualifying Round
Saturday 9 October 1993

At the Synthonia Social Club the beer was a pound a pint. 'Cheapest beer in Teesside, lads,' the gatemen at Central Avenue told us. Steve, a Geordie, came away chuckling because he liked the sound of their voices. The Teesside accent certainly is a unique thing. It somehow manages to be both flat and phlegmy at the same time. Redolent of packets of Senior Service, nights of drinking and years of breathing in noxious fumes, it is a tight-jawed bronchial gargle punctuated with sharp vowel sounds. In the South people said they couldn't tell the Teesside and Tyneside accents apart. In fact the two are as different as Dutch and Italian. Geordie is full of pitches and swoops, the lilting tongue of people who love to talk. The Teesside accent is like the place that spawned it – it isn't pretty, but it gets the job done. Actually, that's not strictly true. When it comes to speech the Teessiders do allow themselves one frippery. They are very fond of polysyllabic words precisely used. Once on the train to Stockton I heard two gravel-voiced gadgies talking about TV programmes. 'Aye,' one of them boomed, 'it was a documentary narrated by Julian Pettifer.' He chewed on the words with lip-smacking relish as if they were a particularly choice pickled egg.

ICI's Billingham synthetics plant looms over Central Avenue Stadium like a giant's chemistry set. Unless you have ever stood near it it is impossible to imagine the vast unnaturalness of the place. Compared to ICI Billingham, Hammersmith

Broadway is a water meadow, the Birmingham Bull Ring a cottage garden in Kent. It stretches into the distance, miles on miles of towers and chimneys and stacks and sheds. Steel brachia and intestinal aluminium tubing swing from its flanks as if it were some huge metallic beast with a multiple hernia. And at night, on the other side of the Cleveland Hills where I was born, the colours it pumps out dye the sky pink and it throbs like a heart.

In the Social Club we sat drinking and eating peanuts. Outside the window there was a women's hockey match in progress. Two coachloads of Gateshead fans had just walked in and were talking to the barman about Boro's flying start to the season. He was saying: 'Hendrie's playing out of his skin. He's unstoppable, like.' I was only half listening. The cheap beer, the accents, the glint of autumn sunlight on the pale thighs of the hockey players, the whole thing had sent me into a coma of contentment and I found myself sliding into . . .

The 1940s. The lights were going out all over Europe, but that didn't bother buoyant Billingham – they were the first amateur team in the North with floodlights! Yet bright though those bulbs shone, they never burned so brightly as the Synners' stars of the post-war era. J. 'Biffer' Smith, a giant of a forward. Sacks of cement for shinpads and a neck so thick he used privy seats for shirt collars. 'Biffer' had a shot like a rocket. In 1942 during a cordite shortage in the Western Desert they got him to punt the shells into Jerry territory. He over-hit one of them and sunk a banana boat off the coast of Barbados. Or Bill McQuarrie, Scottish amateur international, a schemer, a mastermind, a Magnus Magnusson of the plumbline pass. He sold more dummies than Mothercare. And who could forget Christmas Day 1945, when Arthur Rhodes, a beaming, bounding, plum pudding of a man, as fiery as a raw radish, netted eight goals in a 9–2 thrashing of Southbank? A Christmas cracker indeed . . .

Luckily at this point someone farted and brought me back to reality.

Central Avenue Stadium had a look of severe neglect.

The 2,000-seat stand had been built in 1958 and seemed not to have been painted since. The cinder running track that theoretically circled the pitch was pitted with potholes and spotted with lichen, and seemed to disappear altogether once it rounded the curve to the opposite side of the ground. It had been raining heavily all week and there were pools of water everywhere. Across the fence, in one of the gardens on the Cowpen Estate, row on row of prize dahlias were waving in the breeze, as bright and gaudy as cheerleaders' pompoms. In the grey wash of industrial Teesside their colours seemed impossibly bright and incongruous. It was as if a tropical butterfly had landed on the nose of an accountant.

Fortified by by their subsidised beer, the Gateshead fans to our left were kicking up a racket. 'We are Heed, we are Heed, we are Heed,' they chanted. An elderly Synners supporter standing near the touchline turned and looked up at them with the bewilderment of a someone who had woken from an afternoon nap and come downstairs to find Pearl Jam playing a set in his front room. 'The Gateshead, the Gateshead,' they continued, 'He's short, he's square, he hasn't got nay hair, Alan Lamb, Alan Lamb.' Citizens of Rio probably wouldn't have recognised it as such, but in Billingham this was classed as a carnival atmosphere.

The teams ran out on to the field. Gateshead in natty black and white halved shirts, Synthonia in their rather dull green with white collars and cuffs. There had been a time when Billingham played in green and white quartered shirts, something which interested me no little since my junior school football team was equipped with just such a kit. In fact I think ours was Billingham's old kit. The shirts were certainly of ancient manufacture; they had double-thickness, button-through collars and cuffs, and they were so long and voluminous that when we ran out in them the opposition invariably pointed at us shouting, 'Dozy the Dwarf, Dozy the Dwarf!' We lost every match we played in, which was hardly surprising as any time one of us got the ball and tried to run with it he would trip over the hem of his shirt. I was captain. All this job involved was calling for three cheers for the opposition at the end of the game. Not a difficult task, unless of course you are ten years old and have just been caned 11–1 by Loftus Primary. On the way home in the school van from these débâcles, we'd all sit round, going, 'It doesn't matter . . . I'm not bothered . . . who cares . . .? Football's shite anyway . . .' Then I'd get out at my house and run indoors, and my mum would say, 'How did you get on?' And I'd open my mouth to repeat the salient points of this discussion to her, but the only sound that came out was '*Whaaaaaaah!*' I suppose it was all character-building. Unfortunately, the character it built for me was an embittered loser's.

If you've ever wondered what the difference between professional and amateur footballers is, the answer's thighs. The legs of the Gateshead players were uniformly shaped tubes of tanned muscle; Synners' pins, meanwhile, covered the whole spectrum of masculine bunting sticks from pigeon-toed to couldn't-stop-a-pig-in-a-passage. Gateshead were athletes, Billingham were blokes. Gateshead were better organised, too, the result of the extra hours spent training. They were managed by the ex-Newcastle player Tommy Cassidy. Even during his days at St James's Cassidy had been on the tubby side. Since retirement he had swelled to such an extent that the Central Avenue dugout fitted him like an overcoat. On the field Big Tommy had been noted for his delicacy of touch, often supplying the finely judged through balls off which Malcolm Macdonald fed. Gateshead, sadly, were not built in his image (except, rather literally, in the case of the left-back, a man so stocky I suspect that if he stood in the middle of the road traffic would treat him as a roundabout). They were disciplined, hard-working and difficult to score against. I know, just the sound of those words fair sets the pulse racing, doesn't it? In fairness, Gateshead also had a couple of skilful forwards. Sadly, the best of them, Paul Proudlock (formerly of Middlesbrough and Carlisle) was sent off midway through the first half when he was momentarily seized by the notion that he was playing in a rugby match and promptly stamped on a prone opponent.

In the GM Vauxhall Gateshead had kept enough clean

sheets to have gladdened the heart of a Swiss hotelier, so when Paul Dobson gave them the lead shortly after Proudlock's dismissal it seemed odds-on that they would be going into the draw for the next round.

It came as quite a surprise then, when, after forty minutes of total ineffectiveness, Billingham set up Richie Allen for an equaliser that provoked a pitch invasion by three small boys and a Yorkshire terrier. It was Synners' only chance of the afternoon. Denied the space and time they had enjoyed at Dunston, the forward line looked pedestrian and short of ideas. Charlie Butler, impressive at Federation Park and a former Gateshead player, seemed sluggish and out of sorts, perhaps disturbed by the shouts of 'How's the wife, Butler?' from some amateur marriage guidance counsellors amongst the Heed men. He was substituted long before the end.

Paul Dobson missed a couple of chances to win the game for Gateshead at the start of the second half and after that the game more or less fizzled out. Or at least it did for me. I was looking though the gaps at the back of the stand at the ICI plant, all 1,000 acres of it. My grandfather had worked there as a chargehand before and during the war. He cycled everyday from Markse-by-the-Sea, fifteen or so miles down the coast. When the war started my grandfather volunteered for Navy minesweepers, but ICI was a reserved occupation so he had to stay on at Billingham. To help the war effort on the day the men at ICI changed shifts they worked a double stint. On a change-over day my grandfather would get set off for work on his bike at 4.30 a.m., work from six till two, cycle home again, have a nap and something to eat, then cycle back for the night shift. In the space of twenty-four hours he would have cycled sixty-odd miles and worked sixteen hours in a chemical factory. There's no wonder he was always thumping people.

The game ended 1–1. Against all the odds Billingham won the replay by a single goal. They were knocked out in the next round by Leek Town.

Seaham Red Star v. West Auckland Town, FA Trophy Second Qualifying Round
Saturday 16 October 1993

I was standing on the sea front eating a bag of crisps. All along the clifftop there were men fishing. The crisps were Caribbean prawn cocktail flavoured: 'The food of the Caribbean is unique,' it said on the packet, 'Spanish and African cultures have been brought together under the Caribbean sun to add an exciting and unusual accent to the natural riches of the sea.' And here I was munching them in Seaham Harbour, County Durham. Talk about global village.

The fishermen seemed to me wildly optimistic. The natural riches of the Caribbean might have included prawns; the only thing you looked likely to catch in this particular stretch of the North Sea was a used condom and a case of dysentery. The water along the north Durham coast is the most polluted in Europe, the landscape at Seaham Harbour one of the least hospitable anywhere on earth. Old spoil heaps from the collieries spill out into the water, dying it an inky black. The sulphur from the coal poisons the soil. If you've seen *Alien 3* you already know what the area looks like. They filmed the scenes set on the aliens' home planet here. Seriously.

I walked up into Seaham town itself thinking about the state of English football. On the previous Wednesday, in Rotterdam, England had lost to Holland. There had been lots of talk about refereeing decisions but my abiding image of the game was of David Seaman lumbering across his goal, arms flapping, in an attempt to stop Koeman's free kick. He looked like a drunk pursuing a night bus. I recalled a time when goalkeepers were slim, agile men. Cat-like was the usual description. Nowadays the only cat most 'keepers resembled was Bagpuss. They did weight training. They were bulky, top-heavy and looked in constant danger of toppling over. Every time I saw one I was put in mind of the old joke about boxer Joe Bugner: he had the body of a Greek sculpture, but fewer moves. I'm not sure why it was that English goalkeepers became obsessed with bodybuilding. Some people put it down to the influence of Peter Shilton, though, personally, I suspect it has more to do with Sylvester Stallone's performance in *Escape to Victory*.

It was a cold day and Seaham had a Siberian bleakness about it. The town is unspectacularly ugly. There is little grass, no trees; lots of red brick, slate and tarmac. On a street corner a group of lads were buggering about with a Ford Escort. Beyond them, the winding gear of Seaham Colliery stood idle. There was a raw, naked feel to the place I had noticed in other mining towns. It was as if whatever had gone on under the ground had somehow sterilised the surface, so that you felt you were entering a void. The location scouts for *Alien 3* had chosen well. In Seaham, I got the impression, no one would hear you scream. Except in the paper shop, obviously. Which was just as well, as I'd just gone in and asked for a Mars bar. The woman behind the counter, who was wearing make-up so thick she probably had to crack it off with a toffee-hammer, served me, then turned to her friend who was leaning on the counter and said: 'Ah think that new lard's Torkish, mind. Cos ah cannut mak oot a ward worris seein.'

The players were out warming up at Seaham Town Park. As you walked along the path to the ground you saw flashes of them through the gaps between the fence pickets, apparently moving in jerky spasms like figures on an old magic lantern set. Red Star were a comparatively new addition to the Northern League. The club itself hadn't been founded until 1973 and had begun life as a Sunday pub team. Progress from then on had been remarkably swift. Seaham won some floodlights in a football competition in Birmingham in 1979, went up into the Wearside League the same year and did the League and

Cup double before winning election to the Northern League in 1983. They were promoted to the First Division in 1988. Along the way they had produced five players who had gone on to play League football, most notably Nigel Gleghorn (Ipswich and Manchester City) and Bobby Davison (Leeds United and Derby).

West Auckland Town, on the other hand, had been in existence for a hundred years and had yet to see any former players move up into the Football League. Their most famous old boys were Sid Weighell, who turned out for them in the late forties and later became head of the National Union of Railwaymen, and Jack Greenwell, the first Englishman to manage Barcelona. In 1909 and again two years later West Auckland had . . . Ah, but we'll save that till later.

West, as they were imaginatively nicknamed, came into the Northern League in 1922. They won the Championship in 1959–60 and again the following year. By so doing they achieved the signal honour of holding the Northern League title in the year of my birth. They celebrated by losing to Walthamstow in the final of the Amateur Cup at Wembley in front of 45,000 people.

Like most Northern League clubs, the records of Seaham and West Auckland in the FA Trophy were unremarkable. Neither side had ever progressed beyond the third round proper. The reason for the North-East's clubs' poor showing in the Trophy, in contrast to their domination of the old Amateur Cup, was traceable back to the FA's decision in 1972 to abolish the distinction between amateur and professional players. This policy, implemented two years later, had come about largely as a result of lobbying by county associations who were tired of the deceptions and cheating the old two-tier system had produced. With 'shamateurism' gone, all non-league teams were now, theoretically at least, on an equal footing. Clubs which had traditionally entered the Amateur Cup were now to compete in the FA Trophy and the FA Vase. The problem for the Northern League was that as a consequence of the record of its teams in the old competition, all its First Division clubs were entered in the Trophy. Teams such as Consett and Tow Law who regularly played in front of fewer than a hundred people found themselves in the same competition as non-league sides like Barnet, Scarborough and Wycombe Wanderers, whose crowds were large enough to support full-time professional players. Even the FA Vase, by dint of its selection criteria, included among its entrants some very well-supported clubs – that the reborn Aldershot (average crowd nearly 4,000) found themselves playing in the 1993–94 competition is merely one example. The old imposition of amateur status, riddled with deceit and hypocrisy though it was, had served to protect the Northern League's clubs from the economics of footballing success. Just as the abolition of the maximum wage in the Football League destroyed the balance of power which had previously existed between large and small clubs, so the removal of amateur status was to undermine the chances of the less wealthy non-league teams in the national cup competitions. Ironically, the two organisations which had campaigned hardest to bring about this situation were the Durham FA and the Northern League. In the interests of fair play they had cut their own throats.

There were about 130 people in the ground, clustered in the small stand and round the front of the red and white dressing-room and snack bar. Across on the other side of the ground the advertising hoardings touted the services of Mel Cardy – Joiner, Electrician Harry Burnicle and the Elves Fruit Stores – a bijou establishment hidden in a hollow tree in a dingly dell in the middle of the magic wood which sold melons the size of oranges, oranges the size of apricots and apricots so tiny you had to suck them up through a liquorice stick like sherbert. I think there was something in that Mars bar.

Five minutes before kick-off a man with a beatific grin, polyveldt shoes and an eight-year-old boy attached to his hand came and stood just in front of me. He cast his eyes around with the gleeful look of an evangelist who's just spotted a non-believer in an iron lung. Rubbing his palms together (he was wearing those ski gloves with the zips on the back that look like key fobs) he turned to the boy and said: 'Forget Wembley and Old Trafford, Simon. This is the lifeblood of English soccer.' I knew right away I was in the presence of the Master. Most fans consult the Dictionary of Familiar Football Phrases from time to time; the Masters compiled it.

The Master kept up a commentary to his son throughout a game in which 'delicate chips', 'dead-ball specialists', 'subtle probings', 'midfield promptings', 'towering headers', 'defensive lapses', 'clinical finishing' and 'the wily skills of the veteran Paul Walker' 'played a significant role'.

The only thing that raised comment from the rest of the crowd was the refereeing. This was common in non-league football in the North-East. The entry of the teams warranted hardly a clap, a forty-yard volley into the top corner only a murmur, but the instant the referee blew his whistle all hell broke loose. 'Get involved in the bloody game, linesman!' people roared. 'Has someone glued your book in your pocket, or what?' they yelled. 'Are you mental, man referee?' Sometimes I got the impression that many of the crowd would have been quite happy if the two teams stopped in the clubhouse, just so long as they sent the officials out to canter around copping abuse for ninety minutes. The Northern League was the starting place for a number of top referees, including the legendary 'Book 'em' Smith. Listening to this torrent of criticism it was easy to see why Pat Partridge and George Courtney turned out such twisted individuals.

West Auckland, playing in shirts so pale they looked as if Danny Baker had been using them to demonstrate how ordinary household powders fade even colour-fast fabrics, had, according to the Master, very much the better of the early exchanges culminating with their lively number 11 testing the woodwork from twenty yards. Having weathered the opening storm, Seaham gradually clawed their way back into the game. Midway through the half their measured passing style was rewarded when a thunderous drive from the edge of the penalty area buried itself in the top right-hand corner of West Auckland's net, with the goalkeeper stranded.

Red Star's next goal was even better. Struck from well

outside the box, it sent the scorer, a skinhead centre-back, into ecstasy. The Master missed this as he had gone to the Gents' to avoid the half-time rush. Luckily, I was able to inform him that to the delight of home fans a fulminating shot from fully thirty-five yards had cannoned in off the crossbar, so no clichés were wasted.

The second half began in much the same way as the first with West Auckland pressing for an equaliser. The more pressure they applied the more I started to suspect that Seaham's goalie was a relative of the Chorley 'keeper. Built on similar brick-shithouse lines, he had a voice like Oliver Hardy's after Stan Laurel has dropped an anvil on his foot. 'Left!' he howled. 'Right! Inside! Outside!'

'Goalkeeper very much the defensive organiser,' the Master commentated to his son.

'Send him! Channel him!' the goalie continued hysterically. 'Go long! Go short! I'm here if you need me, Micky! If you need me, Micky! Bend me! Shape me! Anyway you want me! As long as you love me, that's all right.'

'It's all about communication,' the Master noted didactically, and for a split second I had a vision of him at a management meeting at some company that makes pop-fasteners or incontinence pants, scribbling on a flip chart with a magic marker and saying, 'We have to seize control of our personal environment and establish credibility at the concept stage. We can't allow the word fear to enter our vocabulary.'

'You must be off your bloody rocker!' a man shouted, probably at the referee.

West Auckland pulled a goal back when the lively number 11, who had long, permed blond hair, a tan that looked more like the product of a blowlamp than a sunlamp, and bore an uncanny resemblance to seventies glamour-boy grappler Adrian Street, was felled inside the penalty area. The ageing McKimm scored from the spot.

'Kept a cool head under pressure,' the Master observed to his son, 'the game entering a crucial period for the home side.'

The penalty marked the high point of West Auckland's fightback. A few minutes later Paul Walker restored Seaham's two-goal lead.

The game ended 3–1. 'A lively contest, with plenty of goalmouth action at either end,' the Master remarked as he and the boy walked down the slope to the car park where their Ford Orion was waiting. The son stopped momentarily and looked up at his father. 'Dad,' he said. 'You're full of shit.'

Only joking.

I followed behind them, then crossed the road to the request stop. I stood waiting for the bus to Sunderland, thinking about Lord Byron. In 1815 he married Anne Milbanke in Seaham Hall. They signed their names in the registry of the local church. I don't suppose Lord Byron was much of a footballer. He had one foot that was totally useless. I know what you're thinking, but I reckon we should leave Lee Dixon out of this.

The next day Middlesbrough played Sunderland in a match televised live on Tyne Tees. My grandad had a thing about TV football commentators. What he particularly disliked about them was the fact they were paid vast sums of money for telling you things you already knew. '. . . And Bell's down injured,' David Coleman would squawk and my grandad would growl, 'I can see that for myself, you bloody tripehound,' as if affronted; as if Coleman was trying to start a barnie by suggesting he was short-sighted.

My grandad would have hated Roger Tames. Tames is the Tyne Tees TV sports producer who doubles as the station's main commentator. A balding man with a swanky moustache, a taste for foppish bow-ties and an uncanny resemblance to the ventriloquist Roger de Courcy, Tames is a commentator of the tell-you-exactly-what-you-can-see school. 'Rash challenge from Pollock,' he says. 'Gary Bennett gives the ball away,' 'Chris Morris falls over.'

To my mind there is something profoundly unsatisfactory about Roger Tames' commentaries, yet this intense obviousness is not it. The real problem is that Tames is just plain dull. Unlike John Motson, he doesn't preface drivelling trivia with the words 'it may be significant'; he doesn't adopt Brian Moore's gambit of making the most obtuse observation sound technical by the use of arcane phraseology (saying 'he's a possessor of good pace' instead of 'he's quick'), he never goes Barry Davies hysterical, or pursues a Tyldsleyesque analogy down a blind alley like a pit-bull scenting fear. In fact, Roger Tames totally fails to fulfil the prime role of the TV commentator, which is, as everybody knows, neither to explain nor to inform, but simply to afford the viewer the regular opportunity to point at the screen and shout: 'Thank you so much for sharing that with us, you sad bastard.'

As a producer Tames has cast his insipid spell over the whole of Tyne Tees' football coverage. Where once the North-East had *Shoot!* we now have *The Tyne Tees Match*. The change of name is in itself instructive – exclamation replaced by exposition. The only nod in the direction of snappiness is that they didn't call it 'The Live Tyne Tees Sunday Football Match'.

This change wasn't made overnight, though. When I first moved back to the region Tames was presiding over a Sunday afternoon sportsfest called *The Back Page*. As its name implies, this covered not only football but every other sport in the region too. With just thirty minutes of airtime available this was the televisual equivalent of trying to squeeze Giant Haystacks into Charles Hawtrey's long-johns.

Where *Shoot!* had offered twenty minutes or so of highlights from one of the region's home games and goals from the away matches, *The Back Page* showed the 'action' involving all seven clubs from the North-East and North Yorkshire in just a quarter of an hour. *The Back Page* was filmed on a set so old-fashioned and flimsy it made the one used for *Clapperboard* look like the Pompidou Centre. One of the programme's great innovations was to have all the available guests sitting on a central sofa right from the start of the programme, even though their turn to speak might not come for twenty-five minutes. As a result the viewer was treated to the edifying spectacle of some expert such as racing tipster Doug Moscrop sitting nervously through the match analysis. What should they do? Chip in with the odd comment? Retouch their nail varnish? Do a bit of needlepoint? In the end they usually opted for staring fixedly ahead, grinning self-consciously like a hitch-hiker stuck in a car with a rowing family.

The Back Page also introduced *The Tyne Tees Match*'s current studio anchorman, Duncan Wood. If Tames is Roger de Courcy, then Wood is the dummy. A whey-faced doughboy with a Marilyn Monroe beauty spot, he is a man with fear in his eyes. His terror stems from never quite being sure which camera he is on, or indeed if he is on one at all. With Wood every cut back to the studio is a moment of wince-making tension. There hasn't been anyone as uncomfortable in front of the cameras since Richard Nixon resigned.

When he finally does decide he's on air, Duncan Wood turns to his main task, interviewing the studio guests. For the Tees-Wear derby these were former Boro captain Tony Mowbray, wearing a suit containing so many different sizes and types of check that looking at it made you go boss-eyed, and Ally McCoist, whose spell at Roker Park had had about the same impact on the fans as an out-of-control 2CV would on the Maginot Line. The appearance of two such notable old boys was largely superfluous, however, because Wood's interviews are strictly rhetorical: 'Lennie Lawrence will be pretty happy with things at half-time, won't he Tony?' 'Terry Butcher will be thinking of making changes, wouldn't you say Ally?' And, heaven knows, you can't blame him. After all, if you asked a footballer a question and didn't tell him the answer at the same time he could say anything. 'What will be going through Don Goodman's mind as he waits to take this penalty, Ally?'

'Well, Duncan, he's probably wondering whether fish burp.'

Producing football coverage as sterile as this in an area like the North-East was a staggering achievement. But then, aside from the games it covered, *The Tyne Tees Match* was devoid of any regional flavour whatsoever. Although the show's main players were happy to trumpet on about 'this hotbed of soccer', none of the authentic atmosphere of football in the region was ever allowed to penetrate the twin vacuums of the commentary box and the TV studio. Away from the clichés the reality of the game in the North-East just seemed to pass them by.

'The Sunderland fans are really getting behind their team,' Roger Tames commented with Boro 4–1 up. And all across the region viewers listened to the Holgate End chanting 'Terry, Terry Butcher, Terry Butcher on the dole.'

It was a telling moment.

Blyth Spartans v. Tow Law Town, Federation Brewery Northern League Division 1
Saturday 23 October 1993

Catherine had been making piccalilli. The astringent odour of hot vinegar and mustard filled the house. Every time the dog went near the kitchen he sneezed. The smell of the piccalilli clung to the furniture, the carpets, our clothes. When I got on the train to Newcastle, people started dabbing their eyes as if someone had sprayed mace. The train was crowded, but I had a whole four-seat section all to myself. It's a useful tip for commuters.

It was a damp autumnal day. Frost had browned the dahlias in local allotments; the remains of the summer cabbages, ravaged by slugs, looked leprous. The gardeners were clearing up for winter. Bonfires of wet leaves burned, the white smoke merging with the mist that clung to the Tyne Valley in an opaque shroud, so that everything, no matter how close, seemed indistinct and distant. It was a scene which would have induced melancholy in anyone who looked at it. Fortunately I was too busy wrestling open a maxi-pack of cheese Quavers to bother.

I was looking forward to seeing Blyth Spartans. They had captured my imagination as a boy, less, it must be said, with their footballing skills, than with their name. As a child my favourite film was a well-oiled Hollywood epic about the battle of Thermopylae,. called *The 300 Spartans*. It starred Richard Egan, which, as students of cinema will know, is a name synonymous with quality. In the film the militaristic Spartans, a mere handful of warriors armed only with swords and impossibly deep American voices, gave the invading Persians a bloody nose, while the rest of Greece dithered about democratically. It was a victory for Spartan freedom over Persian tyranny. Though given that Spartan freedom meant compulsory nights sleeping naked on a frozen mountainside, some might have said Persian tyranny had its good points. Not to me, it didn't. Sparta seemed to offer everything I'd ever dreamed of: a shield, a sword, a spear, and nobody yelling 'Watch what you're doing! You could take someone's eye out with that thing!' every time I threw it at a passing cyclist. The age-old lure of the military dictatorship, I suppose.

Naturally enough, when, shortly after seeing this rubbish, I learned via Frank Bough that there was a team named after Richard Egan and his gallant lads, I was delighted. I had charted their progress ever since, save for a small blip when I discovered that their kit didn't actually include plumed helmets. I suppose they would have made heading difficult.

Formed in 1899, Blyth Spartans spent most of their history playing in the semi-professional North-Eastern League, which also included Newcastle, Middlesbrough and Sunderland Reserves, and clubs which had dropped out of the old Third Division (North) such as Ashington and Durham City. Spennymoor, Consett and North Shields also fielded teams. In light of the strength of amateur football in the North-East during this period it's safe to assume that the standard of the semi-professional game was even higher, given that the prospect of earning extra money must have been particularly tempting for the working-class men who made up the bulk of the players. The fact that Spartans won only one North Eastern League title in half a century compared with the ten Championships they have picked up since joining the Northern League thirty years ago tells its own story. Spennymoor's record paints a similar picture. The absence of any national semi-professional knock-out competition to compare with the Amateur Cup, however, meant that, but for the occasional FA Cup run, the teams of the North-Eastern League toiled away in relative obscurity while their amateur counterparts won the headlines with their frequent Wembley appearances.

After the North-Eastern League folded in 1958, Blyth dithered about for six seasons before finally biting the billy-can and turning amateur. They joined the Northern League in 1964, and severely dented my cast-iron theorising by finishing bottom in their first season. The buggers.

Spartans reached the Amateur Cup semi-final in 1972 and took their first Northern League title the following season. They were champions again in 1975 and 1976, but it was the events of the 1977–78 season that were to bring Blyth Spartans national fame and lead then FA secretary Ted Croker to describe them as 'the most famous non-league side in the country'.

That season Spartans came within seconds of becoming the first non-league side to go through the quarter-finals of the FA Cup. Having already disposed of Stoke City in the previous round, they were leading Wrexham 1–0 at the Racecourse Ground when referee Alf Grey awarded a controversial injury-time corner kick to the Welshmen. Grey then ordered Wrexham to retake the kick three times because the corner flag kept falling over. At the third attempt Dixie McNeil got the equaliser. In the replay at St James's Park 42,000 people saw Blyth go down 2–1. 'It's the only time I've ever cried because we lost,' a fan who was there told me.

That Blyth team included three England semi-pro internationals, Dave Clarke, Keith Houghton and Les Mutrie, former Newcastle United man Ron Guthrie, and Alan Shoulder, who was later to join the Magpies. Alongside them were men such as Eddie Alder, a neat midfielder with a balding pate and facial hair so extravagant it wasn't so much a pair of sideboards as a fully fitted kitchen; Terry Johnson, a prolific goalscorer and Joe Walsh lookalike; and Steve Jones, who scored the goal that knocked out Arthur Cox's Chesterfield in the second round. They rank along with the Bob Hardisty era Bishop Auckland, the Stockton team of R. A. 'Bullet' Smith and Joe Harvey's Crook Town as one of the finest sides the Northern League has produced.

The bus rumbled through the northern suburbs of Newcastle, on into Cramlington, a new town so flat as to be positively subterranean, and out across open fields towards Cambois. Cambois (pronounced 'Cammus') enjoyed a spell of notoriety some years ago because it had the only naturist beach in the North-East. This facility had been set up by the go-ahead local council as part of a tourism intiative that seemed to ignore local conditions totally. The wind howls in off the North Sea along the Northumbrian coast, and in combination with the sharp sand of the beaches it has a strongly abrasive effect. Rumour has it that one hapless nudist had his genitals sand-blasted clean away. Sadly, when the wind isn't blowing off the sea, Cambois beach has another problem. It's right next to a fish-paste factory. The smell's so strong it bleaches seagulls and peels the paint off passing cars.

As the bus approached Blyth I got my first sight of the wind turbines along the harbour wall. A few years before I'd been in the barber's and a bloke who worked for the company that erected them was in getting a basin bill. There had been trouble getting planning permission for the turbines, he said. 'I can't understand it,' he said. 'It's not exactly a beauty spot, Blyth, is it?' And the rest of us laughed knowingly. Walking across to the harbour now I felt ashamed that I'd joined in. After all, it's a pretty threadbare argument. It's like a defence lawyer in an assault and battery case saying, 'Take a look at the plaintiff, ladies and gentlemen of the jury. Who's he trying to kid? He's not exactly Keanu Reeves, is he? Surely no one would possibly notice a few more scars and scabs on a face that already resembles a relief map of Cumbria?'

Blyth wasn't a beauty spot, it's true, but it was a pleasant enough place, although I should point out that being brought up in close proximity to Teesside has given me a very high tolerance of ugliness. Had Perseus been from Middlesbrough, when the Medusa turned her glare on him he'd simply have said, 'Smile, luv, it may never happen,' then tried to pat her bottom.

Croft Park was the first non-league ground I'd been to in the North-East where you could see people in front of you going to the game. It would be an exaggeration to say there was a stream of fans heading towards the ground, but there was definitely seepage in that direction. Blyth are the best supported of the Northern League clubs, attracting crowds of 1,000 and more for big games. For the visit of Tow Law there were around 400 spectators dotted about the stepped cinder terracing, or sitting in the grandstand. Blyth were top of the Northern League. They were unbeaten in their first fourteen games of the season.

Spartans are sponsored by *Viz* comic, the programme carries a picture of Roger Mellie and the Fat Slags on the cover, and the team shirts are the smartest in the Northern League – green and white stripes with neat little lace-up collars. When the deal was first struck it was said that the shirts would carry the sponsor's message, 'Drink Beer. Smoke Tabs'. In the end, fearing no doubt that such a step would result in a whole generation of young North-Easterners giving up mineral water and Tai-Chi in favour of stout and cigarettes, they settled for the comic's logo in red.

The first half of the game was enlivened by a fine display of ill temper by Marc Irwin, the Tow Law centre-half. Right from the kick-off Irwin was stomping about the pitch with a scowl so severe he made Roberto Rivelino look like Sally Sunshine, but when Hallam broke through and crossed for Middleton to put Blyth in front, he went into overdrive. A towering blond-haired man with an angular frame which appeared to contain twice the regular complement of knees and elbows, Irwin was perhaps aggravated by the cries of 'Lurch' and 'Herman Munster' which greeted his every touch. Whatever it was, the goal led to a dispute with the linesman which appeared to conclude with the words 'I'll bloody drop you'. Thereafter, Irwin, who actually wasn't a bad player when he had his mind on the game, crashed about upending opponents, berating officials and fixing anyone who came within range with a glare that had 'Your dangly bits are going in the blender' written all over it in day-glo letters. The referee, a prancing poodle of a man with all the disciplinary control of a French teacher, passed this off as if it were some sort of boyish tomfoolery. His occasional attempts at a crackdown were greeted by the players with the sidelong looks and wry smirks of schoolmates. I could foresee that after the game they would wait until he went into a telephone box and then weld him into it. And he would say in this avuncular, one-of-the-boys voice: 'Come on now, lads, I've got as much of a sense of humour as the next man but— Where are you taking me? Put this thing down. Straight away! Now! I'm beginning to lose my— What's that noise? A waterfall? I think if you actually stop to think about the consequences of what you're about to do, lads, you'll realise it isn't really a very sensible ideahhhhh.' The following Monday, at an assembly of all the Northern League players, the head of the Referees Association would say: 'A joke's a joke, but the boys who drowned Mr Rickerby of Witton-le-Wear in the Wansbeck on Saturday afternoon have gone too far. I expect the chaps responsible to report to my study immediately after hymn practice. And woe betide you if you haven't got some reasonable explanation for your actions.'

While all this wasn't going on the players were engaged in an entertaining game of football. Irwin decided to join in again in the forty-second minute, contributing a blatant trip in the penalty area on Spartans' Don Peattie and following it up with attempted assault when he saw the prancing poodle point to the spot. Steve Pyle put Blyth two up from the kick.

They must have shot Irwin with a tranquilliser gun at half-time because he came out a completely changed man. Ditching the rebel-without-a-ball persona, he tackled cleanly, passed creatively and even at one point essayed a neat back-heel flick. Spurred on by this transformation, the Lawyers pulled a goal back through Barker.

Thirty seconds later Blyth were two goals in front again thanks to a stunning header from Hallam, who dived full length to get on the end of English's cross. Undeterred by the setback, Tow Law continued to attack. Twenty minutes of non-stop pressure produced nothing for the Lawyers but a series of half-chances and near misses. An elderly Tow Law fan standing near me could stand it no longer. Taking a swig from his hip-flask he piped up in a cracked voice, 'Might as well go home now, lads. Blyth are invincible.'

And so, it seemed, they were.

It had been a funny week for Andy Cole. First of all his close friend Lee Clark had been threatened with transfer for toe-ending a bucket during Newcastle's defeat at Southampton, then Cole himself had scarpered before a League Cup tie against Wimbledon. As virtually the whole country spends its time avoiding Wimbledon matches Cole had the nation's sympathy; Kevin Keegan, however, wasn't amused. When Cole arrived back, his boss was standing behind the door, tapping his foot irritably and clutching a rolling pin.

According to the national press, Cole was finding life difficult in the North-East. It was a familiar cry. For as long as I could remember players had been coming up to the region parroting on about football being more like a religion up there, fervour of the fans, sleeping giants, blah, blah, blah, then leaving again a few months later saying they were 'unable to settle in the area'. Personally, I didn't find this a bit surprising. After all, what has the North-East got to offer sophisticated individuals such as Kenny Sansom or Dave Beasant? Picture the scene. The player and his family arrive in the North-East. Their first port of call is the local tourist information centre. It is with an intense feeling of dismay that they discover the region has no opera company, no symphony orchestra, no fringe theatres specialising in challenging dramas from the old Eastern Bloc. Down at the record store there are no Philip Glass CDs, and a request for the minimalist work of Michael Nyman draws only a blank look from the man behind the counter. The player's children pine for *sushi* and lemongrass, and traditional pantomimes updated to include savage indictments of post-industrial economic policy, his wife can't find a rebirthing therapist in the yellow pages and the manager of the local multiplex has never even heard of Jean-Luc Godard. No, the average Northern footballer might be content to live in a land full of golf clubs, racecourses, snooker halls and pubs, but you can't expect his urbane metropolitan counterpart to be satisfied by such rough pleasures. He is a man who craves culture as others would a full steak dinner with all the trimmings.

Having got that off my chest, in fairness to Andy Cole, it must be said that his own situation was exacerbated by two additional factors. First, from being a relative unknown in an unsuccessful Bristol City team, he had suddenly found himself one of the stars in a side so popular that 15,000 people were regularly locked out of their home games. Secondly, he is black.

Because Newcastle train at Maiden Castle in Durham, Cole had moved into a house in nearby Crook. One national broadsheet observed that in such an isolated community the sight of a black man walking down the street was likely to stop the traffic. In some cases they were being too kind. There were a number of drivers in the North-East who would not have braked at the spectacle, but put their foot down and mounted the pavement.

I'm not sure whether racism is more prevalent in the North-East than elsewhere (experience of working in the East End of London suggests not). Certainly, though, racism exists and at times the everyday friendliness of the region's people makes it more obvious and wounding when it does occur. In an area like West Yorkshire, where abrasiveness is a much-treasured virtue, many slights and insults might be passed off as normal behaviour devoid of any other connotations. In the North-East, a place that prides itself on a justifiable reputation for warmth and kindness, any display of truculence, racially inspired or not, stands out like a turd on a trifle.

During his first few games for Newcastle Cole had been barracked by home supporters at the Leazes End. Though the abuse came from a tiny minority of idiots, it was hardly likely to make a quiet and introverted man feel at home. It would be nice to think that the fact that those same morons were now chanting Cole's name showed a change of heart. Sadly, I suspect it would take more than a single individual's brilliance to bring that about. I'm not certain how you radically alter the outlook of someone who takes such a perverse pride in the colour of his skin ('Great news, Dad! I'm white!' 'Congratulations, son. I knew all that hard work would pay off in the end'), though I reckon pulling the pin out of a hand grenade and then forcing him to swallow it might work in the short term.

Middlesbrough v. Peterborough United, Endsleigh Insurance League Division 1
Saturday 30 October 1993

The train chuntered through Heworth. I was eating a sandwich. I was trying to do so as secretively as possible because a friend of ours had once been sitting doing a similar thing by Grey's Monument in Newcastle when a youth with a skin condition that resembled an explosion in a scotch egg factory sat down beside her and said, 'What you got filling your farge, pet?' Our friend, who was from London and didn't know that a farge is a type of flat bread roll, thought the youth was making an obscene suggestion and promptly drove her index finger up his left nostril, while screaming for help. It's the sort of dramatic linguistic confusion that can easily arise in a region with an unusual and distinctive dialect. Fortunately, since the birth of their child the two of them have managed to sort things out.

Anyway, as I was going to say before I decided to make that story up, I was eating my sandwich secretly because it had alfalfa and tahini in it and I didn't want anyone to know. I was worried someone would notice and say, 'Alfalfa and tahini? What's the matter with you, mate? Did your mother want a girl or something?' To fend off this potentially life-threatening situation I had been constructing an alibi based around the old fail-safe male defence of blaming a woman. I imagined someone fixing me with a suspicious look and saying, 'What's that in your sandwich?' And me shrugging and pulling a face and saying, 'Don't ask me, kidder. It could be owt. Since my mam turned fifty she's just gone mental.'

Won over, my questioner would nod understandingly. 'Hormones, probably,' he'd say.

'No,' I'd reply, 'I think it's bean sprouts.'

Sadly no one seemed remotely interested in what I was eating, so I'm unable to report whether my plan worked or not.

Wheezing and rattling like a consumptive's chest, the train pushed on down the Durham coast, through Ryhope, where vandals had set fire to the local Northern League team's clubhouse, and Seaham, where there were goalposts whitewashed on to the gable ends of row on row of terraced houses; on past Easington, Horden and Blackhall. It was a picturesque landscape, but only if the picture you had in mind was by Francis Bacon. This was the eastern edge of the Durham coalfield. In the 1930s there had been close to 140 pits in the county. Now there was one. The colliery towns and villages loitered about the spoil heaps, growing older and gradually falling apart. The coastline here was craggy and topped by grass as white and spiky as a Goth's mohican; sheer cliffs dropped away into the foaming sea. There were no bays or harbours; no ships or boats offering the prospect of escape. Oddly, though, there were plenty of horses. Pie-bald, spindle-shanked drays lolloped about on every patch of waste ground. Some were tethered, others wandered freely, wrenching up hanks of turf with teeth the colour of stained china. I didn't know who they belonged to, or why there were so many of them. I began to suspect that they'd been put there deliberately by some local Enterprise Agency in a bid to encourage a major Japanese glue manufacturer to set up a factory in the area: 'Yes, Mr Yamamoto, high unemployment ensures low wage levels, and as you can see, here on the doorstep are all the raw materials you need. Come on, Neddy, Mr Yamamoto's got a nice apple for you . . .'

There's something about the surname Anderson that invites the epithet 'bloody'. There was Bloody Bill Anderson, Confederate cavalry leader during the American Civil War; Bloody Jack Anderson, the cobbler from Marske my grandad clattered because his dog kept biting our Micky, and then there was

Bloody Stan Anderson, the footballer and football manager who was born in Horden in 1933.

Stan Anderson holds the unique distinction of having captained all the North-East's 'big three' clubs (I use the term 'big' advisedly in the case of the Boro, who could more accurately be described as 'definitely larger than average, but not in a way that's immediately obvious'). He began at Roker Park during the 'Bank of England' era, playing in a side that lost in two FA Cup semi-finals and finished as runners-up in the Championship. He left in 1963 after Sunderland had missed promotion back into the top flight by losing at home to Chelsea in the final match of the season, joining Newcastle for £19,000. Two years later Newcastle won the Second Division Championship. The following April, when Raich Carter resigned as Middlesbrough manager, Stan Anderson left St James's for Ayresome Park, and a side who were about to slide into the Third Division for the first time in their history.

Apart from the blip in his first full season when Boro gained promotion back into the Second, from 1966 until 1973 Anderson presided over an unprecedented period of tranquillity. In those unheady days, excitement was off the menu and the only thing likely to set your heart racing at Ayresome Park was a cappuccino at Rea's on your way to the match.

Anderson built up a good squad at Middlesbrough, but through an unerring combination of player demotivation and the unhappy knack of always selling the key man at totally the wrong moment, he managed to keep them safe from the mean streets of Division 1 for season after season.

Every summer was enlivened by the headline in the local paper announcing that Stan had 'found the missing piece in the jigsaw' above a picture of Johnny Vincent, Hughie McIlmoyle or some other much-travelled goal-machine with faulty cogs and an 'out of order' notice stuck on his forehead. This story appeared so often that had the jigsaw sections been real rather than metaphorical Stan would have had enough for a tasteful 3,000-piece picture of Windsor Castle.

I walked up towards Ayresome Park through the back streets, up past Archibald School, one of those looming Victorian buildings that look as if they should be surrounded by barbed wire and conning towers and run by Anthony Valentine wearing a monocle and a fake duelling scar. Archibald School is where Don Revie was educated. I have always found it hard to accept that Don Revie came from Middlesbrough. Something about his money-grabbing and his lip-licking edginess doesn't seem to fit. I can't reconcile his lack of humour, his paranoia or his dour pragmatism with Teesside. I said this to Bill Brewster. He said, 'I can.' Which was nice of him.

Revie first made his name playing for Hull City. His mentor at Boothferry Park was Raich Carter (see how it all comes together, as if linked by some invisible thread? Thought not). Carter was a snappily dressed chap who bore a striking resemblance to the off-screen Charlie Chaplin and had a pair of cheekbones so high they were partially obscured by his eyebrows. In later years, when his dark hair had turned silver, Carter's alleged fondness for the ladies earned him the nickname 'the Great White Hunter'. Revie, by contrast, was big-chinned, pale and gangly with crinkly hair that appeared to have been applied from a can of shaving foam. A sort of footballing Douglas Hurd.

Revie idolised the great Real Madrid side of the fifties and early sixties. As a player he tried to emulate the intelligent mastery of Alfredo Di Stefano, the 'Golden Arrow'. As a manager he changed Leeds United's kit from blue and yellow to all white. His romanticism, however, stopped short of encouraging his teams to mimic Real's flamboyant playing style. This was what characterised Revie's management. He wanted to do the right thing, encourage attractive football, develop creative players, but something at the back of his mind always stopped him. And that thing was fear. Revie talked a lot about the will to win, but it was the terror of losing that really motivated him. So he selected skilful men, then instilled them with cynicism, just to be on the safe side.

Throughout his career at Elland Road and later as England

boss, Revie was renowned for his shameless opportunism when it came to making money. Probably the greatest legacy of his days in charge of the national side was a kit deal with Admiral that left him considerably richer and Kevin Keegan and co. running round in shirts with a red, white and blue design that appeared to have been copied off the tail-lights of a Ford Zodiac. Greediness, too, was part of Revie's fear. No matter how much money he had it was never enough to make him safe. Over his shoulder he must always have seen Archibald School, and the life he might have led. Revie's upbringing in Middlesbrough frightened him for the rest of his life. As he grew up in the same street as my grandad and his brothers, I can see why.

The Don never had much to do with Middlesbrough FC. His only contribution to the club's history was that he advised Jack Charlton to take on the job of managing it. The year 1993 was the twenty-fifth anniversary of that appointment.

Charlton took over from Stan Anderson, added just one player, Bobby Murdoch, to the squad and led Boro to the Second Division Championship by fifteen clear points. His management style owed much to Revie, and so did his dress sense. The two things dovetailed during Charlton's ritual collection of the tracksuits before kick-off. It was a typical piece of Revie the-boss-looks-after-his-boys psychology. Charlton would stand there laden down with nylon leisurewear, in drainpipe trousers, winklepicker shoes and a belted leather coat. With his angular face and scrape-over hair do he was a dead ringer for seedy detective Frank Marker in the TV series *Private Eye*. He doesn't do the tracksuit collection routine with the Republic of Ireland, I notice. But then, players don't warm up in tracksuits any more. Why did they in the seventies? Was it colder then? Or had the permissive age and the success of the musical *Hair* encouraged everyone to believe that taking garments off in public was deeply therapeutic? If the latter was the case then I suppose we should just be grateful that Alan Foggon and Bobby Murdoch didn't go the whole hog and treat us to a full-frontal rendition of 'The Age of Aquarius'.

Promotion was secured, as it had been from the Third

under Anderson, with a home victory over Oxford, a David Armstrong shot crawling in like a weary commuter.

There wasn't much of a queue to get into the Holgate End, but there was a delay all the same. In front of me a man was arguing with a policeman about a stool. He was saying, 'My son stands on it. If he doesn't he can't see anything.'

'You can't bring it in,' the policeman said.

'Why not?'

'You could throw it at someone.'

The man, who was in his early forties, said: 'Do I look like the sort of person who'd throw a stool at someone?'

The policeman looked him up and down and decided that he didn't. 'All right,' he said. 'Go on.'

As the man thanked him and prepared to go through the turnstiles, someone in the next queue pointed at him. 'Hey, look, Kev,' he shouted, 'it's that bloke that's always throwing stools.'

It was the afternoon's last display of good humour. There were fewer than 11,000 fans at Ayresome Park. Boro were third in the table, but the galloping start to the campaign had failed to persuade anyone that the previous season's relegation had been the result of ill fortune. The 4–1 thrashing of Revie's old club, Leeds United, had been barely twelve months before. It seemed like a lifetime.

The supporters were disgruntled. Middlesbrough had entered the Football League at the turn of the century. In over ninety seasons they had won nothing. They had spent nearly half their time in the old First Division and never finished higher than fourth; they had never got beyond the sixth round of the FA Cup, or the semi-finals of the League Cup. If the trophy cabinet at Ayresome Park was bulging, it was only as a result of malnutrition. Since the opening up of the League pyramid even Middlesbrough's one minor claim to fame had gone: they were no longer the only Football League club to have won the Amateur Cup. Yet despite close to a century of non-achievement, club officials were still counselling the fans to be patient. Personally, I felt we'd been patient for long enough. By this stage even Gandhi would have nutted someone.

At Roker Park Peterborough had never looked likely to score. They didn't at Ayresome, either. Except, of course, when they did. After ten minutes the ball looped over the top of the Middlesbrough centre-backs and the Nigerian striker Dominic Iorfa galloped after it, Derek Whyte trailing behind him with the hopeless, aggrieved tread of someone who's just noticed his pocket's been picked and knows it's too late to do anything about it. Iorfa whacked the ball past Stephen Pears. The crowd was outraged. Even the woolly mammoth of a man who normally spends most of the game in a recumbent position on the concrete terracing forcing beefburgers into his vast maw like some downmarket Roman emperor got to his feet. People were booing and whistling and in the centre of the stand the chant of 'Where's the money gone?' began in earnest.

The game lapsed into much the same pattern as Peterborough's match at Sunderland had done. Middlesbrough attacked, Posh defended. The crowd jeered and howled at every missed chance. Boro hit the post, the bar. Bennett in the Peterborough goal pulled off a brilliant double save from Wilkinson. When Morris overhit a centre the bloke in front of me yelled: 'You couldn't put a cross on a fucking pools coupon!' His face was white with anger.

Eventually, inevitably, Mustoe equalised. Even this hardly lifted the crowd. There was a feeling around that Middlesbrough were in their worst shape for years; that they were sliding back into the mire that had seen them go into liquidation in 1986. Good players had been sold and not replaced, gates were dropping, behind the scenes the club seemed a shambles. You might have expected the anticipation of disaster to galvanise the supporters into some kind of positive action. Perversely, it had the opposite effect. It was as if they knew what was coming and just wanted to get it over with as quickly as possible.

I found myself thinking wistfully about Middlesbrough's first Football League club, the improbably named Middlesbrough Ironopolis. The Nops played, in maroon and green stripes, at the Paradise Field and once entertained supporters with an evening friendly by gaslight. You could imagine them dashing trickily about in the flickering gloom, suede-brush moustaches and cropped heads (it's amazing how closely photos of Edwardian football teams resemble snapshots of a Gay Pride march), shorts like deflated barrage balloons, boots the size of battleships, shirts so stiff with starch they didn't so much flap as vibrate. The referee in jodhpurs and a flat cap blowing the whistle for a goal-kick and the 'keeper, a Desperate Dan figure with a torso the shape of a butter tub, purposefully hitching up his trousers and then running in and hoofing the ball into orbit. The centre-half, a skinny split pin of a chap, getting underneath it. The ball, untreated leather that soaked up water quicker than a camel's hump, dropping from the sky and landing with such force on the top of the centre-back's head that it drives him into the muddy ground like a steam-hammer driving in a rivet, so that only his head is visible above the turf. The foundry and furnace men around the touchline, swaddled in the thick wool clothes that protect them from the heat when they're working and from the cold when they're home, pointing at the centre-half's disembodied head and yelling, 'Away, Billy man, make a contribution.'

Sadly, Ironopolis had folded in 1894, leaving us with this shower.

In the second half, with Boro attacking the Holgate End, I watched Craig Hignett, five yards in from the by-line, fake to pass the ball out to Morris, let it run through his legs instead and sell the full-back so completely he took two yards off him. It was the sort of thing that would normally have gladdened my heart, but in the pessimistic mood of Ayresome Park it only made me wonder how long we'd be able to keep a player that good.

The game ended 1–1. The teams left the field in a blizzard of abuse. I walked down Linthorpe Road to the art gallery. The art collections of towns and cities are odd things. Carlisle's, for example, contains a lot of Pre-Raphaelites, Newcastle's is heavy with early Victorian landscapes. Middlesbrough's prize possessions are a pair of paintings of Purgatory by Hieronymous Bosch. That afternoon I found them strangely comforting.

for example, contains a lot of Pre-Raphaelites; Newcastle's is heavy with early Victorian landscapes; Middlesbrough's

Langley Park v. Esh Winning Albion, Commercial Union Durham Challenge Cup Second Round
Saturday 6 November 1993

The old man standing beside Bill and I groaned every time the ball was hoofed into the air. He was wearing an Asics coat and had a face as gnarled as a bonsai tree. He kept glancing in our direction and I could tell he was keen to talk to us. A decade in London had made me suspicious of strangers who wanted to chat. They might look normal, they might even sound normal – at first. But two minutes into the conversation you could guarantee they'd suddenly grasp your shoulder and hiss, 'Mossad kidnapped me. They took away the left side of my brain. They're holding it hostage in Dorking. It's my brother, you see. He knows their secret. Listen! Can you hear? They're in the sewers. They're under our feet . . .'

Things were tough enough in Langley Park without being bearded by a Zionist conspiracy theorist with a kneb like an oak apple. The place could have been the set for a Karel Reisz film. You felt you should be watching in black and white. Behind one of the goals a group of boys with pale, pinched faces and tight jumpers had abandoned their bikes among the tussocky grass and were kicking a chapped, white casey against a clapboard fence. A flock of flat-capped old codgers was congregating in what appeared to be an abandoned cowshed on the opposite touchline, filling it with tobacco smoke and talk of surgical appliances. To our right was a group of lads in suede jackets and hair gel. The smell of Paco Rabanne was strong enough to stun a canary. After a few minutes of standing near them the skin on my face started to sting. I had become the first-ever victim of passive shaving. The lads were in their late teens and they all had love-bites. If a tangerine face was a must among the youth of Tyneside, then love-bites were the equivalent in County Durham. The teenagers in Bishop Auckland, Darlington and Durham City looked like the victims of a particularly blunt-toothed vampire with only a sketchy knowledge of the pulmonary system: 'Hef patience, my little one. I vill hit ze jugular next time for zer-tain.' Their throats were the hoisted tricolour – red, yellow, blue – of revolting adolescent hormones.

Once, during a trip to Crook, I absent-mindedly conducted an unofficial Love-Bite Championship of the World, marking the bruised necks of the pimply herberts I passed en route for number, coverage and shade. The eventual winner, spotted slurping a Slush Puppy at a bus stop in Brandon, had six hickies strung around his throat, each the size and colour of an Amazonian shrunken head. The youth was spindly, with wispy ginger hair, a velcro moustache and an Adam's apple so prominent it gave him the appearance of a cartoon ostrich which had just swallowed an alarm clock. The look on his face suggested he'd sat on something wet and as yet unidentified. His right index finger was jammed in his ear. It was hard to imagine what sort of desperate creature would have been driven to heights of uncontrollable passion by this geeky plank, though given the choice between kissing his crusty cheek or biting him till he bled I know which I'd have opted for.

'Ooargh!' the man with the bark visage rumbled as the Esh Winning goalkeeper made another attempt to bring down Telstar. He shook his head and looked at me. I pretended to be watching the game. And there was plenty to watch – though not much of it had anything to do with football.

Langley Park were lying fifth in the Second Division of the Northern League. Esh Winning Albion, from a few miles up the road towards Consett, were one place off the bottom in the Vaux Wearside League Division 2. The difference between Gateshead and Billingham had been the thighs. At this level it was the socks. Langley Park's were uniform and clean; Esh Winning's were an odd assortment of styles most of which had the greyish hue that bespeaks senility in a white sock.

Esh had not won a game all season. This was certainly not because they lacked combativeness. Far from it. They bristled with belligerence from the opening whistle, registering their first booking after four minutes, the opening shove in the chest after five; 'You want to back your fucking big mouth up, bonny lad?' made its debut thirty seconds later. In the middle of the fighting a game of football momentarily broke out and Langley Park scored. Albion reacted angrily, one player stamping his foot down so hard he dislocated his knee and had to be carried off. 'Dunno what happened,' he announced to a group of girls in A-line mini-skirts who were shivering on the touchline. 'It just popped out,' he said, managing, despite the pain, to produce a suggestive leer. The girls rocked back and forth on blue legs, cackling insanely.

Esh Winning reorganised. The number 9, a burly, dark-browed individual whose shins were improbably wider than his thighs, and who had accounted for the early caution with a trip so reckless even Ranulph Fiennes would have turned it down, moved back into the heart of the defence where he partnered a centre-half who bore an uncanny resemblance to the late John Belushi, but was marginally less mobile.

'He's either swapped position,' I said to Bill, 'or he's adopting the deep-lying Di Stefano role.'

'Did you see him play, Di Stefano?' It was the old bloke. Bollocks.

'No.' I said firmly.

The man smiled. 'What a player! What. A. Player. Brilliant,' he said. 'Majestic.' He had the same speech patterns as local boy Bobby Robson. His sentences were short, jabbing bursts. Listening to them was the aural equivalent of being trapped in a telephone box with an irate Roberto Duran. 'He just stood. In the centre circle. Directing operations. Like a traffic policeman.' He demonstrated, waving his hands, pointing, kicking out his left and right feet in various directions (it was evidently the Los Angeles traffic police he had in mind).

'Fantastic,' he said. 'Absolutely fantastic.' He was warming to the story. The sentences came rushing out as if under pressure; as if he were a kettle and his words were steam. 'Di Stefano, Puskas, Gento. Eintracht Frankfurt. Hampden Park. Six-three. What a performance! The game as it was meant to be played. Football!' He invested the word with such power and reverence I almost fell to my knees weeping.

'Short passes,' he continued, 'on the ground. What's this headcase doing now?' He gestured towards the field where an Esh Winning player, earlier identified by Bill as 'looking like he might be useful in a pub brawl' was jabbing a finger into the lower ribs of a tall Langley Park defender as if testing to see whether he was wearing a corset.

'Chin him, Kenny,' one of the love-bite lads shouted. 'Drop the fucker!'

The man shook his woody head in disgust. 'Coached him,' he said, throwing out a thumb in the direction of the poker, 'that one. Not a bad player. Prefers fighting to football. This is just an excuse. Disgraceful. Half of them are the same. It's out of hand. And the language!' He looked heavenwards. 'I tell you,' he said, 'I reffed a match here. One Sunday. I warned them. Any swearing. You're going. I might as well of spat at the wall. One lad. Twenty minutes in. He says: "I've had enough of this." And he went. Just like that. Fucked off.' He executed a few short, shoulder-hunched steps away from us, then turned back. 'It's not good enough. Not out there,' he nodded at the pitch where Keith Gardener, Langley Park's skilful young forward, had just been dumped face-first in the mud by another late challenge, 'not on the football field. Bugger off somewhere else. If you want to do that.' He looked at us to see if we understood what he was talking about, and I think we did. For older people like him whose collective memory was scarred by the Depression – 50 per cent unemployment, the chalk crosses of the means test men – it was easy to see why the football field, where everyone started equal and skill and hard work only were rewarded, would come to represent an idealised vision of the world; a place where, as in church, higher standards applied. Victorian gentlemen had conceived a notion that football prepared a chap for life. No game on earth, barring one which involved being whacked repeatedly on the head with a lump-hammer by someone wearing a silk hat, could have been preparation for a struggle as inestimably hard as that of the ordinary people in the North-East during the inter-war years. For them sport was not an education in reality but an escape from it. A glimpse of something better.

The half-time whistle blew. A man came round selling raffle tickets. 'Win a meat packet, lads,' he said.

'What's a meat packet?' Bill said. 'Some type of jock-strap?'

In the clubhouse there were photos of Bobby Robson. He was honorary president of the club. Robson had been born at nearby Sacriston. His family had moved to Langley Park when he was a boy. He'd played junior and senior football in the village, but not for Langley Park FC. By that stage the club, which had been relatively successful in the twenties, winning the Durham Aged Miners Cup and the Durham Hospital Cup and finishing in the top six of the Northern League, had gone out of business after the Crash, crippled by a debt of just £30. In the letter they had written to the League announcing they were withdrawing from it the reason they gave was that they could not raise sufficient funds to buy a match ball. The present club had been formed in 1973.

As a youngster Robson had had a trial at Ayresome Park and been anxious to sign for a club that numbered George Hardwick and Wilf Mannion among its players. He never heard from Middlesbrough again, went instead to West Brom and won twenty caps. It was a depressingly familiar North-East story. Bobby Charlton, anxious to play for the team of his idol, Len Shackleton, watches the Sunderland scout coming across the pitch towards him after a game for East Northumberland Boys. He holds his breath. The scout brushes past and signs the 'keeper instead. Alan Shearer is spotted playing centre-forward for Cramlington Juniors and invited to St James's for a two-day trial. He spends the entire time in goal. Bryan Robson is rejected as too slight. Colin Bell evades everybody and ends up at Bury. Stan Mortensen attracts no interest. Chris Waddle spends a spell as a seasoner in a Felling sausage factory, turning out for Tow Law Town before he is noticed. Even Peter Beardsley has to travel to Vancouver to play before his home-town club show any interest in him. It was the kind of squandering of natural resources that would have Friends of the Earth staging a sit-in.

There was no danger of that on the pitch at Langley Park. If Jonathan Porritt had tried it, Esh Winning's number 9 would have run a tractor over him. He had spent the first half not so much flirting with a sending-off as giving it a bloody good humping. Luckily for him the referee was the same twinkle-toed cherub who'd been in nominal charge of the Blyth Spartans v. Tow Law game. At Croft Park, in front of 500 people, this official's behaviour had seemed ridiculous; here, with forty onlookers, it was farcical. Up and down the pitch he cantered, smiling beatifically as boots flew, fists flailed and the air was filled with language so ripe dogs could smell it in Morecambe, an enthusiastic young vicar in an urban youth club. His uniform was immaculate, his socks were pressed, his whistle glinted in the pale autumn sunlight. Peep! Peep! He blew for a free kick as another player went surfing nose-first through the mud. The perpetrator toed the ball across the field petulantly. The referee wagged his finger. 'You kicked it away. You go and get it,' he admonished. The love-bite lads guffawed. 'Make him go and stand in the naughty corner!' one of them yelled. The player looked at them, confused about what to do next. 'Come on, come on. We haven't got all day,' the referee tutted. 'It's getting dark and some of us want to get this game finished.' The player turned, embarrassed, and lumbered after the ball.

The number 9 continued on his merry way, hacking, chopping and felling like a lumberjack on sulphates. The referee did nothing. Perhaps he hadn't seen, possibly they weren't actually fouls at all, or maybe he'd weighed up the chances of being twatted against the fact that Langley Park were now 3–0 up and decided it wasn't worth risking a red card. As

Northern League referees receive £12 per game, I have to say he had a point. Whatever the reasons that lay behind it, his inaction had a definite effect on Albion's centre-forward. He started to believe he was invisible and therefore capable of getting away with anything. With minutes to go he put this to the test, kicking an opponent on the knee with the ball ten yards away and the ref practically standing on his toes. Faced with no alternative, the vicar sent him packing. The number 9 was stunned: 'What?' he said, as he trudged towards the dugout. 'Can you fucking believe that? What's he sent us off for? Can you tell us?'

The love-bite brigade were quite happy to do so. ''Cos you're a dirty bastard,' one of them shouted.

'I cannot fucking believe that decision,' the centre-forward chuntered, 'Fucking unbelievable.'

'You should have went off for that foul on Keith half an hour ago,' one of the love-bite boys bellowed. The number 9 looked at him, 'Oh, aye,' he said. 'I should have got sent sent off for that. But not just now. No chance.'

The old man turned to Bill and I and pulled a face. 'Brains,' he said, 'in his bollocks.' He looked across the field to the other side of the Deerness valley where the larches were turning yellow on the steep hillside. 'Mind,' he said, 'it's been a canny year for the leaves, though.'

The barber was excited. He flicked his scissors through my hair for about two seconds then stopped and talked for five minutes. My hair was growing faster than he was cutting it. Newcastle had started winning games and the barber was thinking about Europe. He'd been at St James's, along with 59,999 other people, in 1969 when United beat Ujpest Dozsa 3–0 in the first leg of the Fairs Cup final. 'I remember watching the return on telly,' he said. I remembered doing that too.

My cousin Jonathan was staying with us. The TV was one of those old-fashioned ones that were 90 per cent cabinet and 10 per cent screen. The glass was as thick as Mr Magoo's specs. The pictures from Hungary crackled with interference giving the impression that the match was being played in a snow storm. Newcastle came back from 2–0 down to win 3–2. Alan Foggon scored the winning goal. He was young and slim in those days, a mere shadow of the man-butter-mountain Boro fans would later celebrate in a version of 'The Deck of Cards': 'And when I see the nine, I think of the number of pints Alan Foggon drinks before a match. And when I see the ten, I think of the number of pints Alan Foggon drinks before a match.' He had beaky features and his black hair stuck out slightly above his ears, reminding me of the Magellan's penguins that featured in a book I had on endangered animals. When Foggon had the ball he used to feint to pass by flicking out his right leg from the knee as if he was practising the Charleston. His goal satisfied every one of my childhood criteria for footballing excitement: his shot hit the bar, there was a goalmouth scramble, he scored. I was beside myself. Earlier my dad had told me that in European matches away goals counted double. Not quite grasping all the nuances of the system I celebrated Foggon's delirious effort by skipping round the sofa chanting, 'Nine-two on aggregate, nine-two on aggregate.'

The following day we replayed the match on the Subbuteo pitch. Jonathan was three years older than me, so he got to be Newcastle. We used Stoke City for Ujpest Dozsa. The game lasted for one side of a 'Top of the Pops' LP. Newcastle won 6–4, including a three-goal blitz during 'Cinderella Rockefella'.

For some reason the barber wasn't interested in hearing about the second leg (Stoke/Ujpest went down 5–1, demoralised by a controversial penalty awarded in the first chorus of 'A Man Without Love'.) He was recalling great goals in European games at St James's: Robbie Rensenbrink's blaster, Johnny Rep's brilliant solo dribble. Even though they'd put Newcastle out it was obvious from the way he talked that he'd enjoyed them. It reminded me of something Steve had once told me. During Newcastle's struggles in the Second Division in the late seventies he'd been leaving St James's after another pitiful display when he'd heard a man in front of him say, 'I wish we'd get promoted.'

'We wouldn't stop up if we did,' his mate said.

'Aye,' the first man replied, 'but at least we'd see some decent opposition for a bit.'

You have to really love football – not just winning and the vicarious ego-boost it brings, but the game itself – to think like that. And there are a lot of people in the North-East who do.

Bishop Auckland v. Horwich RMI,
Northern Premier League Premier Division
Saturday 13 November 1993

The bus trundled through Gateshead and Felling, past the Naughty Needle Tattoo Parlour, a boarded-up gent's outfitters and a shop called Joymakers, which was shut. I was thinking about *Doctor Who*. I'd just seen a fast-food place called the Pie People and I was imagining a soldier running into the Brigadier's HQ jabbering, 'It's useless, sir. The Pie People are invincible. Our weapons are powerless against the gristle! The soggy pastry just seems to absorb nuclear blasts!' The Brigadier responds with a sardonic twist of his moustache, while outside, in Trafalgar Square, the cardboard-hued invaders splodge about squirting passers-by with glutinous gravy and sticking them to the spot. What kind of world would it be if mankind was enslaved by a race from outer space made entirely from under-cooked shortcrust, bisto and minced meat? A bloody sight better than the current one if today was anything to go by.

I'd been intending to go and see Crook play Whickham. I was going to get the train through to Durham and get the bus from there to the Millfield Ground. But the train was delayed and I missed my connection to Durham by two minutes. The next one didn't get in until quarter to three. I thought I'd get a bus direct from Newcastle instead. I was walking up to Eldon Square when what should I see heaving into view, inevitable and joyful as a wet Monday morning, but the X46 to Crook. Never mind, I thought, there'll be another one. And indeed there was. But not for fifty-eight minutes. So I got the bus to

Bishop Auckland instead. I got on it at two o'clock. A quarter of an hour later we still hadn't crossed the Tyne. We were stuck in traffic on the High Level Bridge and I was craning to see over the parapet in a vain attempt to identify the spot where Hughie Gallacher had been arrested for fighting with his future brother-in-law. There wasn't a plaque.

Gallacher, born in 1903 in Lanarkshire, was arguably the first footballer to become a star in the North-East. He arrived at St James's Park from Airdrieonians in 1925 for the then staggering fee of £6,500. By that stage Gallacher's reputation, both on and off the field, was well established. During Airdrie's Cup-winning season he had scored forty-six times; he had incensed his father, a staunch Orangeman, by supporting Celtic and marrying a Catholic; he had hit five goals for Scotland in a 7–3 win in Belfast and been shot at by a sniper next day for his pains. Wherever Gallacher went people were assured of two things: brilliance and bother.

For Newcastle Gallacher scored 143 goals in 174 matches, 39 of them during the 1926–27 Championship season. Photos show a flat-featured man with crinkly hair, his chin tucked in like a boxer's. Against Spurs we see him heading the ball goalwards, one foot planted firmly on the ground; his limbs swing one way, his body the other, giving the impression of a cartoon character making a swift exit.

An old farmer I met on the riverbank whose elderly corgi waddled about in a large-bottomed fashion that always put me in mind of late-period John Craggs, said: 'We used to play a game of football every Sunday afternoon in a field up by Castleside. There'd sometimes be thirty lads per team we were that keen. And the best of them was this little retired miner, belonged to Leadgate. He could dribble with it, that lad. But by, if you took the ball off him you had to watch out. He was a dirty little bugger. Quick-footed and quick-tempered. You know, like Hughie Gallacher.'

At the time I thought this was funny, that he should think I knew what Gallacher was like. Then later I realised that the old farmer could not have been much more than five or six himself when Wee Hughie left Newcastle. He had no more first-hand experience of him than I had. But Hughie Gallacher was that sort of player: so memorable that even those who had never seen him could recall him vividly.

For three more seasons Gallacher's presence kept St James's packed to the rafters, but despite his goals the Championship win was not repeated and increasingly Wee Hughie's behaviour was becoming a problem. In 1927 he was suspended for two months without pay for shoving referee Bert Fogg into the bath after a match at Huddersfield. In 1929 he was called before an FA investigating committee having been sent off during Newcastle's match with a Hungarian Select XI in Budapest for being 'drunk and disorderly'. In the pubs and clubs of Tyneside, dressed up like James Cagney, he swanked and scrapped, swaggered and staggered and squandered his money. He started to have pre-match drinking sessions with fans in the bars around St James's, often being pulled from a heaving saloon by colleagues moments before kick-off. It is one of the enduring traditions of football that any story involving a wayward genius carried legless from a bar must end with him being decanted on to the pitch a short time afterwards and the words, 'And you know what? He played a blinder.' So it is with Hughie Gallacher. And maybe it is true, too. Perhaps he could still play superbly even with beer sloshing round in his belly like water in the hold of the *Lusitania*. But the certainty was that even if he could do it once, twice, twenty times, he couldn't go on that way indefinitely. Gallacher's drinking meant he was playing on borrowed time and by 1930 Andy Cunningham, the Newcastle manager, had decided that his time was up.

The bus trundled on into Chester-le-Street past a disused Primitive Methodist school. It was 2.40 p.m. now and Bishop Auckland seemed a long way off. How far was it? Fifteen miles, probably. How long would it take? Divide distance by average speed. Average speed, 40 m.p.h. Distance fifteen miles. Six down, carry two. I calculated feverishly. By the time I had come up with the somewhat implausible figure of seventy-seven-and-a-half hours we were there. It was 2.55. The bus stopped and I leaped out. I looked around to get my bearings. I saw a sign on the building in front of me. I had never ever been to Bishop Auckland but – call it an inspired guess – somehow I knew that I wouldn't find Spennymoor Library there. Or Spennymoor Social Club. Or Barclays Bank, Spennymoor Branch. The bus had set off. It was fifty yards away, stopped at some traffic lights. I raced after it, arms waving. Dogs barked, children scattered, old ladies flung themselves into doorways. The lights changed. The bus pulled off. On I charged, breathless, red-faced, loose change spraying from my pockets, size 12s slapping the concrete like kippers. Pensioners pointed, young mums laughed. As I started up a small incline I began to slow. 'Don't give up now, Kidder, you're winning,' a youth shouted from a transit. I caught the bus 200 yards further on, trapped behind a badly parked Nissan Stanza, and hammered on the doors. The driver opened them. 'I knew you got a ticket to Bishop,' he said, 'but I thought maybe you'd lost your nerve'.

It was 3.25 when I paid the gateman at Kingsway. 'You haven't missed much,' he said. But I had. To me coming into a football match late was like missing the adverts at the pictures. It wasn't that you lost anything of the plot, it was just the rhythm of the thing. Somehow without the kick-in and the kick-off I couldn't get into the game. It just didn't make any sense. I suppose if I'd concentrated hard enough I could have caught up. But my chest was aching and my shins were sore from my whistle-stop tour of Spennymoor High Street, and anyway I'd wanted to go to Crook and the programmes had all been sold and the tea had run out and the Cup-a-soup smelled like dog sick . . .

The game, from what I saw of it, was a disjointed affair. Space was so constricted they might well have been playing in one of the old farmer's thirty-a-side matches. The ball seemed to be regarded as a mere irritant by the players, and to cap it all Bishops were not playing in their classic light and dark blue halves but in a hideous modern confection of lurching diamonds that looked like a golfing sweater knitted by a drunkard.

I had come to Bishop Auckland thinking of the greatest

amateur team in history. Eighteen Amateur Cup finals, 10 victories; 19 Northern League titles, 7 Northern League Cup wins, 10 Durham County Challenge Cups, 9 Durham Benevolent Bowls and 27 other trophies won at home and abroad during 108 years of competition. A team which in the fifties regularly fielded ten amateur internationals. The team of Bob Hardisty, Bob Paisley, Bobby Gurney and the imaginatively named (well, he wasn't christened Robert, was he?) Corbert Cresswell. Instead I'd found this dross. For the first and only time during the season, I wondered what on earth I was doing. Why was I standing on this windblown terrace amid these non-league saddos, with their balaclavas, hand-knit bobble hats and baseball caps with the logos of cattle feed companies stuck on the front? I mean, look at them: bearded middle-aged woodwork teachers with real-ale guts who probably enjoyed dialect poetry and at the drop of a clog would stick a finger in their ear and drone out some delightful ditty about famous industrial accidents of the Victorian era; lard-jowled committee men, their hair slicked back with dripping, the collars of their dung-brown trenchcoats frosted with dandruff; unappealing girls whose thick foundation make-up cracked and shifted as if it were designed to demonstrate the principle of tectonic plates; purple-faced pubescent boys; blue-rinsed bag ladies; the loveless; the loners; the loonies. I looked at them all and felt – it's no use trying to conceal it any more – grumpy.

Once I had been travelling on the underground to Upton Park to see Middlesbrough play West Ham. Both teams were near the top of the old Second Division and the train was packed with Boro fans. In our carriage there was a respectably dressed middle-aged man sitting in the corner seat. He had nodded off with his legs crossed. The train stopped at Mile End. The man woke up, looked to see where we were, then jumped to his feet and rushed for the open doors of the carriage. Unfortunately his right leg had gone to sleep. It wobbled slightly, veered numbly off in the wrong direction and then collapsed completely, sending the man sprawling, half through the doors and flat on his face. The doors shut on his waist and bounced open again. The Boro fans in our carriage hooted and whistled and jeered at him. The man struggled upright again and made it out on to the platform, but his leg was about as rigid as over-cooked pasta. It wiggled, it squiggled and down he went again. By now the whole train could see him. The laughter, the cries of encouragement and abuse echoed round the station.

Whenever I'm depressed I recall this incident. That man, befuddled by sleep, betrayed by his limbs and ridiculed by a trainful of Teessiders. It never fails to cheer me up. Aye, there's always someone worse off than yourself. I thought of it at half-time at Kingsway. But it didn't seem to make much difference.

In the eighty-sixth minute Bishops scored the winner after the referee had awarded a free kick for ungentlemanly conduct against a Horwich defender who had been lying on the touchline receiving treatment yet suddenly leaped up to intercept a Richie Bond breakaway. A couple of teenage boys with damp mouths surrounded by nascent bum-fluff celebrated by jumping up and down on the fence, making V-signs behind the back of the Horwich goalkeeper. Every time they flicked their arms in the air their anoraks rode up revealing bluey-white buttock cleavage. A stork-like bloke in his early thirties with glasses so thick they made his eyes look the size of tennis balls, who had spent the whole match whingeing in a reedy voice, 'They're first to the ball every time, look. First to the ball,' yah-hooed triumphantly like a man vindicated.

The win moved Bishops up into the top four of the table. As befitted their history they were an ambitious club; plans were already underway for the switch to the new stadium – a necessity if they were to earn a place in the GM Vauxhall Conference since Kingsway was shared with the cricket club and as a consequence would not meet Football League standards. However, it was hard to see how they'd finance it. Around 350 people had turned up to see Horwich. It was hard to imagine many more being lured through the gate by the prospect of seeing Macclesfield or Stafford Rangers, new stadium or no new stadium.

I walked up into the town centre and caught a bus to Durham. At Durham Station the noticeboard announced that all northbound trains were delayed by forty-five minutes. I paced up and down the platform gazing hopefully down the line and mentally composing letters to the chairman of British Rail that began 'Dear Incompetent Shitehawk' and deteriorated into mindless abuse from there.

My thoughts turned, inevitably, back to Hughie Gallacher. After spells at Stamford Bridge, Derby County and Grimsby Town he'd returned to the North-East to play out the remainder of his days at Gateshead in the Third Division (North). His skills were still impressive. A man I met who'd played against him in a works football match during the war recalled him 'leaping six feet – well, five feet, anyway, in the air and twisting like a corkscrew to get his header on goal', but by now his life was in an accelerating state of collapse. An acrimonious divorce from his first wife was followed by bankruptcy. His second wife died of a heart attack. As his playing career ended, the drinking and the violence escalated. In May 1957 Gallacher's son was taken into care by the NSPCC and he was ordered to appear before Gateshead magistrates on charges of alleged child abuse. The day before he was due in court Hughie Gallacher stumbled down a railway embankment close to his home, placed his head on the track and waited for the Edinburgh train.

Durham City v. Shildon,
Federation Brewery Northern League
Division 1
Saturday 20 November 1993

I once knew a Norwegian who named his favourite musicians as the Sex Pistols, Thin Lizzy and Roger Whittaker. Being an *NME*-reading teenager at the time and consequently as sharp as a safety-pin when it came to pigeon-holing, I protested that it was impossible to like three such disparate musical forms, two of which were also plainly crap. 'They've nothing in common,' I hectored. 'No,' the Norwegian said, grinning, to my mind idiotically, 'except that they are all super.' And, as if to irritate me still further he pronounced that final adjective with an elongated 'oo' sound in the middle, like Penelope Keith praising a particularly successful crème brûlée. 'Soooo-pah'. I didn't have much time for the guitar-straddling antics of Gary Moore, but it was the choice of Roger Whittaker that really got up my nose. Whittaker was evidently popular around the globe, but he hadn't endeared himself to the population of the North-East during the height of his fame in the late sixties. This was not just for the obvious reasons – he was South African, dressed like an art teacher and could whistle in tune – but also because he had taken it upon himself to spread disinformation about the region. 'I've gotta leave old Durham Town,' he warbled, ignoring a large, well-known and rather prominent cathedral. Roger was clearly seeking a rhyme for the word 'down', an adjective chosen to reflect the melancholy of departure. Why, one wonders, had he dismissed the equally evocative and factually more accurate coupling of 'city' with 'shitty'? Not content with reducing Durham's urban status, Whittaker then went on to inform the rest of the world that as a young lad in Durham he had spent his days frolicking along the banks of the Tyne. This may well have been true, but he'd have had to have got the bus to Newcastle first because the river that runs through Durham is the Wear. Talk about irresponsible. The damage Whittaker's warbling did to Durham's tourist industry is incalculable. It was the *Sunday Times* Pergau Dam affair of the sixties. But did the *Daily Telegraph* write a blustering editorial about it? Did it hell. No wonder Northerners are bitter.

One thing Roger didn't mention about Durham, and since it is true, perhaps that's not so surprising, is that it is almost totally spiritually disconnected from the rest of the North-East. In fact, when you're in the centre of Durham you hardly feel like you're in the North-East at all. This is because of the university. Or rather, the sort of students it attracts. As one of them observed on local TV a couple of years ago, 'We don't think of ourselves as being in the North at all. Durham's sort of like an oasis of civilisation.' An accurate summation indeed, though only if your idea of civilisation is wearing striped shirts and velvet Alice bands and sitting around in wine bars saying, 'Yah. But I think the thing is that Hugo's just too immature to commit himself to anything long-term, Lucinda.'

Andy's and Pete Smith's and my world view didn't encompass such activities, which was why we were sitting in a pub in the Tyne Valley rather than in Saddler Street. As a result, instead of being pelted with bread rolls we were being bombarded with insults by assorted Newcastle fans. The Magpies had moved up into the top half of the Premiership. Boro, meanwhile, had slumped into the lower half of the First Division. The next day United would hammer Liverpool 3–0 thanks to an Andy Cole hat-trick, while Middlesbrough lost at home in front of their lowest crowd for seven years.

'Hey, Pete,' the barman shouted, holding up the telephone, 'It's Lennie Lawrence. He wants to know when you can make it tomorrow. Only he's got to fix the kick-off time with the opposition.' A few years before Steve had said he worried that if Newcastle were ever successful again their fans, starved of glory for so long, might become insufferable. I was beginning to see what he meant.

Perhaps Durham's strange atmosphere has contributed to the lack of success of the city's football club. In over seventy years Durham City had won just one trophy, the Durham Benevolent Bowl, in 1955–56. In that time they had been in and out of the Football League (they never finished above eleventh and failed to gain re-election after seven seasons, replaced by Carlisle United), disbanded, reformed, changed their name to City of Durham FC, then back again. Now, at last, things seemed to be on the up. Durham were in second place in the Northern League, beaten only once, and plans for a move to a new ground that would meet GM Vauxhall Conference standards had gone through. The only cloud was that leaders Blyth were thirteen points clear at the top.

According to the Durham programme, Ferens Park ('set in rural surroundings') is one of the most attractive in the Northern League. There are some unkind people who might suggest that this is akin to being voted best-groomed man at a Grateful Dead concert. I am not among them. However, I'd have to say that Ferens Park's claims on the word 'attractive' are tenuous at best. There is a covered section down one side of the pitch, its roof held aloft by so many pillars that an uninterrupted view of the playing area is but a distant dream. The rest of the ground consists of grass banking. The rural surroundings looked to me uncannily like a 1960s housing estate, though it is possible that what I was looking at was actually a cherry orchard cunningly disguised by its owner in order to fool marauding flocks of bullfinches.

We stood on the slope next to the halfway line. Beside us were a group of Shildon fans. Their leader was an ancient figure in a hooded parka which appeared to have been fashioned from the remains of a simulated leather sofa. He was particularly entertained by the referee's baldness. 'Get behind the keeper, referee,' he yelled when Durham were awarded a corner, 'or the reflection off your head'll blind him.' Then, when Shildon's appeals for a foul had been turned down, 'How come you didn't see that, referee? Did your hair get in your eyes?' The ref responded by glancing in his direction and flashing the cheesy grin of someone who knows that his only defence is to play the good sport.

After the disappointment of Bishop Auckland and the primitivism of Langley Park, it was a relief to find myself watching a good game of football. The Northern League has a reputation for producing attractive games between attack-minded teams. It's a reputation that's well deserved. The top Northern League sides all played the same neat, passing football, moving the ball through the midfield with the emphasis on skill rather than strength. It might be that this was a legacy of the old amateur days – the idea of the players' enjoyment of the game taking precedence over the importance of winning it. More likely it had something to do with the social position of football in the North-East. Men who during working hours proved beyond doubt their durability had no need to use a game to advertise their toughness. Instead football was a means to show they were capable of more than their jobs allowed; of brilliance and creativity. That life wasn't just survival. Of course, as with any idealistic notion there were exceptions. One had played for Shildon during their heyday in the 1930s when they had taken the Northern League title five times. His name was Alf 'Whacker' Wild and he was a man so fearsome that even typing out his name has left me with several large welts on my shin. 'He was a right character, was Alf,' men who'd played against him would chuckle. Then they'd work out how many times they'd faced him by rolling up their trouser-legs, counting the scars and dividing by nine. 'On a bone-dry summer pitch Whacker's sliding tackle started from six foot away,' one of them told me. 'So you can imagine what he was like on the wet.' A jack-knifing juggernaut springs to mind.

Durham, who had Bryan Robson's brother Justin chugging about effectively in their midfield, were a capable-looking side. They took the lead when Shildon's goalkeeper, the silver-haired Phil Owers, failed to gather a shot from Steve

Carter. Mickey Taylor, a ponytailed centre-forward with the build of a wildebeest and the rampaging manner to match, scored from the rebound. Shildon equalised through a solid header from Andy Southern. The game flowed up and down the pitch. Shildon were lying seventh in the table and they appeared good value for it. Phil Owers might have looked more like a man you'd buy insurance off than a goalkeeper, but he was a safe shot-stopper. In midfield another Mickey Taylor and the singular Matt Sowden were both elegant and businesslike. Up front Colin Blackburn, who had played a few times for Middlesbrough, showed why he had never quite made it at top level, twisting and turning about on the wing excitingly for half an hour then disappearing from the game so completely that rumours circulated that he'd run away to become a Jehovah's Witness. For all the efforts of these individuals, Durham always seemed the more likely team to score. They were solid at the back and broke forward quickly and in numbers. Steve Carter restored their lead with a good volley.

By this stage the sky had turned the colour of stout and the first hailstones had begun to bounce off Andy Smith's baseball cap with a noise like bursting bubble-wrap. The 120 or so spectators greeted the half-time whistle with cries of joy, and the rush for the warmth of the clubhouse was such that I worried it might tip over from the impact.

Durham had moved to their present home in the early fifties from Holliday Park. It was at this earlier ground during the 1925–26 season that Middlesbrough signed a young centre-forward. His name was George Camsell. Camsell was born in Framwellgate Moor, one of the many pit villages that fringe the city, well out of sight of the bun-throwing Hoorays. His career had begun at Esh Winning in the Northern League, but he'd quickly moved on to Durham, then playing in the old Third Division North. His scoring record at that stage was good without being spectacular. He was marked as a youngster with potential. Middlesbrough, who were destined to finish ninth in the Second Division at the end of that season, brought him to Ayresome Park and put him straight into the reserves. Which is where he might have stayed had it not been for an injury to top scorer Jimmy McClelland at the start of the 1926–27 season.

When I was a boy my grandfather and I would walk along the headlands at Marske and he would tell me stories about the Boro during the inter-war years. In many ways these remain my clearest memories of football: games I never witnessed, played by men I have seen only in photographs. On the edge of the sand dunes, heading towards Saltburn, gulls screaming, wind chasing in off the sea, my grandfather, his cream mac billowing and snapping in the breeze like the sails of a tea clipper, would screw up his left eye and stare out towards the horizon with his right, as if gazing into the past through an invisible telescope. He'd let out a low chuckle, not a laugh of merriment but of pleasure: the laugh of a man who has stored up something – a length of wood, a piece of copper piping – for a long time knowing that one day it will come in handy, and has just now found a use for it. 'Me and our Joe were working as roofers,' he'd say, 'in the Ironmasters district. We could sheet sixty square foot of roof in a shift. I was the rivet man. I brought them up the ladders two buckets at a time. Eighteen pound a piece they weighed. We'd been having some bother with a bloke called Duffy. He was a baloney merchant, a smart alec. So one break he comes over to me and Joe and starts on. Now our Joe was tough. He wouldn't put up with any cleverness. He reaches over and takes the cap off Duffy's head and slings it off the roof. It was about a hundred-foot drop. "Any more out of you," Joe says, "and you're following it." We got no more trouble from him after. That was in 1926, when the Boro had the best forward line in history.'

And he'd go on, talking about the team that had taken the Second Division Championship, scoring 122 goals in forty-two games. The wingers, Welsh international Owen Williams and pale-faced Billy Pease, capped just once by England, and the inside-forward Billy Birrell with his pock-marked cheeks and centre parting, who later managed Chelsea. These men, great though they may have been, were only supporting players, however. Top billing in my grandfather's tales was reserved for two men, Jackie Carr and George Camsell.

Jackie Carr was the best known of the footballing family from South Bank, one of the roughest parts of Middlesbrough, a town hardly noted as the Cheltenham of the North. A genial and skilful inside-forward, Carr played with a permanent grin on his face despite the battering that was often dished out to him by defenders. One opponent recalls him 'spending the whole game laughing and joking and picking himself up off the floor'. In 1925 the offside law had been changed. The new regulation cut the number of defending players needed to put a forward onside from three to two. The alteration put a premium on strikers such as Carr, who were capable of drawing defenders before slipping the ball through to an onrushing centre-forward. For the tactic to work successfully, a centre-forward who was fast, strong and a clinical finisher was essential. It was a role tailor-made for George Camsell. He stood five feet nine inches tall, was stockily built and had wavy blond hair and a gap-toothed smile. The resemblance to Paul Gascoigne is striking. Pictures show Camsell galloping about through the mud and mist in the traditional straight-armed manner of players of the period. Footballers, in fact, weren't fitted with elbows until the late fifties. Johnny Haynes of Fulham was the first to have a pair. Flashy bugger.

Time after time during the 1926–27 season, Camsell would charge across the paddy-field of Ayresome Park on to a through ball from Carr, churn onwards with it at his feet – an early version of Malcolm Macdonald, only without the *Planet of the Apes* sideburns – defenders bearing down on him from all angles, thighs bulging, steel toe-capped boots hammering menacingly on the damp ground. Camsell running on towards the Holgate End, uncovered in those days so that the packed crowd, stacked up to the skyline, looked like a human pyramid, supported by nothing but their own strength; the goalkeeper steaming out to meet him, the defenders converging; Camsell, arms outstretched, cheeks puffing, hitting the ball with his left foot, sending it screaming towards the goal. A split second later the first defender would hit him from the side, the goalkeeper from the front, catapulting him forwards, swallow-diving, so that he landed on his chest and skidded across the wet turf of the penalty area, eyes upraised to follow the course of the ball as it hit the back of the net with the characteristic fizzing noise of the leather scuffing over the knotted rope. The crowd, too jammed in to applaud, would roar approval and Camsell would rise from the dirt, shirt sodden, face besmirched, smiling, triumphant.

'George Camsell,' my grandad would say. 'Now he was a footballer.'

In that memorable season Camsell scored 59 goals in 37 League matches. It was a record, but one which lasted only a year. The following season Dixie Dean scored 60 in 39 appearances for Everton. Boro fans everywhere may now shake their heads resignedly and mutter the word 'typical' in an aggrieved manner.

In the second half Shildon pressed for an equaliser, but with the sleet now streaking across the pitch horizontally into their faces, they quickly tired and the game became increasingly scrappy. It ended without further scoring. On the way back up the A1 we heard over the radio that Blyth had lost at home to Murton. The gap between them and Durham was still ten points, but at least we now knew that Spartans weren't, after all, invincible.

There's an old joke about a stranger sitting in a pub in County Durham when a man comes in who has a flat head and a cauliflower ear. 'Odd-looking bloke,' the stranger remarks to the landlord.

'He's a very brave man,' the landlord replies. 'The shaft was about to collapse in the local pit and that lad acted as a prop and held the roof up while his workmates escaped.'

'That explains the flat head,' the stranger says, 'but how did he get the cauliflower ear?'

'That's where they hammered him to wedge him in,' the landlord replies.

Whenever I thought of Terry Butcher I always thought of

that joke. His most famous performance in an England shirt had been against Sweden, when, with his head swathed in bandages and blood spattering his shirt, he'd captained England to a draw which had helped book them a place in the World Cup finals. That he was brave was never in question, but, like the human pit-prop, admiration of his courage always seemed to be tinged with irony. His behaviour, often excessive (during his time with Glasgow Rangers he embraced sectarian bigotry with such fervour that he had to be spoken to by the police), came across as ridiculously histrionic, like bad Method acting. There was just something wooden about Terry Butcher.

On Friday 26 November he got the chop. It came after a run of six defeats which had begun with a 4–1 beating by Aston Villa in the Coca-Cola Cup. He had been in charge for forty-two weeks. His record as a manager was the worst in Sunderland's 114-year history. Like most sackings in football, Butcher's dismissal was handled with a minimum of finesse. The board reached their decision on the Thursday night. In a bid to spare Butcher's feelings, though, they decided not to tell him about it. He arrived at Roker for work on Friday morning as normal to find journalists gathering for a press conference. Butcher assumed some statement was to be made about the new stadium. The journalists thought differently. 'If I've been dismissed I must have missed it,' Butcher said. An hour later he caught up with it again. Terry Butcher was left to make the announcement to waiting journalists himself.

The club chairman, Consett-born Bob Murray, who had appointed Butcher, resigned at the same time. He remained a director and majority shareholder. Mick Buxton, who had been given the job of head coach by Butcher in July was named as the new manager. Buxton, raised in Ryhope, had previously been manager at Huddersfield and Scunthorpe, but prior to his Roker appointment he'd been in semi-retirement. To describe him as a surprise choice for the job was an understatement. The only picture the *Newcastle Journal* could find of him to put in next day's paper was so blurred it looked like it had been taken by a spy satellite.

Butcher wasn't the first North-East manager to go in the 1993–94 season – Darlington's Billy McEwan had seized that honour. He wasn't even the second. Viv Busby of Hartlepool United had beaten him to the silver medal by a week. Former Sunderland defender John MacPhail had succeeded him. MacPhail was Pool's twenty-first manager since the war. The job at the Victoria Ground didn't have a lot going for it, but it was excellent training for anyone hoping to become prime minister of Italy.

Seaham Red Star v. Gretna,
FA Trophy Third Qualifying Round
Saturday 27 November 1993

It was the first bad weather of the winter. Snow had fallen on Sunday, Monday and Tuesday, thawed briefly, then re-frozen again. The banks of the river were covered with compacted ice, the footpaths as slippery as fish and as lethal as gin traps. The train clattered on through the morning fog, which insisted on appearing over the Tyne despite the fact that it was a bit of a cliché. Through it, you could just make out the dark shapes of gorse bushes rising up the cloud-white hillsides like Apache smoke-signals.

People had been predicting a hard winter since about July. In the North-East they always did. It was a superstitious thing: anticipating the worst in the hope that that would somehow stop it from happening. In late summer the gamekeeper pointed out to me that there were a lot of berries on the hawthorn trees. 'They say that usually means a cold one,' he told me. I nodded wisely, pleased to know that the old country ways, rooted in the steady rhythms of the seasons and the tell–tale quirks of Mother Nature had not yet totally succumbed to the information revolution. 'Though how the bloody hell the trees can predict the weather when the Met. Office can't beats me,' he added before jumping in his Capri and roaring off with Guns 'n' Roses blaring through the windows.

However bad it got the coming winter was unlikely to match that of 1946–47, when snow fell late in the year, allowing only one Northern League match to be played between 1 February

George Cansell, Boro's goal-scoring machine, pretends not to notice that jocular team-mates have filled his socks with concrete

Hughie Gallacher: Are you looking at me, pal?

Len Shackleton, Clown Prince of Soccer and Wearside District Can-Can Champion, puts the finishing touches to a winning routine.

Bobby Robson and his Langley Park team-mates eagerly await the invention of chest-hair and medallions.

Turned down for a part in *The Sweeney*, Big Jack Charlton goes down the launderette instead.

After a few glorious years at Bishop Auckland, Bob Paisley spent the rest of his career somewhere in Lancashire.

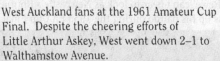

West Auckland fans at the 1961 Amateur Cup Final. Despite the cheering efforts of Little Arthur Askey, West went down 2–1 to Walthamstow Avenue.

Former Esh Winning player, Raich Carter, holds the Cup for Sunderland while two blokes in polo necks struggle to contain their joy.

Carter's protégé, Don Revie, can't bear to look as Newcastle's Ronnie Simpson attempts to mess up his hairdo during the 1955 FA Cup Final.

Brian Clough takes time out during a busy Tyne-Wear derby game to examine Newcastle keeper Gordon Marshall's flaky scalp condition.

Bobby Charlton in Beatrice Street, Ashington: There's always one older boy who insists on showing off.

Alan Foggon braces himself for yet another legend-in-opening-time-style caption.

Desperate to absorb Roman culture, Paul Gascoigne struggles to get the hang of the wolf-whistle.

In a bid to attract Graham Taylor's attention, Peter Beardsley advertises his own qualities.

Lee Clark learns of the critical reception to his latest single.

Former Luton Town keeper, Alec Chamberlain, attempts to yodel his way into the Fullwell End's affections.

Don Goodman *(left)*: Always likely to tip the scales in Sunderland's favour.

Newcastle's Darlington-bound defender, Matty Appleby *(right)*, reacts politely to that last caption.

Andy Cole: Kevin Keegan took Cole to Newcastle, Cole took goals to Newcastle and headline writers everywhere danced in the street.

and 22 March; or 1962–63, which saw only six games between 29 December and 3 March; or 1978–79, when Consett had to postpone an FA Cup tie with Accrington Stanley eleven times. The North-East's footballers have always suffered badly at the hands of the weather. In a game between Chilton Colliery and Stockton in the thirties, one player collapsed suffering from exposure and four more walked off unable to bear the cold any longer. Eventually, after eighty-three minutes, the referee called a halt. And that was on 19 April. In the 1950s Bishop Auckland goalkeeper Harry Sharratt responded to the conditions during a Boxing Day game against Shildon by building a snowman on the goal-line.

I hadn't planned to go back to Seaham (and, let's be honest, who would?), but the weather had wiped out most football in the region. It was only at the grounds near the coast, where the prevailing winds had driven the frost away, that play was possible. It was a choice between Peterlee and Seaham. And that, basically, was no choice at all.

Nothing much in Seaham had altered since my previous visit. The streets were so quiet and deserted you expected at any minute to see a tumbleweed come bouncing down the pavement and from its position on a small hill the disused pit-head loomed over the town like a gibbet. In the shop, the woman in heavy make-up and her friend were in exactly the same positions as they'd been when I'd last seen them. As if they'd been held in stasis, waiting for me to return and reactivate them by asking for a packet of sweet 'n' sour Skips and a bottle of chocolate milk (you can say what you like about us Northerners, but we certainly understand the art of life. *Mais oui*). As I left the friend said: 'You know the ones. They're pink and you have to blow them up first.'

In the little park that surrounds Seaham football ground the local kids had been using the red- and white-striped signs with which the council fence off holes in the road to toboggan on. They'd bent them in half to make a thin sledge and were bombing down the snow and frozen mud slopes which ran from the road to the car park. It had obviously been a popular pastime: the grass banks were littered with discarded and bent signs. They looked like the folded toffee-wrappers of some gigantic litter lout. 'Aaaandy Aaaaarmstrong! And it's gold for England!' one of the sledging kids shouted as he hit the flat at the bottom of the hill and crossed what was evidently the finishing line of the Sliding Down an Icy Incline on a Bent Council Sign World Championship course.

Andy Armstrong was obviously a commentator. In every group of small boys there is always one. It's a natural thing. The greatest commentator of all time was one. He was a Scots lad called Duncan Mackay and I was at school with him. Dunc was seventeen, but for whatever reason he had a mental age of half that. He had blond hair, ethereal blue eyes and bundles of energy. He was our school first XI's greatest fan. Actually, he was its only fan. My school's first XI was crap. You'd see more skill and athletic grace on the dance-floor of a Young Farmers' Club disco after chucking-out time. If a film had ever been made of us a suitable soundtrack would have been a recording of a knock-kneed cat running up and down a glockenspiel. Nevertheless, Dunc attended every game, spending the entire ninety minutes running up and down the touchline burbling breathlessly about the action. Like all the best TV commentators he never once acknowledged that what he was watching was a visualisation of the noise made by dropping a handful of cutlery into a blender.

I played on the right wing, which meant that for half the match I could hear Dunc's description of my every deed (which in the main involved loping up and down waving my arm in the air and avoiding any situation where I might be required to head the ball). On one memorable occasion I received a pass (and that in itself was memorable enough, I can assure you) about thirty yards out, beat the full-back (he was later diagnosed as narcoleptic) and aimed a cross towards the far post behind which our centre-forward was sheltering from the wind in a bid to light a No. 6. In an attempt to intercept, the goalie raced off his line, only for a sudden gust of wind to catch the ball and send it banana-ing into the top left-hand corner of the goal. 'Oh, I say!' Dunc cried from behind me, 'Brazilian skills from the big man.' It remains the high point of my life.

In the ground there were no programmes because the photocopier had packed up and a handwritten sign on the gate said: 'Admission £2 Due to FA Regulations'. The FA regulations part was underlined twice, just so we knew who to complain to. A workman walked past carrying an electric drill. I say he was a workman – he may well have been the Gretna physio putting the finishing touches to a robotic striker. I've had a bit of a thing about robot footballers ever since I was eight and read a story in the *Hotspur* about an English team, Liverchester Wanderers, Arsenham Athletic or some such, who found themselves lined up against a crack Eastern European outfit in the Champions Cup. Eastern European outfits were always 'crack' in those days. I'm not sure what they are now. 'Crap', most likely. Surprisingly enough, the well-oiled footballing machine of the Eastern Europeans – Dynamo Bulgonia? – turned out to be just that: a team of well-oiled machines. Robots. Thankfully, the skipper of Arsenham, 'Squarejaw' Smith, realised this and at half-time came up with a cunning plan to overturn the 3–0 deficit and beat the mechanical men. The robots were programmed to expect high standards, he reasoned, so the way to beat them was not to play well but to play badly. The more idiotically Rovers performed the more the robots would be confused. And it worked, too! Arsenham scraped through 4–3 thanks to a truly woeful display and a last-minute miskick from the knee of 'Rocketboots' Rogers. As a Boro supporter I was naturally delighted with this concept. If only we could get into Europe and draw a few Eastern European Robot XIs to confuse with our dreadful football, we'd be European Champions in two shakes of Stan Webb's tail. Unhappily, finishing sixth in the Second Division didn't seem to qualify you for Europe. So when it came to robots I had to make do with Mansfield Town.

A group of old men were gathered at the back of the covered stand. They were wearing mufflers and overcoats and the cold had turned their skins the colour of mushroom caps. There was a strong smell of drink wafting from their direction. They were well oiled, but plainly not robots. 'Come on, Gretna,' a boy of about ten shouted as his team ran out on to the field. 'Bugger off back to Scotland where you belong,' one of the old men responded with a vehemence that made the boy's eyes fill with tears. I looked round to identify this curmudgeonly codger in time to see him honking into his hankie and then inspecting it. Why do people do that? What are they expecting to find? Did you ever see anyone blow their nose, look at the results and say, 'Bugger me! That's where the shed key got to'?

The hankie man proved to be the second commentator of the day. Only in his case he was that most ubiquitous of footballing beasts, the time-delay expert. The time-delay expert is to be found in most grounds across the country. He has perfected the art of making his comments moments after the action, but in such a way as to suggest he has made them before the event took place. Thus, a split second after a forward has wellied an attempted volley into a neighbouring allotment, the time-delay expert will say: 'He'll never score from there!' As a pass goes astray: 'That won't come off!' As the opposition bulge the back of the net: 'This is dangerous!' Quite why he does it is open to doubt. Some suggest it is an attempt to boost his standing in the community, others that it stems from a desire to feel he is shaping rather than merely reacting to events. For my part I think the delay comes because of the unusually long distance the thought must travel from his brain to the part of the body he speaks out of. About three feet in most cases.

Gretna were the only Scottish club playing in English competitions, the first to do so since Queen's Park in Victorian times. Gretna had, in fact, played only one season in Scottish football, in the Dumfriesshire Junior League, before looking south of the border for opponents. After thirty-five years in various Cumbrian leagues they'd eloped to the Northern League in 1982. They won the title in 1991 with ninety-five points, a total only once bettered, by Blyth in 1974–75 (I'd pay attention if I were you – there's a quiz at the end with a range of top prizes, including a meat packet, to be won), and again in 1992 when they became the first, and at the time of writing, only Northern League team to be promoted into the Northern Premier League through the auspices of the pyramid. During the course of the 1993–94 season Gretna applied to become one of the new teams in the expanded Scottish Second Division. They were turned down, perhaps because their crowds were too small, but more likely because the Scots couldn't handle the thought of all the 'It's a Marriage Made in Heaven for Gretna' headlines such a move would have provoked.

The crowd was much the same as it had been for the tie against West Auckland in the previous round: about 120 regulars plus a small group of players and officials from nearby Horden, whose match had been postponed. 'Thought we'd come and have a watch of Walker,' one of them said. 'He's getting on a bit now, like, but he's still got all the moves.'

At thirty-five, Paul Walker, Seaham's player-manager, was still one of the best midfielders in the Northern League. He'd begun his career as a junior at Sunderland, played professionally at Hull and Doncaster and then returned to the North-East to join Blyth. He was part of the Spartans team which won the title five times in a row in the eighties; the last Northern League player to win a cap with the England semi-professional team. Off the field, Walker, with the kind of waistline extension that must have troubled local planning officers, receding hair and an aged cherub's face, looked more like the man who'd take the title role in an amateur dramatic society's production of *Pickwick Papers* than his team's star performer. On it, though, things were different. He'd pick the ball up on the halfway line and swan around with it, looking up all the time, considering the options. Opponents would close in and he'd seem oblivious to them – an absent-minded professor too intent on weightier things to notice. Then, suddenly, without ever once glancing in their direction, he'd accelerate or turn away, or make a neat five-yard pass to a team-mate, always delaying it until the last moment, when the tackler was committed, so that seconds later Walker would be picking up the return and his opponent would be picking himself off the floor. His passing was consistently accurate and thoughtful. He'd keep getting the ball and knocking it into spaces around the penalty area, gently, testingly; as if he were a doctor examining a patient, and every pass was a gentle prod with the question 'Is that where it hurts?'

I have always found the skills of a player like Paul Walker intensely puzzling. The flourishes of outrageous talent such as that of Gascoigne, paradoxically, seem easier to explain. We know we could not imitate what he does, but we can see how it is done. But how could you do the simple things that Walker does? Make a packed midfield seem suddenly full of space, or sense an opponent's presence without seeing him? It was like watching a great chef. There were skills here that could be learned, but there was also a knowledge that could never be passed on, an understanding that could never be taught. Paul Walker never played at the highest level. There are many possible reasons for that. Perhaps he was too slow or wasn't committed enough; maybe he couldn't stand card games and George Benson records. Whatever they were, they didn't alter the fact that Paul Walker knew football in a way that I, and millions of others like me, would never know it. We could appreciate the picture, but the brush-strokes remained invisible to us.

Despite Walker's skills Seaham were unable to get the better of Gretna. They attacked for much of the first half, creating plenty of chances, but at the back something was wrong. Their goalkeeper, a competent if noisy presence against West Auckland, seemed oddly out of sorts. In the previous round he'd come early for crosses and dominated in his penalty area. Now he seemed hesitant, treating his six-yard box as an agoraphobic rabbit would its burrow. You could tell he wasn't playing well by the amount of shouting he did at his defenders. It's a rule of goalkeeping that the more mistakes you make yourself the greater the rocket you must deliver to your team-mates. There's a famous clip of a German goalkeeper throwing out the ball and delaying the release of it so long he ends up lobbing it into the back of his own net. Any normal person would have reacted to such a blunder by blushing to the roots of his hair then running home and hiding under the bed. Not a goalkeeper, though. His response is immediately to start yelling at the left-back. Goalkeepers never admit to their mistakes. If it wasn't for their athletic abilities most of them would have gone into politics.

After half an hour Gretna's centre-forward, Les Armstrong, a man with the swarthy features and immaculate moustache of a Victorian cad, swaggered through the heart of the Seaham defence and struck the ball into the net. 'Here's a goal!' the time-delay expert wailed accurately. 'Get bloody stuck in there Seaham, man,' one of his friends roared, 'and stop fannying about.' This was typical of the sort of advice football crowds give to their teams. Ninety-nine per cent of it is destructive: 'Get rid of it', 'Put him under', 'Welly it'. Never once do you hear anyone shout, 'Use a bit of creativity, man' or 'Play an intricate series of passes and finish it with a viciously swerving half-volley, why don't you?' If the players did what the crowd told them to do the ball would be either one hundred feet in the air or disappearing over the roof of the stand for the entire game, while half the players would have been sent off or carried away on a stretcher inside the first fifteen minutes. And what would the crowd shout then? 'Two quid to watch this shite? It's bloody robbery,' of course.

After the goal Seaham went back on the attack. Walker prodded and poked, but if the Gretna defence was feeling any discomfort they didn't show it. Marshalled round a slender, dark-haired centre-half, they looked resistant to most things. And when they broke forward, they did so swiftly and accurately. On the hour Les Armstrong added a second goal. 'This'll be number two,' the time-delay man groaned. 'Get up his arse next time, number five,' his chum added imaginatively.

By that stage you could tell it was pretty much all over for the North-Easterners. Gretna were cruising. Seaham, even at full throttle, were still chasing the game. The Scotsmen got a third with ten minutes left. By then I was on my way. It might not have been frosty on the coast, but the wind off the sea had come uninterrupted from the Arctic Circle. My feet usually went numb at some point during a game. Now I had lost all feeling from the knees down. I passed by the Red Star Social Club and crossed the road to the bus stop with the bandy-legged stride of someone who has just wet his trousers.

Gateshead v. Stafford Rangers, GM Vauxhall Conference
Saturday 4 December 1993

It was a short walk from the Metro station to Gateshead International Stadium, down an alley between two factory walls and round a council estate where every other house seemed to be fitted with steel shutters. The winter had gone into temporary remission and there was washing flapping damply in the gardens of the occupied houses. I clunked across a metal footbridge spanning the four lanes of the main Newcastle-Sunderland road and down the other side, past a drive-in McDonald's, a service station and a car-wash. Traffic thundered along the A194. This part of Gateshead had the look of a place by-passed. It had all the charm of the outskirts of small American towns without the cheap petrol and the hot butterscotch sauce. There was a hand-printed sign strapped to a streetlamp which read: 'The Tuck Inn. "Hot Food" Third Left'. Maybe it's just me being fussy, but I don't think I'd ever eat at any place whose owner puts the word 'food' in inverted commas. The area was grim and grey, the only splash of green left over from the night before by someone who had unwisely chucked a carton of mushy peas down on top of ten pints of Exhibition. Worst of all, though, as I walked along by the high mesh fencing of a used car lot, a police siren blared and for a brief, stomach-churning moment I thought I was back in New Cross.

The Gateshead International Stadium is immaculate. It has comfortable seats with adequate leg-room, excellent sight-lines, easy access, a roof that keeps out the rain rather than funnelling it down the back of your neck, a snack bar that doesn't smell like the biggest burp in history and clean toilets. In short it's a completely unsuitable place to stage a football match. Call me a romantic, but unless I've waded up to my ankles in urine, got wedged behind a pillar and had boiling hot Bovril spilled down the back of my legs by a fat bloke who's been poorly advised on the breath-freshening qualities of fried onions, I just can't settle down and enjoy myself. Jane Seymour's exactly the same, apparently.

Only the main stand is open for Gateshead's matches. It holds over 3,000. Today there were about 350 people in it. The crowd, such as it was, was much noisier than it would have been at a lesser non-league game. As if they reckoned paying £4 entitled them to chant a bit rather than just abuse the referee. I took a seat at the end of a row in front of four elderly men who were arguing over who should sit where. 'I'm not going next to him,' one of them said. 'He smells like he's slept with a badger.'

I sat looking northwards across the running track, to the other side of the Tyne where the white bulk of Byker Wall dominated the skyline, rising up from the red-brick surroundings like the last great monument of a once mighty civilisation. Socialism, probably.

'Can we get past?' a grey-haired man in a melton overcoat said. I stood up and let him and his cronies by, then sat down again musing vaguely on T. Dan Smith and the Venice of the North Plan. Unfortunately I'd forgotten about the tip-up properties of the stadium's seating, with the result that I landed flat on my arse on the concrete. I sat on the ground for a moment, wondering if I mightn't be able to pass this off as something I'd meant to do all along. Some sort of one-man protest against the Taylor recommendations, or a demonstration about the unwarranted presence of Wagon Wheels in the tea huts of every football ground in Britain. By the time I'd considered these options people were gesturing at me and laughing anyway, so there didn't seem much point.

Gateshead had spent much of the season in the relegation zone of the Conference. As a result big Tommy Cassidy had been handed his P45. His replacement was Colin Richardson. Richardson, a large avuncular-looking man, had been manager of Whickham when they'd won the FA Vase and he'd kept his lucky bubble-perm and 'tache ever since despite the fact that they had become terminally unfashionable. Since his Whickham days he'd also managed North Shields who, under his guidance, had won the North Eastern Counties League (the League below the Northern Premier in the original pyramid), and captured the Northern Premier League First Division title and the FA Vase again with East Yorkshire club Bridlington Town. In Richardson's first game in charge Gateshead had been hammered 6–1 by Macclesfield, but they'd won the next two matches and were now edging up into the kind of mid-table position which had been their usual resting-place since they made it into the Conference in 1990.

Gateshead's history was not exactly echoing with the tunes of glory. They'd started life eight miles away in South Shields where, unsurprisingly, they'd been known as South Shields FC. South Shields played in the North-Eastern League, winning the Championship in 1914 and 1915. In 1919 they were invited to join the newly extended Second Division. South Shields stayed in the Second for nine seasons, but by the late twenties, when that part of south Tyneside now designated as Catherine Cookson Country by the local council was in danger of becoming Soup Kitchen Country in the eyes of the rest of the nation, the club was in financial trouble. Relegation to the Third Division (North) followed and two seasons later South Shields closed down altogether. Their ground, at Horsley Hill, was briefly turned into a dog track, then demolished. A housing estate was built on the site. The following year, however, they were back in business ten miles further west at Redheugh Park, buried amongst the gas-holders and foundries of Dunston. Now known as Gateshead FC, they took on the unique distinction of becoming the only club to change both name and location while members of the Football League (fair sets your heart pounding, doesn't it?). Like their forerunners at South Shields, Gateshead made a bright start, beating Doncaster 2–1 in front of 15,545 cheering Geordie fans (last phrase copyright the author) and finishing ninth. The following season they tied for top place with Lincoln City, losing out on promotion to Division 2 on goal average. It was a high point. By 1937 they were applying, successfully, for re-election. The following year Gateshead's redoubtable chairman Bill Tulip signed Hughie Gallacher from Grimsby for £500. Gates soared and Gallacher netted five goals in a 7–1 rout of Rotherham. By October, however, the mercurial Scot was too ill to play. Gateshead's promotion challenge faltered and crowds dwindled. By the time Gallacher had made his comeback the chance had gone.

In the fifties, a Gateshead team which featured the Callender brothers, Jack and Tom, a pair of dark-haired, rugged individuals who would not have looked out of place on a Sicilian wanted poster, finished as runners-up again in the Third Division (North) and made it to the quarter-finals of the FA Cup, where they were beaten by eventual finalists Bolton Wanderers. In 1958 they became a founder member of Division Four. Two seasons later they were again forced to apply for re-election for only the second time in their history. This time they were unsuccessful. They were replaced in the Football League by Peterborough United. Some have described this as the most unjust decision in football history (though personally I'd have thought that honour went to the man who decided to hand a microphone to Elton Welsby). When you consider that Hartlepool, who finished below the Tynesiders, were applying for re-election for the sixth time, you can see their point. It's hard to know what to say about the clubs who voted against Gateshead, but the word 'shitehawks' leaps to my lips.

Gateshead limped on for ten years in non-league football before calling it a day. Redheugh Park was demolished and nothing whatsoever was built on the site. Which just goes to show how things have improved since the thirties, really.

The programme announced that games between the Tynesiders and Stafford had usually been dour, low-scoring affairs. This proved to be a sadly accurate summary of the afternoon's match, which provided all the rousing entertainment normally associated with that moment at a neighbour's house minutes after the words 'holiday' and 'video' have conjoined. Rangers had plainly come looking for a draw, and Gateshead seemed intent on helping them find one, even if it involved sticking their hand in among the crunchy bits down the back of the sofa. The afternoon wasn't without its moments, however. Alan Lamb, Gateshead's former England Under-16 international, who was, as the chants at Billingham had suggested, short, square and lacking in hair, showed some neat touches. The Conference's top scorer, Paul Dobson, went close a couple of times. Time passed, as is its wont.

On the side of the running track one of the ballboys kept himself warm by doing those spotty-dog exercises. He went bounce-step-bounce-step. He was wearing a yellow baseball cap and had pulled his arms out of the sleeves of his tracksuit and folded them across his front, so that with the peak, the bulge and the empty sleeves bouncing up and down he resembled a pregnant penguin desperately trying to take off. The sun came out. Mother-of-pearl clouds skated across the ice-blue sky. It was quiet. You could see the cranes of the doomed Swan Hunter shipyard further down the river at Wallsend. Have you ever wondered whatever happened to the *Blue Peter* baby? Or why there's always a single white slingback shoe on top of a bus shelter? And what happened to the other one? No, neither had I, but an afternoon at Gateshead International Stadium gives you space for such ruminating. There's a calm serenity about the place that invites us to look inwards rather than outwards. The man in front of me was similarly moved to self-examination. 'Four quid for this shite,' he postulated philosophically at one point. 'I must need my head looking at.'

At half-time I went down to the snack bar and bought a bag of crisps. I got spring onion because I felt I needed to eat some vegetables. I loitered about behind the stand for a moment wondering whether to bother with the rest of the match. Shameless hedonistic thrill-seeking is all very well, it's just that sometimes you've got to face up to your responsibilities.

I had some ironing to do at home. But I stayed for the second half anyway.

The game finished 0–0.

A sculptor friend of mine was working at the Amarc retraining centre during the 1990–91 season. Amarc is in the old British Shipbuilders' yard at Hebburn on the south bank of the Tyne. One day the foreman told my friend there was something he thought he should come and see. He took him over to one of the huge fabrication sheds in which the hulls of ships were once built. There, in a clearing amid the discarded cogs and cable, rising out of the rusting detritus of industrial history, was a bronze statue of Jackie Milburn, 'Wor Jackie'. A man was kneeling, bent before it as if in obeisance. He was carving an inscription on the marble plaque.

Normal practice when installing a sculpture in a public place is to erect the plinth first, then bring the statue along later and fix it into position. The statue of 'Wor Jackie', though, was going to be erected in one of Newcastle's busiest shopping areas. Building the plinth in situ would cause too much disruption. Instead the statue had been fitted to its plinth at Hebburn and that night the whole thing would be taken by lorry and concreted into Northumberland Street. It seemed apt that the bronze effigy of a great goalscoring centre-forward should, like the man himself, suddenly materialise as if from nowhere, so that the first anybody noticed of his coming was when he had already arrived.

My friend asked the stonemason if he had seen Milburn play. The stonemason said he had, many times. He didn't think the statue looked much like the man he'd seen.

'It's funny,' the foreman said. 'Nobody thinks it looks like Jackie Milburn except for his family. They reckon it's the spit of him.'

'I suppose,' the stonemason said, 'we never saw him that close to. Not really to know his face. I tell you what, though – the stride's dead right. I'd recognise him from that.'

Milburn did have a distinctive stride. In the old Pathé newsreels when he hits top speed his body seems to sink slightly so that his hips are on a level with his knees. In 1951 in the FA Cup final at Wembley he powers away from the Blackpool defence, low-slung as a sports car, to score his second goal. The statue shows him in mid-sprint, right foot cocked back ready to strike the ball. Like his nephew, Bobby Charlton, Jackie Milburn had a powerful shot. Photos show the follow-through, his foot as high in the air as a can-can dancer's, his jaw looking in imminent danger of being dislocated by his fast-rising thigh, head tilted forward, eyes staring along his shin as if down the barrel of a bazooka. He got 199 goals for Newcastle in 398 appearances. Not many were scored with his head.

It is unusual for a player to come to epitomise a football club in the way that Jackie Milburn does Newcastle United. For all Manchester United's stars, it is the manager Sir Matt Busby who is the figure most associated with the Old Trafford club, just as it is Bill Shankly at Liverpool, Jock Stein at Celtic and Herbert Chapman at Arsenal. It is hard to think of another side for whom a footballer is so symbolic: Bobby Moore at West Ham, perhaps, or Danny Blanchflower at Spurs? Fitting, too, that in an area which has produced so many footballers, it is a player who is the most revered figure of that region's biggest club.

In truth Newcastle had never had a guiding hand like that of Busby. They were the last professional side in England to appoint a team manager. Even during Milburn's era, when United won the FA Cup three times in five years, there had been a succession of managers at St James's Park, a high degree of boardroom hurly-burly and heroic figures like centre-half Frank Brennan had departed in acrimony. The Ashington-born Milburn stuck with United through it all. He never played for another English club. The son of a miner and a colliery worker himself when he was young, Milburn was a quiet, modest man. Other great Newcastle players, from Gallacher to Keegan, had been hero-worshipped; Jackie Milburn was liked. Which doesn't sound like quite so power-ful a thing, until you stop to think about it.

'A canny fella,' the shopkeeper admitted. 'Even if he did

play for Newcastle. But I'll tell you something funny about that statue. It's running away from St James's rather than towards it. You see, even a lump of metal has more sense than a Geordie.'

The statue of 'Wor Jackie' was paid for by public subscription, one of the few artworks to be financed in such a way since the war. It had cost in excess of £20,000. The money had been raised in a matter of days. At the same time as the statue was being sculpted and cast Newcastle United were going through one of their greatest upheavals. The Sir John Hall-led Magpie Group were attempting to wrest control of the club away from Gordon McKeag. The McKeag family, along with the Seymours, had owned Newcastle United for generations. Gordon McKeag had memorably described United as 'part of the family silver'. The Magpie Group were pledged to democratising the club; to redistributing that silver to the fans who over the years had paid for it. So, while Jackie Milburn could be said to personify Newcastle United, the statue of him, and the way that it was financed, might be seen as the symbol of something else: the moment when the club he had served so faithfully and so well finally started to be handed back to the people to whom it really belonged.

When my friend had finished looking at the sculpture he noticed another one being fabricated across the shed. It was Claes Oldenburg's work 'Message in a Bottle'.

'Where's that going?' he asked the foreman.

'Teesside,' he replied. 'It's for outside Middlesbrough Civic Centre.'

Newcastle got a footballer, the Boro got a giant bottle. You can draw your own conclusions from that.

Whickham v. Bamber Bridge, FA Vase Third Round
Saturday 11 December 1993

The train was packed. Newcastle were playing Manchester United, but that wasn't where most people were going. 'Who says two weekends before Christmas is a time for shopping? They don't on Tyneside,' said the man who presents *Match of the Day* when Des Lynam and Ray Stubbs are unavailable. (You know the one. He's got blond, side-parted hair and looks like he might have been in the New Seekers.) He obviously hadn't seen the hordes bulging the Metro Centre, or flooding Eldon Square that lunchtime. No one on earth shops with the manic ferocity of Geordies. If Henry V had had any Tynesiders with him on the Agincourt campaign he could have dispensed with all that high-flown rhetoric about 'Once more unto the breach' and just shouted: 'Half-price sale in Harfleur!' They'd have knocked the walls down and the French with them. A week before Christmas venturing within 200 yards of a shopping complex in the centre of Newcastle is fraught with danger. You walk down Haymarket minding your own business and suddenly you've been picked up by a tornado of humanity and dumped in the ladies' gloves department of Fenwicks. When you go in search of presents yourself any attempt at a plan is useless. You just throw yourself into the surging torrent of humanity and buy something wherever you happen to fetch up. Last year my mum and dad got a gorilla mask, two bri-nylon pillowcases and a wind-sock.

Happily I wasn't going anywhere near the centre of Newcastle. I was going to Whickham, a suburb high on the hills to the south of Blaydon. The bus crossed the Tyne on the Redheugh Bridge and hammered on past the factories of Team. Steve and I talked about Bobby Robson, who'd been sacked the week before by Sporting Lisbon, and the hapless Graham Taylor (just what the hell is a 'hap'? And why is it a disadvantage not to have one?), who'd resigned after England's triumph over San Marino. Steve was worried Kevin Keegan would get the England manager's job. Jimmy Armfield had been championing Keegan's cause on Radio 5. Armfield had just been appointed special adviser to the FA international committee, so it was reasonable to assume he was expressing the same view to them. Newcastle had been struggling for years and now, just as they had started to revive, it seemed that the man responsible was going to be taken away from them. Steve was fed up. He said: 'What have England ever done for the North-East? They don't come and play here; they don't even send the B team. And they'll take Keegan and we're supposed to say thanks for the honour. Well, bollocks.'

It was the old club-versus-country debate which taxes many football fans. Thankfully, as a Boro supporter, it's never had much relevance to me. I tried to imagine myself in Steve's position. Middlesbrough, piloted by a charismatic and dynamic ex-player, have cantered to the First Division Championship, spent millions on players and ground developments and are now fifth in the Premiership, having set the top flight alight with their brand of dynamic attacking football. Then suddenly the England manager resigns and . . . No, it was too difficult. Even Baron Munchausen would have struggled with it.

I knew what Steve meant, though. In the North-East, England, or rather the notion of England, seems a long way off. The North-East is at the far corner of the country but it is separated by more than just miles. There is the wilderness of the Pennines to the west, the emptiness of the North Yorkshire moors to the south and to the north, the Scottish border. The nearest major city to Newcastle is Edinburgh, and that is in another country. Sometimes the

North-East seemed more like an island than a region. And there was more. As a boy I can remember looking through one of those colour illustrated encyclopaedias and coming upon a full-page picture that caught my attention. There were cottages festooned with hanging baskets, burgeoning gardens, white picket fences, a village green, a duck pond, a cricket match, a district nurse on a bicycle and, doubtless, a future prime minister sitting outside a thatched pub sipping warm beer. The caption underneath read: 'An Everyday English Village Scene.' This got me very excited indeed. I knew that a mistake on a stamp made it much more valuable and so there seemed a pretty good chance the same might be true of encyclopaedias. And this caption was clearly a mistake. Because I lived in an English village *and it didn't look anything like that!* Strangely, neither my primary school teacher, Miss Thom, nor my mother seemed particularly interested in my potentially money-spinning discovery. So I went back to the encyclopaedia and looked up Peru instead. I was very fond of Peru. It was where Paddington Bear and Hector Chumpitaz came from.

Twenty years later I went to see a friend of mine in Sonning-on-Thames. It was a hot June day and as we walked across the churchyard I realised that this was, spiritually if not figuratively, the village in the encyclopaedia. There were rambling roses growing up the white-painted walls of the houses, lupins nodding and bees buzzing. You half expected to see Mrs Miniver waving to a cycling vicar, or Joan Hunter Dunn on her way to a tennis party. This *was* England. England, their England. It wasn't like the North-East at all.

Whickham is an inner suburban mix of massive Edwardian villas set in tree-lined avenues, and council estates. The Glebe Road ground tilts down towards the Tyne as if nodding at an old acquaintance. On the other side of the river Scotswood appears to be nodding back. Though knowing Scotswood it's more likely it's attempting a head-butt. In Whickham's clubhouse we paid our admission ('In case there's a rush before kick-off,' the gateman said optimistically) and got a programme. There was a drawing of the local hero, 'Lang

Jack,' on the cover. In Victorian times 'Lang Jack' had achieved regional fame for his ability to carry several large pieces of stone over long distances. You had to be able to do something to become a celebrity in those days.

A busload of Bamber Bridge fans had already taken up residence in the bar. Bamber Bridge was in Lancashire, so there was the usual assortment of Cyril Smith lookalikes and fluff-topped senior citizens filling the air with their jocular Hobson's Choice tones. One of them had a hunting horn which he blew at regular intervals to guffaws of merriment from the rest of the party. So the noise in the room went something like: Aymildanbittergraciefieldswiganpiertripeanonionsmorecambe*paaaarp*hahahahahadandelionanburdockrochdalehornets*paaaarp*hahahaha . . .

We bought Federation Bitter and stood looking at the photos of Whickham's 1981 victory in the FA Vase which lined the bar. Whickham had been in the Vaux Wearside League then (they were promoted into the Northern League in 1988). Two down to Willenhall at Wembley, they'd fought back to win in extra time. A photo from the *Chronicle* showed the team celebrating after their semi-final win over Windsor and Eton. They're in the dressing-room, drinking and singing, a Nolan Sisters poster on the wall behind them. Colin Richardson is in the middle of his team, bubble-perm damp, mouth open, looking like a clumber spaniel after a particularly enjoyable swim. P*aaaarp*hahahahahaha . . .

Outside it was freezing. Winter had returned and the slate-grey sky carried the threat of snow. A wind was whipping diagonally across the pitch, flattening the corner flags and making the telephone wires on the red-brick semis that lined the north side of the ground whistle. We were debating whether to go out there at all. You could see all but a quarter of the pitch from the window and – P*aaaarp*hahaha.

'I wish someone would shove that bloody thing up his arse,' I said.

'Aye,' Steve replied, 'but the really worrying thought is that somebody already has.'

P*aaaarp*hahaha . . .

At that moment a man appeared in front of the window and started jumping up and down and gesturing wildly at us. 'Who's this nutter?' Steve said.

I said, 'It's a friend of mine from Teesside.'

Pete Smith's appearance forced us outside. The teams were already warming up. Strutting about in the black and white shirt of Whickham was a player of about thirty with a bleached curly perm, Zapata moustache and skin the colour of condensed tomato soup. His shirt was outside his shorts and he was holding the cuffs in the palm of his hands in a manner pioneered by Len Shackleton and made famous by Denis Law. 'Away, Monkey, man,' someone shouted from the touchline. Without looking over to where the shout had come from the curly permed player waved a hand nonchalantly in acknowledgement. 'Got to be the temperamental ball-playing genius,' Steve said.

When the game got underway it quickly became obvious he'd hit the bullseye with Jocky Wilson-like accuracy. Monkey flitted about round the edge of the Bamber Bridge penalty area feinting, chipping and flicking, with the apparent contemptuous leisureliness of someone who is really rather pleased with himself. The only time his insouciance deserted him was when the actions of an opponent offended his sensibilities. He was a passionate aesthete, the Bamber Bridge defenders mere Philistines. Around him his Whickham team-mates constructed a series of neat, short passing movements. They hit the bar and post in quick succession, a header fizzed six inches wide of the post. Bamber Bridge countered by hoofing the ball down the field at every opportunity. As they were kicking into the gale this usually resulted in it ballooning over the touchline and scampering off across the adjoining cricket square pursued with gradually diminishing enthusiasm by groups of youngsters, several of whom had brought bikes with them for the purpose.

In the forty-third minute Whickham went in front. A quick exchange on the edge of the D saw David Cleary round a defender, draw the 'keeper and clip the ball into the net. It was a deserved reward for their efforts, but one goal hardly seemed enough. Bamber Bridge would have the wind at their backs in the second half and for all the lack of imagination they'd shown in the first forty-five minutes they were in Division 1 of the Northern Premier, two divisions above the home side in the league pyramid; fitness if nothing else would surely tell. We scurried off in the direction of the tea hut without much confidence in Whickham's chances.

Outside the Corner Kick Café, housed in a brick and concrete bunker, there was a hand-painted tin sign detailing the goods available inside. The last line read: 'Dogs, crisps, sweets etc.' A young bloke emerging through the doorway said, 'Aye, and the cats are canny, too,' and took a bite out of an evil-looking bun.

The Lancastrians had already eaten all the gerbils, so we had to make do with sausages.

It was warm inside the Corner Kick. Great puffs of steam sneezed from the tea urn and the hot dog pan. There were Formica tables and little wooden chairs with red leatherette seats. It was like a set from a 1960s *Play for Today*. You felt at any minute a RADA graduate with a blond bouffant and white mac would come in, smoking prodigiously, and say: 'Ey oop, old cock. How about a chip booty for our Dad's tea?'

In the wall opposite the serving hatch was a brick fire-surround, painted pink and engraved with the legend 'Whickham 1954–55' . . .

1955! What a year that was! The Magpies were at Wembley again. One for sorrow, two for joy, three for the goals they rattled past Man City. The cry went up across Tyneside, 'Get out the silver polish, lass! The Cup's coming home once more.' And that wasn't the Geordies' only triumph. Plucky little Whickham, then still known as Axwell Park Colliery Welfare, had also carried off a lesser-known national amateur knock-out competition. After the FA Cup, the FA Trophy and the FA Vase came the FA Fireplace (the equivalent of today's Dimplex Sunday Shield). Whickham's victory over the Norfolk village side Ottoline Morrell was the North-East's only success in this venerable contest (Darras Hall Casuals, a blue-blooded squad of chief accountants, had reached the final in 1924–25, but scratched from the competition following the infamous cottage pie incident). The Tynesiders owed much to the skills of one man, the legendary 'Croggy' Clemmy Noble. A schoolboy player of some repute before the war, Noble tragically lost his left leg at sea, in what he later described as 'the wildest game of pontoon I ever played in my life'. Despite his wooden limb and the fact that his love of food and drink had swelled his weight up to the eighteen-stone mark, Noble played successfully on the wing for Whickham for many years. The sight of his vast frame hopping up and down the touchline on his pointed left peg made him a hero at the Glebe Ground. As long-serving manager Reg Dobson observed, 'Croggy may not be quick, he may not be skilful, but he's a hell of a help with the drainage.'

By the time the second half got underway a lumpy rain had begun to fall. Actually, that's not strictly accurate. It wasn't falling at all. It was sort of whipping past, parallel to the ground, heading in the general direction of Norway. Pushed on by the howling wind Bamber Bridge attacked incessantly. Every time they got the ball they hoisted it into Whickham's penalty area and charged in after it. The home side defended manfully, marshalling themselves around a massive centre-half who may have been a descendant of 'Lang Jack' and certainly looked well capable of carrying several large opponents long distances. Or kicking them there, if needs be. Their plight became increasingly desperate, however. Even when they won the ball back, they couldn't clear it – the wind simply boomeranged it back at them. 'Monkey', so influential in the first half, now had to content himself with trotting about in the centre circle and having the occasional violent disagreement with an opposing defender. The match increasingly came to resemble a game of attack and defence. They could have switched off the floodlights in Bamber Bridge's half for all the action they were illuminating. And the more one-sided the contest became, the more surely I found myself being drawn into it. It was like the Sunderland v Leeds Cup final. The more Leeds attacked, the more hopeless Sunderland's situation seemed, the greater hope it seemed to generate. As if wishful thinking was being drawn into the vacuum by a process of emotional osmosis. So it was at the Glebe Ground, as the lumpy rain turned to more solid sleet and Whickham's rotund young 'keeper slithered across the mud after a deflected shot, clinging on to the retrieved ball with all the ferocity of a starving chocoholic grabbing a two-pound Creme Egg.

And so it went on. The ball hovered around the Whickham penalty area. Men in black and white flung themselves at it from all directions, but it wouldn't seem to budge. The hunting horn sounded in one long fanfare. The Lancastrians roared encouragement. A cross came in again; under pressure the goalie tried to punch, but succeeded only in waving it into the path of an onrushing forward. It dropped at his feet eight yards out. The goal gawped. He hammered it as hard as he could. I closed my eyes, waiting for the swish of the ball hitting the net, the blast of that bloody bugle. Instead I heard the crash of corrugated iron and a burst of derisive laughter. The shot had cannoned off the roof of the stand.

Looking back, this was the turning-point of the game. It was Jim Montgomery's double save; the moment when Bamber Bridge saw the game going away from them; when Whickham rallied. Viewed from a distance it was about this time that Bamber Bridge's attacks became increasingly unco-ordinated and Whickham started to threaten on the break. Epiphanies are only recognisable retrospectively, however. At the Glebe Ground there were still fifteen minutes of agony to be endured. And then the injury time. Three minutes. Five minutes. The ball dropped on to the edge of the Whickham six-yard box again. The 'keeper caught it this time and wellied it downfield with all his strength. It travelled about forty yards, stopped, took five paces back and dropped to the turf. In it came again. Eight minutes. Ten minutes.

'Away, referee, blow your fucking whistle!' someone, perhaps even me, shouted.

'He's adding it on for all your time-wasting,' one of the Lancastrian aldermen said.

'What bloody time-wasting?' Steve retorted.

'You keep kicking it off,' the Lancastrian said. 'You should have ballboys to chase it.'

'You bloody chase it yourself,' someone, possibly me again, said. 'You look like you could do with the exercise.'

And finally the whistle blew. Monkey and the rest of the Whickham players danced about in the sleet, boots squelching on the sodden grass, wet faces gleaming under the floodlights. Club officials stood by the dressing-room doors grinning broadly and applauding.

'Well, you did it, lads,' the Lancastrian said sportingly.

And just for a moment I thought, 'Yes, *we* did.'

In the next round Whickham were beaten in a replay by Dunkirk of the Notts Football Alliance.

Sunderland v. Millwall, Endsleigh Insurance League Division 1
Tuesday 28 December 1993

Standing with my back to the barrier at the Fulwell End I felt a bit queasy. That morning I'd had my traditional Yuletide breakfast of four liqueur chocolates, a handful of mint Matchmakers and a cold roast potato. I'd also had a couple of segments of Terry's Chocolate Orange because it had been frosty and I knew I needed vitamin C to fight off colds. So it clearly wasn't anything I'd eaten that was making me feel ill. Most likely nausea was being brought on by the overpowering odour of aftershave and new gloves that was wafting round Roker Park, combined with the sight of all the strident box-fresh shellsuits. There'd been a bit of controversy in the papers about shellsuits. Apparently, some of them were highly inflammable and could burn to a cinder in thirty seconds. Questions had been asked in the House of Commons, because plainly this just wasn't quick enough.

My neighbour had predicted a big gate. He'd also forecast two large doors, a cat-flap and thirty yards of larch-lap fencing. I got that one out of a cracker.

My neighbour thought there'd be a big crowd, which was why we had our backs to the barrier. The Fulwell End was steeply raked and the prospect of being shoved up and down it by men wearing over-decorated sweaters and Blue Stratos who'd been made over-exuberant by several schooners of sweet sherry and the relief of escaping from the bleeping choirs of Gameboys in their front rooms evidently didn't appeal to him. 'We'll be leaned back on this and get a good view of the pitch,' he said.

And we did get a good view of the pitch, too. Unfortunately we didn't get much of a view of the game because at 2.55 p.m. a bevy of Genuine Supporters arrived, shoved in under the barrier and came up in front of us. I could tell they were Genuine Supporters because one of them said so. 'Away out the road you bloody part-timers, and let the Genuine Supporters in,' he said. There were always people like this at football. Barging in at the last minute bellowing, 'Where were you lot at Plymouth Argyle away in 1977, eh?' They always pushed. Even if there was only one other bloke in the end he'd get a bloody good shoving when the Genuine Supporters arrived and they'd all be pointing at him saying, 'He hasn't been for donkey's years, that fella. He just asked me why Jackie Mordue wasn't playing.'

I have a facility for names. I can tell what someone's name is just by looking at them. The bloke who'd come and stood in front of us was called Fat Bugger. He was enormous. He was like Rockall in a waxed jacket. He had a voice so reverberating and powerful that every time he spoke far out in the North Sea herds of female elephant seals came over all broody. He parked himself in front of my neighbour's son. He was as wide as a tank. 'We Will Rock You' by Queen came over the tannoy as Sunderland ran on to the pitch. 'We will, we will FUCK you!' Fat Bugger roared in tones reminiscent of the noise produced by a Firebird Trans-Am with a cracked exhaust.

My neighbour shook his head. 'What a moron,' he said, a bit too loudly for my liking.

Fat Bugger had half a dozen mates with him. Combined they probably weighed about as much as he did. There was a goofy one, a short-arse with a mouth full of mintoes, a ratty-faced redhead, a beanpole with a bum-fluff moustache, a belcher and a curly-top with a Walkman who stared vacantly at the pitch, occasionally saying 'Newcastle still losing,' to a chorus of 'The bastards!' from everyone within earshot.

I can't understand how anyone can listen to one thing while watching another. It must be very disorientating. Especially when you're listening to local radio, which is fairly confusing to start with. The North-East's local radio stations have some of the most baffling football commentators of all time. This is mainly because despite the fact they start off trying to play the calm neutral, they quickly become embroiled in the game. After about fifteen minutes of anything remotely exciting the commentary has deteriorated to the point where it begins to sound as if it's being simultaneously translated from Arabic by someone with a surreal sense of humour and several pages missing from his phrasebook. 'And in this sandy goalmouth,' a commentator blathered during Sunderland's Cup tie at Stamford Bridge a few years ago, 'a 'keeper could easily lose his feet.' Later, as the hysteria mounted, he said: 'And Chelsea, being pushed forward by this big house, are literally crucifying the Wearsiders.' Which, even given the Shed's reputation, seemed a little unlikely.

If the game's a real thriller, then any attempt at fairness goes out of the window and the men in the box become rabidly partisan. 'Bryan Robson,' one of them yelled during Boro's League Cup semi-final with Man United, 'the biggest moaner in British football. Why don't you just shut up and get on with it, you baby?' Listening to something as hysterical as that while watching Horden versus Easington must send some really contradictory signals to your brain. And then there's the problem of how to stop yourself getting carried away. Later in the season I was at Willington when amid the eerie silence of Hall Lane a dark-haired bloke standing on his own behind the goal suddenly yelled, 'What are you on about now, you stupid twat?' then suddenly started looking frantically around him for someone else to blame it on. There would be nothing worse than dishing out some such caustic observation on a packed yet silent terrace. Though I suppose being dropped head-first into a threshing machine would come close.

Peeping out from around the corners of Fat Bugger I could see that Sunderland were more co-ordinated than they'd been against Peterborough. Since Butcher's departure and the arrival of Mick Buxton they'd put together a good enough run to pull away from the relegation zone and start talk about the play-offs. They looked a competent enough side now, certainly as good as Millwall, who'd been in contention for much of the season and were currently lying third. Even though Phil Gray put them in front after ten minutes, their main problem still seemed to be converting possession into goals, a difficulty the sight of Don Goodman limping off after seventeen minutes seemed unlikely to alleviate.

On the way over we'd been talking about another Boxing Day game at Roker Park thirty-two years before. That day there'd been an injury to a Sunderland striker too, but one that was far more serious than Goodman's thigh strain. Brian Clough, a £45,000 signing from Middlesbrough the previous year, had collided with Bury goalkeeper Chris Harker and smashed the cruciate ligaments in his knee. Charley Hurley had missed an earlier penalty and the Rokermen lost 1–0. To all intents and purposes they also lost Brian Clough. He played three more games for them two seasons later, then retired. He was twenty-nine.

Nowadays it's hard to view Clough's playing career as anything more than the prologue to his story. We know what will follow – the Championships, the European Cups – so that moment when he is carried in agony from the pitch at Roker Park seems less like the end than the beginning of something. Yet at the time it must have been a sickening blow. Clough was the leading goalscorer of his day. He hit 197 for Middlesbrough in 213 appearances; 63 for Sunderland in 74. In photos he always seems to be hovering several feet above the ground, staring intently after a ball he has just blasted in the direction of the net. His face is thin and there's a pale brightness about it. Other great North-Eastern football managers had successful playing careers: Bobby Robson and Don Revie were both capped by their country; Bob Paisley was in the successful Liverpool side of the immediate post-war years. None of them was as popular as Clough. He was the local boy made good, a Steve Bull figure. Over 20,000 people turned up at Roker Park to see his comeback match for the reserves.

Brian Clough was born in Grove Hill in Middlesbrough.

Unlike Revie, it was easy to imagine Clough on Teesside. He had a recognisable, sharp-featured face and in the tone of his voice you caught that characteristic mix of avuncularity and abrasiveness, so that every witticism was a mixture of joke and taunt; an invitation to laughter or fisticuffs, which ever took your fancy. I was once in a local pub with my grandfather, who was about seventy at the time, and the landlord came to serve us. He was a huge man who must have weighed in excess of twenty stone. 'I've been away on holiday,' the landlord said, 'in case you're wondering why you haven't seen me for a couple of weeks.'

'Really?' my grandad said, looking him straight in the eye. 'I thought you'd run away to become a jockey.'

I'd been living in London a long time and my grandfather was dead before I heard that same tone of voice again. It was during the 1986 World Cup. Bobby Robson's England side had played pathetically in their first two games and back in the studio the panel of experts was debating what had gone wrong. Mick Channon was burbling on about the English players' failure to 'get by people'. 'The Brazilians do it,' he said. 'The French do it, the Danes do it . . .' From off-camera you heard a voice say, 'Even educated fleas do it.' Clough. The look on Channon's face, queasy, humiliated confusion, was an exact replica of that on the fat landlord's.

If it was easy to picture Clough on Teesside it was easier still to imagine what people would have made of him; a slight, young man with a quick mind and a fondness for giving people a piece of it. He'd have been a cheeky bastard, a big-mouth, a clever bugger. In Saltersgill and Belle View they must have been queuing round the block blowing meditatively on their knuckles. You could see, too, how when that physical pressure was gone his self-confidence would bulge out like bread dough from the fridge set on a warm stove. He'd get bends of the ego.

Millwall equalised through Roberts, who struck a weak shot goalwards from twenty yards. Chamberlain went down for it so slowly he appeared to be defying the laws of gravity, and the ball trickled into the net. Alec Chamberlain had been one of Butcher's close-season signings. There was always a murmur of complaint about him bubbling around the Fulwell End: 'He's not worth what we paid for him, this get.'

'I thought we got him on a free.'

'Aye, that's what I'm saying.'

Like his predecessor, Tony Norman, Chamberlain was, usually, a good shot-stopper, but when it came to collecting crosses he had more in common with Pat Coombs than Pat Jennings, dithering hysterically on his goal-line before flinging himself at the ball with all the brimming confidence of someone attempting to catch a grizzly bear in a butterfly net. Ironic cheers went up every time he caught a centre and you'd hear people saying, 'Bloody hell. Two in a row. It must be Christmas.' Poor old goalkeepers, eh? No wonder they're all as mad as Bob Wilson.

There was more urgency about Sunderland at the start of the second half. They charged about furiously launching themselves into tackles. There were a number of chest-slapping incidents. 'Don't argue, fight!' the Fat Bugger roared diplomatically, and across the North Sea off the coast of Norway she-whales nudged their partners and smiled saucily.

'Newcastle still losing,' the Walkman lad said.

'The bastards!' everyone rhubarbed.

It made me think of another incident that had occurred on Boxing Day. It was in 1946 at Ayresome Park. Boro were playing Arsenal and genial Leslie Compton, the Gunners centre-half, a man so uncompromising he made Stalin look like the Pilsbury dough boy, had fouled our 'keeper, David Cumming, for the umpteenth time. Fed up with it, Cumming got to his feet, felled Compton with a haymaker, chucked his sweater into the goalmouth and stomped off the field. Compton rose at the count of eight. At which point my grandfather's cousin Davey decided it was high time one of the family made his mark on professional football, and that the place to leave it would be on Leslie Compton's face. Jumping over the advertising hoardings, he ran on to the pitch. Shortly afterwards Compton hit the deck for the second time. Davey was led away by police. Later he was banned from Ayresome Park for five years. The judge said if he caused any more trouble in the meantime he'd reduce it to six months. Chortle, chortle.

Behind us a chant about ex-player Gary Rowell started up to the tune of 'The Twelve Days Of Christmas'. Seaham-born Rowell held the Sunderland scoring record jointly with Len Shackleton. Like Clough he'd retired early through a knee injury. 'Seven Gary Rowells,' the supporters sang, 'six Gary Rowells, fiiiive Gaaaa-ry Rowells, four Gary Rowells, three Gary Rowells, two Gary Rowells and a Gary Rowell in a pear tree.'

Then Craig Russell scored. It wasn't a particularly good goal, but it produced one of the most electrifying moments of the season. What happened was that someone played the ball into the path of Russell, who was running into the penalty area. He seemed certain to score and the crowd began to yell in anticipation. When he got to the penalty spot, Roberts slid in from the side and knocked the ball away to the right, bringing Russell down. The crowd, appealing for a penalty, increased the volume. The ball rolled out to Armstrong, who sidestepped a defender and struck a cross over the head of Keller in the Millwall goal. The noise went up another notch as Russell appeared again, unmarked at the far post. When the ball hit the back of the net the roar was so huge you couldn't hear it any more, it just crackled round inside your head like static. It blared up from the Fulwell End, hit the roof and bounced back down again. A steward near me put his hands over his ears. It went on and on and on.

Finally it subsided. 'Newcastle still losing,' the Walkman lad said.

The gates at Normanby Road were locked, but someone had helpfully bulldozed a hole in the wall a bit further along, so I walked in. The terraces were overgrown with weeds, the clubhouse looked like a pill-box after a flame-thrower attack, the ground was frosted with broken glass. Along one touchline there were two piles of rubble which had once been the dugouts. The goalposts were scabrous, the bollards which had held the crash barriers empty. Local kids had obviously been using the pitch for kickabouts – the goalmouths were solid mud. Now, though, it was spring and the uncut grass had risen to the height of a vicious tackle. The only player who'd go on a surging run here would be one armed with a machete. Over in the corner a small boy was whacking a tennis ball in the air with a baby cricket bat. Beyond him the vast bulk of Dorman Long, the engineering company that built, among other things, the Sydney Harbour Bridge, squatted by the River Tees. This was the home of South Bank FC, the oldest football club in the North-East, founder members of the Northern League, entrants in the first-ever Amateur Cup. George Elliott of Middlesbrough and England, the first player my grandfather could remember watching, had begun his career here. Blond-haired and handsome, Elliott was a skilful centre-forward. 'A brainy player,' my grandad would say. 'He didn't have to huff and puff all over the place waving his arms about like that tripehound.' He'd point at the television. It was switched off. I'm not sure which player he had in mind – obviously one we'd watched on *Match of the Day* or *Shoot*. I'd like to think it was Emlyn Hughes.

Jackie Carr had also started out at South Bank. Four of his brothers had played there, too. My grandad could remember one of them, Billy, or Pudden as he was nicknamed, being knocked unconscious heading a ball at Ayresome Park. And not just once. 'He was stretchered off three times in a game against Sunderland,' my grandad would say admiringly. No wonder Pudden was cross-eyed.

The Bankers had won the Amateur Cup in 1913 and unsuccessfully contested the finals of 1910 and 1922. They'd been Northern League champions on three occasions; won the League Cup twice and the North Riding Senior Cup seven times. Now their ground was unfit for football of even the most basic kind and they were about to be expelled from the league they had co-founded.

An old man was looking in at the ground too. He was in

his late sixties, shaped like a breezeblock. As I walked past him he said, 'I've seen some games in there.'

'There used to be allotments behind yon goal,' he went on. There were council houses now, many with steel-shuttered windows to keep out vandals. 'My grandfather had one, like. And when I was a lad the pair of us would sit on his shed roof and watch the game. The shed roofs over there would be covered in blokes watching the match. They were a top side, South Bank.'

I mentioned Elliott and Carr to him. He said: 'There's been more professionals come out of there than anywhere, internationals.' He was thinking, perhaps, of George Hedley and Fred Priest of Sheffield United, of Ted Catlin of Sheffield Wednesday, John Calvey of Nottingham Forest and Bob Turnbull of Bradford PA, all of whom had won England caps after leaving Normanby Road.

'The main stand was over there,' he said, indicating the far touchline down which in pre-war years a twenty-stone winger named Barney Mole had jinked mercurially. 'It would be packed. They got good crowds then. I lived just behind it. The houses aren't there now, they knocked them down to widen the road. I used to finish work at South Bank Steel – that's gone too, like – on Saturday morning, get my dinner and I could tell when the game started by the roar. I'd finish up and run round, maybe five minutes late. Sometimes, if I was off, I'd go and watch a game down the road, one of the boys' clubs, St Peter's or them, then I'd come racing back up for the kick-off here.'

We drove away, back in the direction of Middlesbrough, past the chemical works, the steelyards, the tower cranes and the container ships, and the council sign that said 'South Bank. Beauty, Business, Leisure.'

People who don't follow football think of it as just a game, something that can be packed away when it is finished and forgotten about. But the game, played out by twenty-two men in an hour and a half, is only the kernel of something greater. The game is the core, you might say, of the Game. In the North-East people wound the strands of their everyday life around it – childhood, youth, work, friendships, relatives, experiences, memories – until football became inextricable from existence itself; like the cardboard formers in one of those woollen pompoms parents wind from left-over yarn and dangle above the cribs of babies.

'We had good players, good crowds, good times here,' the old man had said. 'Whenever I come past I feel like crying.'

Spennymoor Utd v. Great Harwood Town, Northern Premier League Division 1
Saturday 8 January 1994

There had been a heavy frost. I phoned Brewery Field to check the game was still on. The phone was picked up and I could hear papers rustling, but nobody spoke. I said: 'I wondered if the game was on today.' There was a long pause, then someone said, 'Yes.' Only it wasn't quite like that. It was delivered in a fey, high-pitched swoop of the sort Spike Milligan adopts when playing ancient butlers. 'Yayyyys.'

Puzzled, I persisted. 'Spennymoor,' I said, 'against Great Harwood. It's going to be played?'

'Yayyyys.' It sounded like the speaker was far away in a vast and empty place. Which isn't what Spennymoor's like at all. Not unless it's early closing day, anyway.

'It's going ahead, then?'

'Yayyyys.'

'Definitely?'

'Yayyyys.'

I put the phone down and dialled another number. The receiver was lifted at the other end. 'I was wondering if the game's still on today?'

There was an eerie silence. 'Yayyyys,' the voice said.

An icy fog lapped around the towns and villages of County Durham. The day was so cold even the sun was wearing a balaclava. The bus spluttered along through Gateshead, past a pub whose sign advertised 'Real Ale for Real People' and another one that might have been offering surreal ale for unreal people ('Three pints of distended elephants' feet.

And I want them in a straight glass an' all, Salvador. And while you're at it I'll have a melted stopwatch sandwich and a packet of deep-fried bathroom fitments'); past the Pie People ('It's lunch, Jim, but not as we know it') and on into Birtley. The bus stopped near Bimbis Chip Shop ('All fish fried in our secret batter'), an old man got on, came up the stairs, sat down beside me and began to talk. I'd seen him once before, on television. He was a *Mastermind* contestant. His specialist subject was 'The comparative prices of beer throughout the United Kingdom'. He didn't pass once.

'Where are you from, like?' he said.

I told him.

'I know it, I know it. Now,' he said, 'work this out if you can. The pub near the castle has Exhibition (I'm going back a few years now, mind) at ninety-four pence a pint. A hundred yards down the road at the spot near the station it's ninety-one pence a pint.' He fixed me with much the same look Pythagoras must have sported when he first presented his theorem to the Academy. 'That's three pence difference!' he said brilliantly.

Well, knock me down with a feather.

'So do you belong there, then?' the man said. Meaning was I from there originally.

'No.'

'So where are you from?'

I told him, reluctantly.

'Ah, Camerons beer. Strongarm. I tell you, here's a thing. In the Masham Hotel . . .'

He was the reason Walkmans were invented.

The bus chugged on through Chester-le-Street, birthplace of Bob Hardisty, Alan Suddick, Colin Todd and Alan Foggon. At least one of whom would have been better placed to join in this conversation than I was. Not that I haven't sunk some beer in my time, mind. Last Friday I had forty-eight pints and I never went to the toilet once. I'm a right nutter, me.

'. . . the lad said, "It's Country & Western night. A pound admission." I said, "Will you let us in for nowt if I promise not to listen?" Now they had Banks's bitter. And I'd had that in Wolverhampton not three months before and there it was . . .'

The man left the bus just outside Tudhoe. He'd have done so a lot sooner only the collar of his shirt snagged on the handle of the emergency window.

The pitch at Brewery Field was frozen solid. The players' boots clattered on it as if it were a school corridor. In the circumstances it was incredible that Spennymoor produced any kind of football at all, let alone of the quality they did. They were top of Division 1 and it was easy to see why. Moors knocked their passes about crisply and always seemed to have men over; they were skilful on the ball and ran well off it. They were easily the best non-league side I'd seen. The codgers watching from the touchlines knew it, too. They had that sparkle in their eyes old men in the North-East get when they are enjoying themselves but don't want to risk anything as namby-pamby as a smile. Great Harwood were seventh in the table. They were totally outclassed.

I walked round behind one of the goals, past a youth in a pale suede jacket who was shovelling beefburger into his mouth and saying 'I've had about ninety fucking sausages since then, like,' and stood behind a man who was wearing a simulated leather trenchcoat with a pale grey fur collar. He looked like Paul Damon in an early episode of *Spycatcher*. Every time he turned his head in my direction I expected him to whisper, 'Thanks to Mavis, the Big Top's dancing bear is wearing a tutu, and her unicyclist has custard in his saddlebag. The matinee should prove most illuminating. And by the way, I also have the formula for Bimbis' secret batter.' The man next to him had long, black, centre-parted hair and darkly tanned skin. He might have been an Apache Indian except for the fact he was dressed in a chocolate-coloured quilted anorak and brown crimplene bell-bottoms. You see a lot of people at non-league football who seem to have bought radical wardrobes and haircuts when they were eighteen and never ditched them since. There were DAs, Ziggy Stardust quiffs, mop-tops, feather-cuts, triangular sideburns and Van Dyke beards; loons, bum-freezers, Oxford bags, brothel-creepers, ponchos and crocheted waistcoats. Glancing round a ground was like looking at a living reconstruction of those drawings displayed on the walls of barbers' shops. The ones you never see anybody point to and say, 'I want it like that, please, Mister.' Thankfully my own asymmetrical peroxide wedge is one of those classics that doesn't go out of fashion, otherwise I might have looked as if I belonged there.

Brian Healey put Spennymoor in front, side-footing in from ten yards after a good move down the right. The fans behind the goal at the far end waved flags and chanted in a vaguely disjointed way. When there are 1,500 people singing it doesn't really matter if one or two of them are slightly out of time; if there are fifteen it makes quite a difference. It was the first time I'd ever heard 'United! United!' done in rounds.

There were about 300 people in the ground altogether. Like Blyth, Spennymoor United had been one of the better-supported Northern League clubs. Like Spartans, too, they had come out of the North-Eastern League when it collapsed in the early sixties. They'd had more success as a semi-pro outfit than any of the other teams from that League who'd later turned amateur, winning the Championship four times. They'd had a fine team just after the war, taking the title in successive years. Three of the players from it, Jack Oakes, Tommy Dawson and Bert Johnson, went on to appear in FA Cup finals with Charlton Athletic. Moors finished top again in 1957 when the club was managed by Johnny Spuhler, a handsome broken-nosed gent who'd played for Sunderland as an outside-right and later for Middlesbrough at centre-forward in a team that also included George Hardwick, Micky Fenton and Wilf Mannion.

Spennymoor had been the dominant force in the Northern League in the seventies, winning the title five times and finishing as runners-up to Blyth on three occasions, establishing a rivalry with Spartans that, on the terraces at least, was often far from friendly.

Moors joined the pyramid in 1990 and spent three seasons in Northern Counties (East), struggling against the likes of Ossett, Belper and Brigg before sneaking the Championship on goal difference from Pickering and progressing into the Northern Premier. North Shields, another old rival from North-Eastern and Northern League days, had achieved a similar feat the previous season and gone bust in the process. Spennymoor seemed to be on firmer footing.

Except on the icy pitch, where Keith Gorman, their shaven-headed forward, had just executed a triple salchow prior to bouncing off an advertising hoarding. The half-time whistle blew. Spennymoor were still only 1–0 up despite the pressure. They'd spent the entire forty-five minutes in Great Harwood's half and could hardly have tested the woodwork more if they'd gone at it armed with chainsaws.

I wandered round the ground looking in vain for a programme and crunching ruminatively on a mouthful of tea. Great Harwood was in Lancashire, but their fans were strangely subdued, normal even. Perhaps the sub-zero temperatures had quelled their strange passions. They didn't have a klaxon, a bugle or even a rattle among them. The comedy grannies and rubicund bald roisterers had stopped at home. Which was rather mean-spirited. Some traditions are worthy of preservation. What was the sense of having Lancastrians if you couldn't sneer at them?

Their team got off to a better start in the second half, but the Moors defence was as solid as the clubhouse tea. After a Great Harwood attack broke down, Craig Veart raced off down the right and crossed for Healey to get his second. Veart teased the away team's back four sadistically all afternoon. If the left-back had had a pigtail he would undoubtedly have tugged it. He was short and dark-haired and there was a sparkling neatness about his work. He nipped in from the wing soon afterwards and curled a sharp left-foot shot inside the post. It was the best goal of the day. The pleasantly named Petitjean added a fourth five minutes from the end from a cross by Gorman.

I left before it hit the netting. It was freezing. I had an

unnerving feeling that if I farted it would drop out of one of my trouser legs as an ice-cube. There was a bus in two minutes. I trotted to the stop and stood waiting. The bus roared round the corner. Its windows were steamed up. A haze of heat radiated from its roof. I stuck out my hand in the prescribed manner. In a moment strangely reminiscent of the title sequence of *Whatever Happened to the Likely Lads?*, the bus tore past, the driver studiously avoiding my imploring stare. I stomped up into the town, glowered at a timetable fixed to the shelter, then grumbled round and round in circles.

Bonny Bobby Shafto was from Spennymoor. He'd gone to sea. I couldn't say I blamed him. The town centre wasn't very inviting. The shops' window displays were skimpy, as if they didn't have enough goods in stock to mount one. Times would be hard for traders in Spennymoor, their customers lured away by Morrison's superstore in nearby Bishop Auckland or sucked into the whirling vortex of the Metro Centre. There were lots of places in County Durham which had once been towns in their own right but now seemed more like a series of suburbs clustered around out-of-town shopping malls. The football clubs were often one of the few left-over reminders that these had once been communities rather than places where people happened to live.

Another bus came. Outside Brewery Field a youngish bloke got on and came upstairs. He nodded at me. 'Canny game,' he said. 'We played brilliant.' I'd noticed him in the ground, tall and thin, dressed in grey, standing heron-like on the edge of the terrace. I asked him if it was the best he'd seen from them this season. He shook his head. 'No, against Marine in the League Cup. Won three–nil. Slaughtered them. They were jammy. Lucky to get nowt. We could've got a boat-load. And they're top of the League. Miles clear. We caned them, man.' We talked about the game, the season, Andrew Fletcher, whom Spennymoor were supposed to be signing from Synthonia, and the time in 1974 when Moors had tied on points for the Championship with Blyth and beaten them in the play-off game at Ashington against the run of play. 'It was great,' he said. 'Like winning money on a horse instead of working for it. And I'm glad it was them. I've got nothing against Blyth, like, but they're big-headed bastards.' He got off somewhere near Durham, in a place so dark you could barely make out the shapes of the houses against blue-black sky. 'See you later,' he said.

The bus rolled on through the frosty North-Eastern night. All the villages it passed through were deserted. It seemed like everyone in Durham had gone indoors.

On the train back from Newcastle after the Spennymoor game I'd sat in a carriage full of Carlisle United supporters. The Cumbrians had been playing Sunderland in the FA Cup that day and they'd got a 1–1 draw at Roker. The fans were optimistic about their chances at Brunton Park in the replay. They were singing, 'If you're proud to wear trousers clap your hands,' and the contingent of their supporters from across the border in Dumfries and Galloway were whistling and jeering. The two police officers travelling with them looked on sternly.

Carlisle had a special relationship with the North-East. In fact many people seemed to think it was part of the region. 'Have you been to Carlisle yet?' they'd say when I told them about my book. When I pointed out that the 'Great Border City', as it likes to bill itself, was actually in the North-West they'd nod thoughtfully and say, 'Aye, I suppose it is, really,' as if they'd never noticed before.

The confusion was easy to understand. I'd suffered from it myself periodically. The main cause of it were the TV companies. The ITV regional network in the North-East, Tyne Tees, took in North Yorkshire, Cleveland, Durham, Tyne & Wear and Northumberland, while the BBC's North network covered all these plus Cumbria. As a result at least half the regional sports programmes you watched as a child covered Carlisle's matches. 'And now,' Tom Kilgour, the presenter, would say, 'let's have a look at how the rest of the region's clubs got on. First to Brunton Park where . . .' He was talking about the BBC region, of course, not the region I lived in, but the distinction was a fine one and certainly too subtle for me.

The North-East's football authorities also served to aggravate matters. Penrith from Cumbria spent nearly thirty years in the Northern League, while Carlisle United and Workington both played in the North-Eastern League before gaining Football League status. In addition there was an almost constant procession of players trooping back and forth across the Pennines between Brunton Park and the North-East. The first man to make the move may well have been Ivor Broadis. The striker from the Isle of Dogs was player-manager of Carlisle for a while, but then decided he was surplus to requirements and put himself on the transfer list. Sunderland offered him £18,000 for himself, which he happily accepted. Peter Beardsley started his career with the Cumbrians too, playing there under Bobby Moncur, the ex-Newcastle captain and round-Britain yachtsman, and Bob Stokoe, the Sunderland manager whose courageous attempts to make the combination of red tracksuit trousers, tan mac and brown trilby a hot fashion item will surely be remembered by Roker fans long after the 1973 FA Cup win he inspired has faded from their memories. The original Bryan 'Pop' Robson, arguably the best North-East-born player never to win an England cap, played out his career at Brunton Park; so too did Britain's first £100,000 teenager, the deftly skilful Tommy Craig. Former Middlesbrough winger Joe Laidlaw went to Carlisle and played in their Second Division promotion side. Before the next season began he stated that his new club would finish higher than Jack Charlton's Boro team, who had been promoted with them. Joe later went on to predict that Slick would be bigger than the Beatles and that no one would vote for a political party with a woman in charge of it. In the 1980s Carlisle sold Mick Buckley to Middlesbrough. Least said soonest mended. The mutual exchange list, in fact was pretty near endless: Hughie McIlmoyle, Gary Rowell, Don O'Riordan, Eric Gates, Kevin Beattie. I could go on, but it would only be a pointless and facile way of filling space. Des

McPartland, Malcom Poskett, Archie Stevens, Peter Garbutt, Wilson Hepplewhite . . .

So there was really no wonder football fans were confused.

On the train a Cumbrian took out a penny whistle and began to play 'I Can't Help Falling in Love With You'.

'Mr Flute's Barmy Army, Mr Flute's Barmy Army,' the Carlisle fans chorused.

Sunderland won the replay.

West Allotment Celtic v. Newcastle United Reserves, Northumberland Senior Cup Quarter-final
Saturday 15 January 1994

The bus went up through Killingworth, where George Stephenson had lived while working as a brakesman at West Moor Colliery. His first locomotive had been built in the wagon shops. Andy Sinton was born here, too. Which is probably less important historically, but more relevant to the subject of this book.

The two men in front of me were talking about the former Newcastle captain Kevin Scott, who had recently fallen out of favour at St James's. One said, 'He's moved into rented accommodation, so he must be twigging something.'

'Aye, well,' his mate said, 'What I heard is . . .'

Tyneside was always oscillating with gossip about Newcastle Football Club: Cole was going; Ferdinand was coming; this one had twatted a nightclub bouncer; that one's lass had run off with a Betterware salesman. Someone always knew; an uncle definitely reckoned; a lad at work's brother-in-law's nephew went out with a girl whose cousin lived with a bloke whose best man's ex-wife worked at the cobbler's where the woman who cut the hair of a friend of Lee Clark's mam got her stilettos sharpened and she said . . . People chatted about the players as if they were a cross between characters in *Coronation Street* and members of the Royal Family. They were a cornerstone of conversation; something everyone held in common.

There was some kudos to be gained too from being the one

who said, 'Well, you know why that is don't you?' especially if you paused long enough to let everyone shake their heads and admit they didn't. With the result that much of what you heard was, if not deliberately false, a mongrel sort of truth. In the dungeons of the city the facts and fittings had been severed from the corpses of long-dead tales, stitched together, given life and sent out at nightfall to lumber around the streets, frightening old ladies and befriending the lonely.

'Someone was telling me, whose mate's lad's an apprentice,' someone whose wife was married to a cab driver told me shortly after the start of the season, 'that, apparently, the day after this Nicky Papavasiliou signed they had a training session at Maiden Castle. And the players are all lined up and Keegan holds up the ball and points to it and says, "Ball. Ball." Then he points to his head and he says, "Head. Head." Next he points to the goal, "Goal. Goal." Points to his head, "Head," points to the ball, "Ball," points to the goal, "Goal." "Head, ball, goal!"

"Away, boss," one of the players says, "Nicky's English isn't that bad."

"I'm not talking to Nicky," Keegan says. "I'm talking to Brian Kilcline."'

A funny story. Though not as funny as the first time I heard it, in a pub in Cleveland, from a man whose uncle was a director at Ayresome Park, when the protagonists were John Neal, newly arrived Yugoslav Bosco Jancovic, and Billy 'The Bear' Ashcroft. Not as funny, but probably just as true.

You might say that in the North-East football was an everyday source of magic, and the clubs were Camelots around which a modern mythology was spun. Though you'd sound a right prat if you did.

West Allotment Celtic played in the Northern Alliance, a mixed bag of clubs ranging from inner-city Walker to the isolated North Tyne village of Wark. West Allotment itself was a more or less self-contained oblong of terraces (Maud, Buddles, Eccles) overlooking the old Rising Sun Colliery in Wallsend. The club played at nearby Backworth Miners' Welfare Ground. Backworth was more Gatcombe Park than

Langley Park. There were eighty-five acres of tree-fringed parkland; dew sparkling on the greensward, birds twittering amid oak and beech; an early Georgian house in glowing, golden stone with a pillared doorway and a flight of steps leading up to it. The estate had once belonged to a relative of Lord Grey of Fallodon. Now it was the property of the pitmen – nominally, at least. The NCB had just announced the impending closure of Ellington Colliery, the last colliery in the North-East. By a sad irony the current owners were swiftly becoming as much of an anachronism as the aristocrats who'd preceded them here.

The football pitch was to the west of the house. There were about 2,000 people arranged along the touchlines. Beyond, coveys of golfers strode loudly about on the immaculately manicured course. Football could learn a lot from golf. The PGA's decision to impose a five-stroke penalty on any player not dressed like Coco the Clown had certainly brightened up an otherwise dull game.

The Newcastle players were ferried from the changing-rooms in the mansion to the pitch by minibus to save them from being mobbed. West Allotment walked. Newcastle were playing in blue, but you could tell they were the professionals. They had longer shorts. It's a strange reversal of trends, the lengthening of the football short. I have an unnerving feeling that one day I will sit looking at my old football annuals with my grandson and he'll keep tittering and pointing at pictures of Barry Endean saying, 'Eee, look, Grandad, you can see his knees.'

Grandsons and sons were much in evidence around the pitch at Backworth. Their elders were busily pointing things out to them, and being children they were watching open-mouthed, believing it all. The Jesuits are renowned for saying, 'Give us the boy and we will show you the man.' This is usually seen as an indication of their unsurpassed powers of indoctrination. Compared to the work put in by a football supporting father or grandfather, however, the Jesuits' efforts are as nothing. A desultory wipe with a damp J-cloth compared to a total brainwash and wax. My own father wasn't interested in football. He'd been to a Grammar School and played rugby. When I was a boy I would suffer terminal agony if a football ever landed in his vicinity, because he would always dink it back in the prescribed rugby manner and after he had gone my friends would say, 'He toe-poked it! He toe-poked it!' – which, as everyone knows, is the way babies, girls, mothers and other sad unfortunates kick a ball. For a long while I thought my father was the only man in the North-East who couldn't kick a football properly. Then Newcastle signed Alan Gowling.

My grandfather, though, *was* keen on football. He first took me to Ayresome Park when I was five, presumably on the grounds that a trouble shared is a trouble halved. All through the game and the journeys to and from the ground he told me about Middlesbrough Football Club, flooding my head with such exaggerated accounts of valour and triumph that it washed any doubts or objections straight out of my ears and on to the back seat of his Morris 1100. I have never recovered my mental equilibrium. To this day I find myself during the long winter evenings gazing into the fire, sighing wistfully and saying, 'When will those glory days return?' Even though I know that logically and grammatically a thing cannot return to a place it has never been.

All around me at Backworth similar acts of callous mental manipulation were being carried out; the seeds of fandom sewn and given a liberal top dressing of horse manure. The man next to me – whose two small boys were so cranked up with excitement they wore the wide-eyed, drooling grins of hospital patients after the pre-op injection – not content with a quick recap on the deeds of Tudor and Supermac, was also inflating the reputations of some of Newcastle's reserve team to the point where any carelessness with a match might have resulted in a rerun of the *Hindenburg* disaster. 'Here's Liam,' he announced, every time Liam O'Brien crossed the halfway line. 'He could have a dig from here. He's scored plenty from this range.' And the boys would suck in their breath and wait expectantly for the Irishman to unleash an unstoppable forty-five yarder. Often they went quite blue.

'Nicky's got the ball, he could dribble round him,' the man said a couple of times, but soon gave up. Nicky Papavasiliou was wearing the sulky look of a child attending the birthday party of someone he doesn't much care for. Earlier in the season he'd been playing in the first team at Old Trafford. Keegan had called him 'my little gem', which was presumably not a reference to lettuces. Now, here he was turning out in the Northumberland Senior Cup. Papavasiliou kept running with the ball up to the West Allotment right-back, then stopping and pushing it out towards him as if to say, 'There it is. Try and take it off me.' Unfortunately, the right-back, unaware that he was cast in the role of dupe in this display of professional trickery, kept doing just that. Eventually, fed up with being upstaged by the volunteer from the audience, Papavasiliou whacked him on the back of the leg.

'He kicked him, Dad,' the small boys squeaked, outraged.

'Aye,' their dad said sagely. 'It's his Latin temperament.'

For the first half-hour Newcastle attacked non-stop. Mike Jeffery, signed in the autumn from Doncaster, hit the bar, while the peroxide blond Alun Armstrong, a local lad widely tipped as a future star, fluffed a series of chances. The length of shorts wasn't the only contrast in the two teams. In boxing it's said that the difference between a good amateur and a good professional is that the amateur always hits along the recognised channels, while the pro delivers his blows from varied and unexpected angles. It seemed that the same was true of football. West Allotment played well, they tackled fiercely and had good skill on the ball. When they went forward, though, their moves seemed stiff and pre-programmed: the ball went into the central strikers, they fed it out to the wings, the wingers crossed it. It was what you imagine English football was like in the fifties before the fiendish Continentals upset everything with their fancy theorising. Newcastle, on the other hand, were fluid. The complicated geometry of passes they created seemed to come naturally, not as part of some imposed plan, but as if the game was an extension of the players' imaginations.

And then West Allotment scored.

It was probably a grave mistake. At 0–0 Newcastle had seemed unconcerned; now their reputation had been called into question. The lead lasted seven minutes, then Papavasiliou equalised. Four minutes later Peter Cormack added a second. Three minutes after that Liam O'Brien hammered one in from thirty yards, thus ensuring that the father would be thought of as a font of footballing wisdom by his two sons for ever – or until they reached adolescence, at any rate. By that stage I wasn't standing near him any more. It had started to rain so I'd gone to stand under the commentary gantry. Newcastle first team weren't playing till Sunday and neither were Sunderland, so Metro Radio was running live commentary on the game. I'd never realised before that commentators have an assistant who calls out the names of the player on the ball to them, and spots others who are moving into dangerous positions. It's a responsible job and one that must offer an almost irresistible degree of temptation.

Newcastle got a fourth ten minutes from time when Aardvark tapped in Pot-Noodle's cross.

Blyth Spartans v. Bishop Auckland, FA Trophy First Round
Saturday 22 January 1994

Past Cramlington, across the fields to the south, I could see Seaton Delaval Hall. This had once been the home of the 'Gay Delavels', a family usually described as 'eccentric'. This is because they had a lot of money. If they'd been poor they'd have been described as 'mad'. One of their number had been something of a practical joker and had rigged up a series of trapdoors and pulleys which catapulted house-guests out of their beds and into tubs of freezing water. He also installed collapsible walls between bedrooms, thus pioneering a practice still used to this day in flat conversions. Catching on to this spirit of devil-may-care jiggery-pokery, the government played their own little prank on the Delavels this century – they built a massive power station right opposite their front windows. Oh, how we laughed.

About 800 people were at Croft Park. Before kick-off there was a minute's silence for Sir Matt Busby. There was a close bond between Busby and Bishop Auckland. During the war Sir Matt had become friends with Bob Hardisty, Bishops' most celebrated player, out in the Western Desert. Hardisty had played in Bishops' 1939 Amateur Cup final win over Willington, but his time in the forces made him as a player. He'd entered the army an ordinary half-back with a full head of hair and emerged from it a balding midfield genius. People might have been forgiven for suspecting some bizarre footballing variation on the old Blues legend – a crossroads, a guitar-player, a deal with the devil – in which Hardisty had swapped not his soul but his scalp for the ability to play. In truth the difference had been brought about by his involvement with Busby. Hardisty was a player with the kind of skills usually self-effacingly described by the English as 'Continental'. He could glide round opponents like a slalom skier between posts and spray passes accurately around the field all afternoon; tackling and defensive duties, though, were not his strong suit. As Busby was to prove later on with the likes of Bobby Charlton, it was players such as these he got the best out of. Hardisty went on to captain the Great Britain side which played in the London Olympics, a team managed by Sir Matt. During the fifties he would earn a reputation as the finest amateur footballer of all time. He retired from the game in 1957, but the following year, in the aftermath of the Munich air crash he, along with Bishops team-mates Derek Lewin and Warren Bradley, helped United fulfil their reserve team fixtures by turning out for them as amateurs.

The clash between Spartans and Bishops – once the two most successful amateur sides in the North-East – had been eagerly anticipated. When the draw had been announced a month before I'd thought Spartans would stand a good chance of winning. Bishop Auckland hadn't impressed me when I'd seen them, while Blyth had looked, as the man said, invincible. Since then, though, Spartans had been vinced on a number of occasions. Their form had begun to wobble like a jelly on a spin-drier. They'd lost four of their last nine matches and Durham had cut their lead at the top to nine points. Bishops, meanwhile, had plodded on, losing just two games out of twenty-two and sidling into fifth place in the NPL Premier Division. Manager Tony Lee had taken over at Kingsway the previous October from Harry Dunn. He'd played for Leicester City and shared a kind of gum-chewing grittiness with his namesake and fellow Filbert Street alumnus, Gordon. Gordon Lee had endured a spell in charge at St James's Park in the late seventies (I was going to say 'enjoyed', but that's not a word that sits easily in the same sentence as Gordon Lee). He was more of a soccer puritan than a soccer purist. Despite the fact that he took United to a League Cup final in 1976, supporters never forgave him for selling Supermac shortly afterwards. A Newcastle fan on the train once summed up his two-year reign thus: 'If football were sex, he'd be a a rubber glove and a copy of *Farmers' Weekly*.' Under Tony Lee, Bishop Auckland played a similar type of low-thrills, unromantic soccer; a pragmatic percentage game that was irritatingly efficient. Still, at least Bishops had ditched the awful diamond-pattern shirts in favour of more traditional raiments: light and dark blue halves.

They had some good players, too: most notably Richie Bond, a tanned, dark-haired striker who stood hunched forward with his hands on his hips in a manner reminiscent of Trevor Francis. Bond had started his career with Blyth before moving on to Blackpool, then Carlisle. He was very fast ('quicker than hot snot', someone opined, charmingly) and when he picked up the ball and cut in from the wing he sent such a huge wave of panic rolling through the Blyth defence that Patrick Swayze turned up and tried to surf on it. Luckily for the home side Bond shared another characteristic with Francis: most of his runs ended when he got in the penalty area, at which point he went strangely weak at the knees and fell over. Afterwards he would gesture at the referee, plainly frustrated by the debilitating effects of this mysterious and evidently incurable ailment. In Francis's case medical opinion, from Dr Brian Moore to Professor Ronald Atkinson, was united in the view that it was 'something he'd picked up in Italy'. Probably from eating foreign food, which as everyone knows is a dangerous business. A friend of mine once had a tin of alphabetti spaghetti and it spelled disaster.

Shaun Elliott, the youngest-ever captain of Sunderland, now considerably older and playing on knees that creaked like the deck of the *Flying Dutchman*, succeeded where Bond had failed by winning a penalty towards the end of the first half. The resultant goal was the one shot on target in the entire forty-five minutes. The two teams had done their best, but conditions were horrible. A freezing west wind was blustering as fiercely as a politician who's been caught with his pants down, and the pitch, sodden by a week of rain, was increasingly goose-bumped with divots. All week the local press had been building up the game as a classic encounter, though the one they had in mind probably wasn't Act 1, Scene 1 of *Macbeth*. 'When shall we three meet again/ In thunder, lightning, or in rain?'

'When the day is raw and dark/ then we'll set off for Croft Park/ Eye of newt and blind toad's caul/ I'll sell these off to the hot dog stall.'

John Borthwick, an old hand who'd seen service at Hartlepool and Darlington, put Bishops two up shortly after the start of the second half. Blyth were struggling. The one bright spot was the performance of Mickey English. A short, straw-haired figure in the centre of the Spartans midfield, English controlled and passed the ball with a neat accuracy that confounded the efforts of the rutted playing surface. He was slim and pale and he held his shirt cuffs in the palms of his hands. He reminded me of Colin Suggett, the Sunderland player from the sixties who had recently resigned as youth team coach at St James's. I'd always had a soft spot for Suggett, and not just because of the part he played in the controversial West Brom goal which denied Leeds the Championship in 1971, nor the startling enthusiasm with which he'd embraced the bubble-perm craze while at Norwich. When I was about six my mum had gone to Jack Hatfield's sports shop in Middlesbrough and bought me my first football kit. When she came back she said, 'I thought the Boro top was a bit boring, just plain red, so I got you this nice red and white-striped one instead.' It was a Sunderland shirt. If she'd done the same thing nowadays I could have claimed mental cruelty and gone on the *Oprah Winfrey Show*. Actually, I was quite excited by the shirt. Because (I'm gonna unburden myself of something now, OK?) my mum was right: the Boro top was boring. A fact which Jack Charlton, something of a style guru, rectified soon after his appointment as manager by incorporating a white boob-tube into the design. (And Jack really had to fight to get what he wanted. Some of the Boro's fuller-figured players were simply not keen on wearing hoops. 'It's just going to make Foggy and Craggsy look soooo ample!' Stuart Boam protested in *Jimmy Hill's Football Weekly*. 'And Bobby Murdoch will appear positively Rubenesque.' Eventually Charlton pulled a master-stroke, agreeing to an away kit of flattering blue and black stripes. Everyone was happy. Except for Frank Spraggon; his colour therapist said that for a Sagittarius none of these were positive tones.)

So I'd go out to play in my red- and white-striped shirt, pale, fair-haired and skinny, and passers-by, ignoring the clear evidence that I possessed all the speed and two-footed skills of a grass snake, would point at me and shout, 'Colin Suggett!' Naturally, I was pleased as pickle to be compared to any professional player, let alone one who featured in the Barratt Bubblegum Soccer Star Card Collection, and waved back enthusiastically. It was only years afterwards, when I'd grown six inches and the Sunderland shirt was serving out its dotage as a washcloth, that I realised that what people had actually been saying was not 'Colin Suggett!' but 'Colin Suggitt?' They weren't drawing attention to my resemblance to a silkily skilful young striker – they'd been asking me if I was the ice-cream shop-owner's nephew.

After which pointless digression Mickey English pulled a goal back for Blyth, collecting the ball on the edge of the area, skipping round a tackle and driving a low shot into the right-hand corner. For a short while recovery for the home side seemed a possibility. The crowd began to buzz. The Northumbrians around me were shouting. Behind the far goal an old lady in a pink anorak vibrated a Presto carrier bag excitedly. Spartans shuttled the ball swiftly about in front of their opponents' defence, jabbing away, looking for an opening. Bishops remained steadfast. They were nothing if not durable. And they had a sucker punch in their armoury. Shortly after Blyth had fluffed a couple of half-chances, the ball was wellied out of defence. Bond sped after it with the sure, springing tread of a lurcher on the trail of an elderly rabbit. The ball hopped erratically across the pitted surface, began to tire. Bond swooped, chivvied it goalwards. A defender backed off and fell over. The 'keeper advanced half-heartedly. Like the crowd he seemed to sense the dull inevitability of what was about to happen. Bond scored.

There was no way back for Blyth.

Kevin Keegan was keen to sign a new central defender. The press speculated that the man he was after was Ulrich van Gobbel, Feyenoord's highly rated Dutch international. Reports on van Gobbel centred on two things: his pace and his party trick of wrestling against two team-mates. 'I have seen him do this many times,' a coach at the Rotterdam club said admiringly, 'and not once have they defeated him.' No one I spoke to in Newcastle knew if van Gobbel was a good player or not, but they were all agreed he'd be a great asset in the Bigg Market on Friday nights.

If he signed, van Gobbel would be joining a small band of overseas stars who'd played at St James's. The most notable of these were the Chilean brothers Jorge and Eduardo Robledo. Known more prosaically as George and Ted during their days in England, the pair were brought to the North-East from the exotic climes of Barnsley in a double transfer deal worth £26,500. Ted Robledo was a right-half and appeared in United's 1952 FA Cup-winning side, but it was his brother who was the better player. Playing up front alongside Jackie Milburn, George Robledo was what Spanish-speaking fans term 'a rabbit-killer' (amazing how some foreign words look just like English ones, isn't it?) which roughly translates as 'someone who kills rabbits'; in other words a goal-poacher. Most of the ninety-one goals Robledo scored for Newcastle, including the winner in the 1952 Cup final, were put away from closer than ten yards, often in manoeuvres that involved illegal traps and moonlit forays into the opposition penalty area.

George Robledo's spiritual successor was undoubtedly Mirandinha, signed from the Brazilian club Fluminese in 1988 with the aid of the international brokering skills of Malcolm Macdonald. The little forward's arrival at St James's was commemorated with the immortal chant: 'His name is Mirandinha, he's not from Argentina. He's from Brazil. He's fucking brill. Na nah-nah na. Na nah-nah na.' Sadly, the diminutive Brazilian failed to match the poetic achievements of his fans. He scored one memorable goal, almost inevitably against Middlesbrough, in which he samba-ed through the entire Boro defence, waltzed round the 'keeper and danced a saucy lambada with a passing policewoman before knocking the ball into the net, then seemed to spend the rest of his time at Newcastle trying to repeat the trick, and failing. Newcastle manager Willie McFaul's decision to recruit Dave Beasant and Andy Thorne from Wimbledon hardly helped the little Brazilian's cause. The sight of Mirandinha staring wistfully up into the sky as another mighty clearance sailed into the stratosphere was tear-jerkingly reminiscent of the final frames of *ET*.

The Robledos and Mirandinha were not the only South Americans to have turned out in the North-East. During the days following the success of Ossie Ardiles and Ricardo Villa at Spurs, when it seemed that every agent in the country was out scouring the pampas for anything in football boots, Sunderland signed Claudio Marangoni. Marangoni went on to play in the side which defeated Liverpool to win the World Club Championship. Unfortunately for Sunderland fans, he had to go back to Buenos Aires to do so. Since those heady days the Roker Park management have put their faith in Europeans. Thomas 'The Tank Engine' Hauser was pre-eminent among them. A massive German, he arrived at Sunderland from Switzerland where, rumour had it, he'd dressed in grey and set himself up as a rival to the Matterhorn. His early days at Roker were marred by a slight misunderstanding of German history among certain sections of the crowd, who chose to make Hauser feel at home by sieg-heiling whenever he scored. Hauser complained in the local press and thankfully the practice stopped. Attempts to come up with something that was more representative of modern Germany foundered when an inflatable Chancellor Kohl got wedged in a side street causing severe traffic congestion.

In the end van Gobbel didn't go to St James's. Keegan toyed with the idea of buying Philippe Albert of Anderlecht,

Dragan Lukic of Real Madrid or Marc Rieper of Brondby. In the end he signed Darren Peacock instead. He wasn't a foreigner, but he was from Herefordshire, which is practically the same thing.

Darlington v. Scunthorpe United, Endsleigh Insurance League Division 3
Saturday 29 January 1994

Scott Fitzgerald once said: 'A ride in a train can be a terrible, heavy-hearted or comic thing.' Which was remarkably prescient, considering he never travelled on British Rail. I'm not sure in which category Fitzgerald would have placed a railway journey that involved being surrounded by PhD Philosophy students. My own preference would be for all three at once with a dash of irritation thrown in. The group, bound for a conference in Birmingham, flocked on to the train at Newcastle and filled the carriage with the fluting, arch tones of academe. 'First define your terms, Alan,' one of them said as he flopped down into the seat opposite me. Alan, a short man whose greying beard held enough crumbs to keep a family of sparrows safe from starvation through a Siberian winter, tittered. 'Oh, the classic retort,' he said. The two men laughed and looked at me. I had no idea what they were laughing at. It was like being in the audience at a Tom Stoppard play. I laughed too.

Across the aisle a lone philosopher in grey shoes with quilted fronts had come to rest next to a large youth who appeared to have a can of superlager welded to his right hand. His face was the consistency and colour of concrete. The philosopher smiled at him and said, 'Is the train in motion?'

The youth looked out of the window, then back at him with a glare that had 'What the fuck are you on about?' typed on it in triplicate and signed by his probation officer. There was a pause. 'No,' he said.

'Could we prove that with a mathematical formula?' the philosopher said, grinning cheerfully, 'or are we entirely reliant on empirical observation?' The youth stared at him. Inside his head a Socratic dialogue was in progress:

'What's he saying?'

'I don't know, but crack him one just in case.'

He took a swig of lager.

'They are important areas of study, you see,' the philosopher continued blithely. 'Perception and sensation. Reality and illusion. How, for example would you prove your existence to me?'

The youth studied his can of lager for a moment. It was one of those cheap, generic brands they sell in corner shops. The ones with spurious Teutonic names (Pilsner von Pist) whose advertising slogan would be 'Beer – it gets you mortal'. After a few seconds he looked up. 'Why would I bother, like?' he said.

The youth got off the train at Darlington. Which wasn't so surprising. Darlington has a bit of a reputation for producing hard cases. My father works for a steel company there. During the mid-eighties there was a series of games between Middlesbrough and Darlington, all of which seemed to culminate in mass fighting. The day after one particularly bloody FA Cup encounter had ended with a pitch invasion and a punch-up that resembled the pool-room brawl in *Mean Streets*, only without the Motown soundtrack, my dad was unsurprised to find that a proportion of the workforce were missing due to court appearances. 'The funny thing is, though,' he said, 'quite a few of them were in their fifties.'

This riot was not the first incident of its type at Feethams. That had occurred way back in 1893. In a Northern League game with Bishop Auckland the referee was forced to hold up play for six minutes after the crowd ran on to the pitch to join in a brawl between the players which had been sparked by a savage foul on a Darlington forward. The trouble continued at half-time, when another outbreak of fisticuffs involving spectators, players and officials broke out in the pavilion. The *Northern Echo* described the scenes as 'shameful, detestable, dirty and brutal'. Strangely, the paper didn't go on to blame a lack of discipline in schools and the breakdown of traditional family values for the fracas. In the days before violent videos and the abolition of corporal punishment in schools you just had to face up to the sad truth: some people like fighting.

It's hard to see quite why Darlington should turn out these rock-hard reprobates. Perhaps it comes from the town's peculiar feeling of isolation. It's a nice enough place: part Georgian market town, part Victorian railway town, part modern toytown, but it seems oddly cut off from the rest of the North-East; physically in Durham but spiritually leaning towards the wide open spaces of North Yorkshire. When I was a teenager, Darlington seemed to exist in some kind of a youth cult time-warp. In the mid-seventies on a Saturday afternoon you used to see groups of teds, mods, skinheads, Ziggy Stardust clones, hippies and heavy-metal fans loitering on every corner. And then there were the Northern soul boys in their star-patterned tank-tops, flapping about the place in Oxford bags with the button-shut pockets running from hip to ankle. Once, in a record shop in Darlington, I heard one say to another, 'Well, how many spins can you get off a push then, kidder?' It was the only time I've ever heard one man threatening another with dance steps.

Pretty is not a word you normally see attached to football grounds, but it's certainly applicable to Feethams. You buy a ticket at the entrance to the sports grounds, walk around the cricket pitch, pausing for a while to watch the hockey match that's in progress and admire the gaily painted pavilion, and in through some intricate iron gates where stewards proffer canvas bags into which you drop your ticket. It's an arcane system. Why do they collect the tickets? Is it to prevent someone paying to get in, then sneaking off to spend the afternoon asleep in the scorebox rather than watching the match? At half-time do they count the gate receipts and tickets, match the two up and say, 'Sod it, Bob, there's twelve pounds more here than we've got tickets for. That means two of the buggers have escaped. Give me the shotgun. I'm going in behind that sightscreen'? No, I don't think so, either.

I paid a quid extra and went into the paddock. It was a good choice. The paddock had the high codger quotient I need to really enjoy a game. There were men with rosy faces and caps the colour and shape of cowpats all around me. In France, to appreciate a region fully you must eat the local cheese and drink the local wine. In England you should go to a football match and stand among the codgers. The codgers are the authentic taste of an area. In an England that is increasingly smooth and homogeneous, they still have their corners.

The codgers at Feethams were *premier cru*. A lot of them must have come from across the Tees in the North Riding because they had the peculiar accent of that part of Yorkshire – a kind of rook-like cawing noise coupled with a seeming reluctance to open the mouth any more than is absolutely necessary and an insatiable desire to insert extra syllables into everything. The older farmers in the village where I grew up spoke this way. One of them once pointed at his dog, who was bounding off in pursuit of our spaniel, and said, 'Door-ent my-ind 'im 'ees fond as a gaaaart.' Tempered by frequent visits to the metropolis of Darlington, the accents at Feethams weren't quite as strong as that, nor as impenetrable, but the bewildering similes (I mean, is a goat stupid?) remained. Five minutes after kick-off the man next to me said, 'Way, look at our defence. They're stood there like grapes.'

Darlington were struggling near the foot of the table, but their new manager, Alan Murray, seemed to be pulling them round. Taking the reins at Feethams was not the most secure position in football. Since the war the club had employed twenty-four managers, a total which suggests that in the case of the Quakers any heat in the hot seat had been created by the friction of rapidly shifting bottoms. Among them had been some illustrious names from North-East football history: Frank Brennan, a beef mountain of a man who had played in Newcastle United's FA Cup wins in 1951 and 1952 and managed the North Shields side which won the Amateur Cup; Billy Elliott, a team-mate of Len Shackleton in the Bradford Park Avenue side, later to join him at Roker Park as a £27,000 winger in the Bank of England club; and Cyril

Knowles, another Yorkshireman, who'd begun his career at Ayresome Park in 1964 and was to die twenty-seven years later in the General Hospital that overlooks the ground.

Despite their fame, none had lasted long at Feethams. Alan Murray was as prepared for such situations as anybody could be. He'd previously been the boss at the Victoria Ground, Hartlepool – a place that could hardly have been less stable had it been built on the slopes of Mount Etna. Murray had taken Hartlepool up into the Third (now Second) Division and on to the highest League position in their history. It was a minor achievement, but in the context of the financial problems of Hartlepool it was probably the equivalent of winning the European Cup with Blackburn Rovers. Since arriving at Feethams, Murray had encouraged Darlington to play a short passing game and he had secured the services of Matty Appleby, on loan from Newcastle.

Appleby had been one of the young stars of Ardiles' struggling United team. Playing at centre-back, he'd picked up so many North-East Barclays Young Eagle of the Month Awards his front room must have resembled an aviary. Since Keegan's arrival, Appleby had been displaced in the team by Steve Howie. He remained an excellent player. That afternoon at Feethams, whenever he got the ball, the codgers purred appreciatively. He always seemed to have yards of space around him and every headed clearance he made went to one of his team-mates. He was solid, reliable and there were the occasional flashes of brilliance from him, too – notably when he broke from the halfway line and spanked a thirty-yarder inches over the crossbar. Darlington couldn't scrape the money together to buy him, though. He would be back at St James's within the month.

Appleby wasn't the first classy player to make an appearance at Feethams. While Darlington hadn't produced the same number of top-class players as the region's larger clubs, or indeed some of its better non-league sides, there have been a few over the years. David Speedie, a putative Scot, born in Hartlepool, had spent a couple of seasons at Feethams in the eighties, scoring twenty-one goals before moving on to

Chelsea, where he lost his hair and his temper with equal rapidity.

Goalkeeper Ray Wood had been signed from Darlington for Manchester United by Matt Busby. Wood played for United in the 1957 Cup final. For him the game ended prematurely when he was knocked senseless by Aston Villa's Peter McParland. On the newsreel of that final the incident is described as 'a stiff shoulder-charge', though to modern eyes it looks more like a prototype for ram-raiding. Wood suffered concussion and a fractured cheekbone. The following year he would be more fortunate, surviving the Munich air crash with only minor injuries.

The first black player in the Football League turned out for Darlington, too. He was a goalkeeping Ghanaian named Arthur Wharton who had been a professional with Preston North End in the 1880s.

Darlington had already had one goal ruled as offside ('There's some ten-bob gets around,' the grape man commented, waving in the direction of the linesman) when Lawrie Pearson volleyed them into the lead in the thirty-eighth minute. They were playing good football on a glue-pot pitch, passing the ball around quickly and accurately. In attack they had the slim Robbie Painter, an ex-Burnley player with a good touch and a pair of sideburns that would not have disgraced the cheeks of John Tudor himself.

Pearson's shot inspired the crowd. Behind the goal one of the great chants of world football began: 'Quaker aggro, Quaker aggro.' I'm not sure what exact form Quaker aggro would take, but having been educated by the Society of Friends myself I would guess it would probably involve inviting opposition fans for a post-match cup of tea, then making them feel guilty for moaning about the lack of biscuits by asking them to sit silently for five minutes thinking about Somalia. And it would work too, because the Quakers are experts at making people feel guilty. When you're a follower of a pacifist religion, guilt's about all that stands between you and the sledgehammers. Our school football team played in the Teesside League – not a place for pacifism, you might think. However, our cunning use of self-protection strategies developed over the centuries stood us in good stead. We never tackled for the ball, we just used to say, 'Have it by all means. I realise that your need for this leather spheroid stems from some terrible childhood trauma which you have totally repressed.' We didn't win many games, admittedly, but many of the boys we played against subsequently had nervous breakdowns.

Five minutes into the second half Scunthorpe equalised through Carmichael, an energetic individual in cycling shorts. 'Typhoo put the tea in Britain, you put the cunt in Scunthorpe,' one of the codgers yelled.

Like Darlington, Scunthorpe was low down on the list of suspects when the authorities set out to discover who set the footballing world alight, but they had rescued Kevin Keegan from the obscurity of a bathroom fitments factory. He'd signed as an apprentice with them in 1968. Three years later, Bill Shankly took him to Liverpool in a £35,000 deal. The received wisdom about Keegan the player was that he was not naturally gifted; that he had achieved everything by hard work. Certainly that was an opinion modestly endorsed by the man himself. Without doubting the amount of effort Keegan had put into improving his game, this had always been a deeply troubling judgement to me. Not just because of some romantic notion that to become European Footballer of the Year would require more than application and elbow-grease, but also because of the weird picture of humanity it conjured up. Imagine all those people slogging their guts out in factories and kitchens and offices and shops who, had they but chosen to, could have applied the same effort to professional football and now be earning twenty times as much money for working a fifteen-hour week. If mankind really is this strange, then I don't think there's much hope.

Darlington got the winner in the fifty-seventh minute. It was the best goal I had seen all season. Himsworth surged through from the halfway line, his boots splattering across the sticky surface, played a one-two with Gary Chapman, then slid a pass through to Painter, who neatly lifted the ball over the advancing 'keeper. 'That's football, that is,' the grape man said, beaming.

I was irritated. Billingham Synthonia had played Woking in the replay of the FA Trophy quarter-final the previous night and the *Independent* had inverted the scores. They'd printed the result as 2–1 to Billingham whereas, in actual fact, it had been 1–2 to Woking. I had gone through the whole day celebrating Synners' achievement – the first Northern League team to make the semis since Spennymoor in 1978, only Enfield between them and Wembley, ee-aye-oh, ee-aye-oh etcetera. I had just bought a *Northern Echo* to read the match report and found out the awful truth. I was standing beside the car, railing on about this terrible abuse of press freedom, while Catherine searched through her bag for the keys. It was about five o'clock, the sky was black with rain clouds and the streets of the town were deserted. I was sure the bloody Ombudsman would be too busy protecting the privacy of various toffee-nosed trouser-droppers to do anything about this latest life-wrecking travesty of disinformation. I said so to Catherine, who was still rooting out the car keys. I didn't hear her reply because by that stage I had caught sight of something out of the corner of my eye. It appeared to be a red- and white-striped armoured personnel carrier.

When we moved from the Old Kent Road we hired a removal company from Longbenton in Newcastle. They sent two men, the driver, Clem, who was young, with dark Hispanic features, and his mate Davey, older, moustachioed, teeth that resembled a blitzed street. I travelled back in the lorry with them to save a coach fare. We talked about football, mainly. Davey had been a keen Sunday player but he'd had to give it up.

'Why's that, Davey?' Clem asked.

'Well, it wasn't fair on our lass and the bairns, was it?' Davey said. 'I mean, I was going out to football at ten on Sunday morning, playing a game, having a shower and by the time I'd finished it was twelve o'clock, so I've went down the club. I'd get home about half-three, sit and watch a bit of football, fall asleep and wake up for tea. Then it'd be time to go down the club again. I'd be back about midnight. Our lass hadn't seen us all day. Eventually she started playing war. So I give up the football. What else could I do?'

'You could've give up the club,' Clem said.

Davey looked at him as if he'd just announced he was a woman trapped in a man's body. 'Don't talk daft, Clem, man,' he said.

The two of them knew the town we were moving to. They went out drinking there on Saturday nights. It was wild place of beer and bouncers and bundles. Clem said, 'You'll have to watch out for the Sunderland Skinhead. He's a total psycho, that lad.'

'Aye, he must be,' Davey said. 'He's out on Saturday night with all West End lads from Newcastle in there and he's wearing his Sunderland shirt.'

'Wouldn't make any difference even if he didn't,' Clem said. 'He's got Sunderland AFC tattooed on his forehead.'

'He's a size,' Davey said. 'He's as big as a tree.'

'He took a pop at our kid,' Clem said. 'Give him a right fourpenny one.'

'Why'd he do that?' Davey asked.

"'Cos our kid's big,' Clem told him. 'If he sees a big lad, he just wades into them.'

They looked at me. I am six foot five.

'He's bound to have a go at you, mate,' Davey said gleefully.

Sitting in the lorry, eating midget gems, swigging American cream soda and with the endorphins produced by humping a high percentage of our furniture down four flights of stairs bouncing round my veins like valium, I received this information with much merriment. After all, up until that minute I had been living in the Old Kent Road. I had heard the gunfire and the sirens; seen the groups of bulky middle-aged men in their Lacoste polo shirts, Gucci loafers and gold ID bracelets cruising down the evening streets like schools of killer whales; stepped over bloodstains, broken glass and discarded teeth, and once witnessed a punch-up in a baker's shop at 11.15 on a damp Monday morning. Was someone who had lived through such times, who had trodden the gore-encrusted tarmac of London's toughest street, really going to be intimidated by some provincial knuckle-scraper? I gave my thigh a metaphorical slap: you're damned right he wasn't! I was sealed in a speeding lorry, 250 miles from the Sunderland Skinheed, and I was brave as all get-out, I can tell you.

Besides, our house was miles outside the town and I had no intention of going in there drinking on any night, let alone Saturday. I imagined, therefore, that when I did eventually see the Sunderland Skinheed it would be on a market day afternoon in midsummer, in full sunlight, the streets thronging with shoppers and coppers, and I would be able to point him out to friends who were up from London and say, 'Ah, look. The Sunderland Skinheed. Frightfully funny. Chap terrorises the whole neighbourhood, apparently,' and we'd all laugh condescendingly, as if this was Provence and he was some terribly amusing rustic. I scanned the streets for him every time I went into town that first summer, but I never saw him once. When the leaves started to fall I stopped looking. By the following spring I had forgotten him altogether.

And now here he was, the Sunderland Skinheed, looming up like major surgery on a prematurely dark autumnal evening when everyone else in Northumberland, including the entire police force, was inside eating their tea and watching Mike Neville.

'Yes,' Catherine said, fishing the keys out of her bag at last, 'it is a bit of a pity.'

The Sunderland Skinheed's nostrils flared as he scented us. He was so large that when he stepped backwards his hazard lights flashed automatically and he made a wa-ah wa-ah noise. 'Get in the car,' I hissed.

'What?' Catherine laughed. She had her back to the action. The Sunderland Skinheed was now swivelling round with all the lumbering majesty of an aircraft carrier and locking his sights on me.

'Open the door!'

'Is something the matter with you?'

The Sunderland Skinhead was coming my way. I wasn't looking at him. I could just tell from the vibrations. 'Open this bloody car, woman!'

Catherine flipped the catch. I jumped in, slammed the door and locked it. A pointless gesture, I knew. The Sunderland Skinhead would rip the door off and send it bouncing across the street like a McDonald's carton in a gale. Steel was no protection. We should have got a reinforced concrete car, wrapped it in barbed wire, bought a bazooka . . . The Sunderland Skinhead rolled past.

'What's got into . . .' Catherine paused as he crossed her line of vision. 'Christ,' she said as he disappeared into the gloom, 'his neck's wider than his head.'

Hartlepool United v. Reading,
Endsleigh Insurance League Division 2
Saturday 12 February 1994

The Reading fan had cropped hair, a thick gold earring and a bump on his forehead the size of a goose egg. He was wearing a denim shirt. He was a bit of a lump. He said, 'What a morning! The wife's out. Thought I'd have myself a nice little cooked breakfast: sausage, mushroom, tomatoes, you know. So I'm frying my bacon and egg and my contact lens pops out. Does it fall on the floor? Does it bollocks. Straight in the pan. Hot fat. Psisssss! Melted. Hundred quid down the spout. Can you believe it?'

I said, 'What, that a tubby bugger like you'd be too vain to wear glasses? No, frankly, I find it totally incredible.'

Only joking.

The Reading fan lived in Sunderland. He liked it up North, he said, and houses were cheaper. The only thing he couldn't stand was the rivalry between Sunderland and Newcastle. 'When I first come up I thought it was a joke,' he said, 'but it isn't. It's totally fucking serious.'

I told him about the blokes on the train arguing over which place had the best shopping facilities. He said, 'Yeah. I mean, stupid, right?' then scratched his head, "Cos Sunderland's only got the Lanes, whereas in Newcastle you've got Eldon Square *and* you've got the Metro Centre.'

We got off the train together in Hartlepool. The Reading fan rushed off. He was meeting his mates. 'The missus is away at her sister's,' he said, rubbing his hands together gleefully. 'I'm going to have a real good night.' He raced across the road into an evil-looking pub. There was a sign in the window advertising cocktails. It looked like the sort of place where the barman's speciality would be a pint of black and tan with a pickled egg floating in it. Shaken not stirred.

Hartlepool looked like a set from *Mad Max*, only it was colder. Outside the station there was an empty Victorian hospital, the ornate red brick stained black, the windows smashed. The shop fronts across the road from it were boarded up. There were enough burned-out buildings to suggest that someone in Hartlepool was running a restart scheme for prospective arsonists. I walked up the road. A wind whipped in off the sea, sending a school of sweet-wrappers scurrying off around a crumpled traffic cone. The shops that weren't boarded up looked grubby and furtive, as if they were desperately resisting the urge to leap across the pavement and ask for 20p for a cup of tea. Even the minicabs were Ladas. Poor old Hartlepool. It had once been the busiest port in County Durham, a prosperous place. Now its notoriety lay in high unemployment. And, of course, the monkey. People in Hartlepool are a bit sensitive about the monkey business. At a hotel I was working at in London a new luggage porter started and, recognising his North-East accent, I said, 'I'm from Middlesbrough, where are you from?'

He said: 'Hartlepoolanddon'tmentionthatfuckingmonkey.'

The latter part of this outburst is, in fact, a bit of catchphrase in the North-East. Whenever Hartlepool comes up in conversation (which is not that often, admittedly) someone is bound to smirk and say, 'Don't mention the monkey.' So I won't.

Oh, all right then. Allegedly, a French ship was wrecked off the coast during the time of the Napoleonic Wars and the ship's mascot, a monkey dressed in a striped sailor's shirt, was washed ashore at Hartlepool. No one in the town had ever seen a Frenchman before, but they knew from hearsay that they were small and dark and gibbered unintelligibly, a description which fitted the monkey perfectly. So they put him on trial as a spy, found him guilty and hanged him. An unpleasant fate for an innocent simian – though personally I think the ape asked for it. He should have heeded the words of that other naughty monkey, Brian Clough, who said 'You've got to be daft to go to Hartlepool in the first place.'

I walked up the A19 towards the Victoria Ground. Signs everywhere pointed in the direction of Hartlepool Marina. Hartlepool Marina. Don't those two words just fill your head with glamorous images? A flaming sun in an aquamarine sky; the azure sea lapping against the glistening white prow of a schooner, its poop-deck astir with a shoal of bikini-clad blonde beauties, while down below Tom Selleck shakes up the pina coladas and . . . why, who's that over there? My old friend Quincy, Frisco's top medical examiner . . . Sarcasm, I know, is the lowest form of wit, but it's the only sane response to this kind of madness. Millions had been spent on Hartlepool Marina. It was all part of an expensive marketing strategy: brighten up the image of the town and encourage investors. Perhaps the zenith of the campaign came a couple of years ago, after a grim yet sympathetic piece about Hartlepool, written by an American journalist, had appeared in the *Independent on Sunday*. A reply from local MP Peter Mandelson pointed to the town's many delights, including the marina, a selection of good restaurants and the fact that there was excellent skiing in the Pennines just a short car journey away. Mandelson was a member of the Labour Party, but his thinking owed more to Marie Antoinette than Nye Bevan. Trying to cure the problems of Hartlepool using leisure facilities and advertising was like tackling leprosy with a bagful of cosmetics and a couple of Benetton vouchers.

I stood looking over a wall at a stretch of waste ground behind the station. It was littered with broken pallets and other debris; torn polythene flapped limply from rusted re-enforcing rods; a crow struggled for balance on a fractured stave. 'You've got to be daft to go to Hartlepool in the first place,' Cloughie had said, but he'd gone anyway, taking up the position of manager during the 1965–66 season. He was the team's sixth manager in as many years. It was never going to be an easy job. As if Hartlepool's financial problems were not enough, the club also seems to be cursed with ill fortune so severe if one of its players buys a banana there's an evens chance when he peels it it will be empty. In 1916, for instance, the Victoria Ground's main stand was destroyed by bombs jettisoned from a burning Zeppelin. The club claimed £2,500 compensation from the German government. After numerous letters asking if they intended to pay up, the board of directors finally got a reply twenty-five years later, when the Luftwaffe bombed the ground again. They voted unanimously to take this as a no.

If Clough had thought his presence would put a stop to such bad luck he was mistaken. Shortly after he took over police turned up at the training ground and arrested one of his top players for non-payment of maintenance. The roof of the boardroom leaked, the average home gate had halved in ten years, and the club had applied for re-election five seasons out of the previous six. Nevertheless, aided by his former Middlesbrough team-mate Peter Taylor, Clough succeeded in lifting the club from twenty-third place to eighth. His team included the only Hartlepool player to win an international cap, Irishman Ambrose Foggarty; a prolific goalscorer from Bolton, the brilliantly named Ernie Pythian and a local midfielder, John McGovern. Other ex-Hartlepool players have earned footballing fame – Andy Linighan headed Arsenal's winning goal in the 1993 FA Cup final; W.G. Richardson is still in the record books after scoring four times in five minutes for West Brom and a man named Forman was signed from Workington for football's most unusual transfer fee – £10 and a box of kippers. McGovern's achievements easily eclipse these. A player with gifts so modest as to be barely discernible to the naked eye, he accompanied Clough from club to club like some kind of talisman, along the way picking up the kind of medal collection normally only seen on the chests of octogenarian Russian generals.

There was a bigger crowd than usual in the Victoria Ground. Reading were the runaway leaders of the Second Division. More than that, Hartlepool were supposed to have a new chairman. According to the local press the buy-out by businessman Harold Hornsey had gone through the previous day, which meant that Garry Gibson's reign was at an end. From what I'd heard, Gibson was about as welcome in Hartlepool as a rattlesnake in a bran-tub. The club's financial problems had obviously been a contributing factor. Creditors including the Inland Revenue and ex-manager Viv Busby were claiming over £70,000. That in itself might not have raised the campaign to such heights of vilification (after all, there was nothing new in Hartlepool having money problems) had it not been for certain exacerbating circumstances. The club had banned players from talking to the press after their wages cheques had not been honoured; the popular Alan Murray had been sacked just months after presiding over a famous FA Cup win against Crystal Palace; a testimonial cheque handed over to Cyril Knowles' widow had bounced not once, but three times. Rightly or wrongly, a lot of people held Garry Gibson responsible for this; a view that was unlikely to be altered by his own apparently off-hand and unrepentant attitude to the whole affair. Gibson wrote a weekly column in the *Northern Echo* which could have provided the ideal platform from which to explain the situation. Instead he spent the bulk of it addressing the topic 'Why are the press telling lies about me?' invariably concluding, 'because it sells papers'. Which demonstrated, among other things, a considerable overestimation of the public's appetite for Hartlepool United stories. Fans who had paid hard-earned money at the turnstiles in the belief that it would go to the bereaved wife of a popular man, only to find it had been sucked up to furnish company debts, were unlikely to feel any sympathy. The irony was that Gibson had presided over the most successful spell in Hartlepool's history. Perhaps the turmoil was just another example of that infamous bad luck.

The Victoria Ground is not so much a theatre of dreams as a Punch and Judy stall for insomniacs. One side of the ground is missing entirely, the pitch separated from a busy road only by a line of rickety corrugated iron and a couple of portakabins. The most solid structures in the whole stadium seem to be the dugouts – two Benny Arentoft-shaped brick edifices which look as if they've been picked up from the pill-box department of the local Army Surplus Store. Unopposed by anything too substantial, the wind howled towards the home end, ensuring that whichever team was kicking in that direction had the kind of advantage an opera singer might enjoy in a blow football match with a pneumokoniosis victim. Reading foggied first go with it. Under former Newcastle favourite Mark McGhee they were alleged to have been playing attractive football all season. At Hartlepool it was hard to envisage such a thing. Seduced by the power of the wind, they limited their attacking manoeuvres to whacking shots at goal from improbable distances. Jimmy Quinn had a bash straight from kick-off; Mick Gooding wellied a volley from ten yards inside his own half; soon even Shaka Hislop in the Reading goal was getting in on the act, punting a clearance downfield and watching expectantly as it bounced a couple of feet over the Pool crossbar.

'Royals! Royals!' the away fans encouraged, totally ignoring the fact that Reading's historical nickname is 'The Biscuit Men'. They were so called after the large Huntley & Palmer factory in the town. This may well no longer exist, but that seems a poor excuse to adopt The Royals as a sobriquet. After all, what's royal about Reading? The Hexagon? The M4 by-pass? If the club was looking for something more up to the minute in reflecting the nature of the community which supports it, why didn't they opt for the Commuters, Overspill or the Software Programmers? Actually it seems probable to me that no Reading fan has ever called his or her team the Biscuit Men. Some club nicknames just never seem to catch on with supporters. Sunderland are supposed to be the Black Cats, for instance, but I can't imagine anyone chanting it at Roker Park, and Newcastle were always the Toon even though the club and the media have only recently acknowledged the fact. Many of these old 'official' nicknames seem to have been invented solely to help sub-editors write headlines: 'Biscuit Men Crumble', 'Black Cats Make Own Luck', 'Two For Joy – Magpie Cole's Goal Double'. Sadly, no one ever seemed to be able to make much out of Leeds United's moniker, the Peacocks, though

I'd have thought knocking off 'The Pea' and sticking an exclamation mark after what remained would have served a multitude of circumstances at Elland Road.

Reading bombarded Hartlepool's goal from a bewildering variety of angles and ranges, but it was the home team who scored. A corner was swung in from the left and centre-half Ian McGuckin hurtled in from the edge of the box and smacked a header into the top corner. It was the sort of goal central defenders always get from corners. Unless, of course, they are playing for your team, in which case it glances off an ear and bounces a yard behind your top scorer, who is left staring drop-jawed at the gaping goal like an old man who has just opened a cupboard and now can't for the life of him remember what he wanted out of it.

It was the only goal of the half. Hartlepool deserved their lead. Reading's vaunted attack had been subdued by the veteran defender Mick Tait, an individual from Wallsend whose birthplace also served as an accurate physical description, while up front another old campaigner, Keith Houchen, had linked up well with the lively youngster Nicky Southall. Predictably, the situation was too good to last. Twelve minutes into the second half Reading equalised. Six minutes later they had taken the lead.

By that stage any sympathy I might have had for the home side had evaporated. On the touchline five yards in front of me, Hartlepool's left-back, Anthony Skedd, a teenager with cropped hair who still looked young enough to con bus conductors into charging him half-fare, committed one of the worst fouls I have ever seen. Leaping in two-footed, over the top of the ball, he caught Kevin Dillon just below the knee with a sickening crunch. Dillon collapsed to the grass with a shriek. A little old man in front of me with a benign face under a black felt cap turned away, shaking his head and sucking air between his teeth. Players rushed in from all over the field. Ray Ransom, the Reading defender who'd spent three seasons with Dillon at Newcastle, was fuming. It was easy to see why. He and Dillon were both edging towards their mid-thirties, and a serious injury now would end a career.

'Break his fucking leg next time, Skeddy,' a bloke a few yards along the terrace shouted. He was tall and rangy with straggly hair and a ginger Zapata moustache. He looked like the sort who'd turn up as a wall-eyed psychopath in a spaghetti western spitting out streams of red tobacco, grunting and maniacally muttering, 'Son of a whore,' before catching a slug in the chest from Lee van Cleef's Buntline Special. He'd deserve it, too. 'Fuck off, you big-nosed cunt!' he yelled at Ransom when he came to collect the ball for the free kick. Dillon was still lying on the ground, his face contorted with pain. The referee had only booked Skedd. Earlier he'd taken similar action against Jimmy Quinn for complaining to a linesman about an offside decision. Ransom was plainly furious. A lump of chewing gum flew past him. 'You stupid wankers,' he said.

'He's swearing, referee,' ginger 'tache shouted, transforming from brutal gunslinger to self-righteous prig before you could say 'twat'.

The referee called Ransom over and had words. Kevin Dillon eventually got to his feet. In his Newcastle days, I had always thought of the Sunderland-born Dillon as something of a midfield lounge lizard – elegantly stylish, but ineffectual. A few minutes after the foul he showed that there was more to him than that, getting the ball on the halfway line and cutting through three players in a marvellous flash of mindless bravado. The foul had a similar galvanising effect on his team-mates. They scored two more before the final whistle.

'Ten out of ten for effort, Pool,' a middle-aged man in a blue anorak shouted as the players trooped off. 'Nought out of ten for skill.'

It had hardly been the new beginning Hartlepool were looking for.

As it transpired, Hornsey hadn't taken over the club that weekend. His bid was delayed by the legal wrangle over the unpaid tax bills. The affair dragged on like extra time in a dull Cup final. As the season drew to a close the reluctant incumbent, Garry Gibson, was still in charge at the Victoria Ground.

*   *   *

Sir John Hall, Newcastle's chairman, said he had a feeling in his bones that this was United's year in the FA Cup. It must have been rheumatism. The Magpies were beaten 2–0 by Luton Town in the fourth round replay. Things had suddenly started to go awry at St James's and no one seemed to know who or what to blame. Except the fans.

Mike Hooper had been bought from Liverpool in late September for £500,000. He'd replaced the popular Irishman Tommy Wright between the posts almost immediately. Shortly afterwards, Wright had been sold to Nottingham Forest. The red-headed Hooper had done well enough to start with, then in New Year his form had begun to dip. By the time Newscastle lost 4–2 away to Wimbledon he was in such a state of jitters that when he ran out to collect the ball he looked like Jacques Tati imitating a nervous myopic crossing the Champs Elysées during rush-hour. You got the impression at the end of the game that the only reason he didn't put his head in his hands was for fear of dropping it. All season Newcastle's fans had been entertaining themselves by baiting opposition goalkeepers with the chant, 'Dodgy 'keeper! Dodgy 'keeper!' Now they had one of their own. They soon let Hooper know it. The goalkeeper lost his form completely.

'It's probably in the back of the net,' the shopkeeper said maliciously, 'That's where everything else seems to end up.' He was in a good mood for the first time since August. Newcastle hadn't won for six matches; Sunderland, meanwhile, were creeping up the table. The shopkeeper had taken bets down at the Social Club that the Rokermen would finish higher in Division 1 than United did in the Premiership. Suddenly, it had begun to look like he might collect after all. An elderly woman in a mauve mac, who'd been hoping to buy a bottle of Domestos but was now – after a prolonged anecdote about how Shack's first football boots had been made by his father from an old pair of brogues, some rubber off-cuts and a packet of carpet tacks – contemplating a way of cleaning the toilet with a couple of leeks and a packet of savoury rice, said, 'I think the supporters ought to get behind him.'

'The only thing that'll get behind him is the ball,' the shopkeeper scoffed merrily.

'Well, I think it's cruel,' the old lady said. 'He's a nice young lad doing his best.'

'He's a nice enough lad, I'm not doubting that,' the shopkeeper said. 'Apparently he's a keen environmentalist.'

'Is he?'

'Oh aye. He just joined Greenpeace. He wanted to save the whale. But the whale went under him.' He chuckled gleefully, clasping his hands together and rocking backwards dangerously close to a stack of tinned pease pudding.

'Ah, bugger off,' the old lady said and walked out.

'Right, what can I get you?' the shopkeeper said when he'd finished cackling. I asked for a packet of soda crystals and a pair of tweezers. I fancied beans on toast for lunch, so I figured it was worth a try.

Kevin Keegan was not happy about the treatment meted out to Hooper. He went as far as threatening to resign over it. In the end, though, he settled for bringing back Pavel Srnicek. Srnicek was hardly a model of reliability himself, but he was foreign and as a consequence his frailties were treated as exotic eccentricity rather than home-grown incompetence.

Middlesbrough v. Wolverhampton Wanderers,
Endsleigh Insurance League Division 1
Saturday 5 March 1994

Pete Smith was taking his lucky A1 route to Middlesbrough. We cut left at the Sedgefield turn-off and headed south past Sir John Hall's estate at Wynyard. On Tees FM the studio anchorman said, 'Now, David, putting aside today's game for a moment, I'd like to talk to you about history.' Sadly, it turned out to be the history of Middlesbrough versus Wolves fixtures the anchorman was talking about, so the thoughts of David Mills on the trade policies of Sir Robert Peel will remain under wraps for the time being. Wolves, it seems, had not won at Ayresome for many a long year, which, said Mills, popping on his Freudian slippers, would be an immense psychological advantage to Lennie Lawrence's men. Football pundits are fond of making such pronouncements. They seem to believe historical events hold some peculiar sway over the present. 'Newcastle, of course, haven't won there since 1952,' they intone dramatically, as if to say 'Let's see Peter Beardsley scurry about knocking incisive final passes into the danger areas with the weight of that historical baggage on his back!' I suppose we should be grateful that John Motson doesn't have the ear of the Prime Minister, otherwise we'd almost certainly have invaded Germany by now. After all, they haven't had a result against us since the Angles invaded Mercia in the seventh century, 'and that's certain to be preying on Chancellor Kohl's mind, Des.'

We crossed the Newport Bridge, the Cleveland Hills rising up behind the industrial sprawl of Teesside. At one time the riverside area had been the heart of the North-East's steel industry. There had been twenty-seven blast furnaces belching out flames and smoke. People said that driving into the district was like riding into hell. The blast furnaces had all gone now. If you wanted to find hell on earth you'd have to go elsewhere. If it was limbo you were after, Ayresome Park was fifth on the left.

We parked in Acklam Garden City, a place which ties with Greenland for bottom spot in the Aptly Named Places of the World League. My grandfather's first job when he left school had been as a messenger boy for the company who were building Acklam Garden City. He used to tell how the site managers cut costs by buying up cheap Army surplus doors. The only problem was the door frames were too small to fit the holes that had been built for them. They had to botch the whole thing up with cement. 'One kick,' my grandad said, 'and the whole lot would fall out.'

After he finished work on Saturday lunchtime my grandad would nip back to Parliament Road, have something to eat and then he and his brothers and cousins would go to the match. They only paid one entrance fee between them. While Joe, the eldest, fiddled about giving his money to the gateman the others would crawl through his legs and under the turnstile.

My grandad was pretty much an archetypal Boro supporter. After forty years' service at Ayresome Park he was saturated with disappointment. As a result he was predicting disaster from the moment the game kicked off. As soon as the opposition crossed the halfway line he'd say, 'I don't like the look of this.'

When they'd advanced ten yards: 'This could be dangerous.'

And when they got to the edge of the penalty area: 'Here's a goal.'

He'd go on like this throughout the entire game and if the opposition did finally score in the eighty-ninth minute he'd nudge me and go, 'What did I tell you? I could see that coming a mile off.'

We used to sit in the 'Bob' End, opposite the Holgate. It was where all the codgers congregated. If Boro lost my grandad would walk up to the top of the steps, hands drilled deep into the pockets of his mac, then turn, look at the pitch and say, 'Well, that's it. That's me finished, that is.' And he wouldn't be the only one. There'd be a queue of old blokes behind him shaking their fists at the tunnel and yelling, 'I'm never coming back. So you'll have to find someone else to pay your wages, you useless pack of buggers.'

The Holgate End was half empty when we got in. Pete was telling us about the glorious heyday of the Ayresome Angels, arguably the only group of football supporters ever to have a plastic ball named after them. I had one. White, they were, with the words 'Ayresome Angel' writ on them in red. And I'll tell you something for nothing: a football was a football in them days. It was a substantial thing. Not like these flimsy modern so-called footballs. Way, they'd burst on a stick of rhubarb.

Peter had been an Ayresome Angel himself. He attended matches splendidly decked out in a white umpire's coat with 'Boro' painted on the back and sleeves in red. He carried a red and white frying pan which a mate of his used to hit rhythmically with a red and white mallet. Once, at a night game in Barnsley in the mid-sixties, Pete, immaculately coutured and brandishing his frying pan, had led a coach load of Boro fans in the direction of Oakwell. Turning left into a side street he'd found himself marching against a grim-faced tide of West Yorkshire hard men. Emerging unscathed from his foray through this evil mare, he turned to see how the rest of the party was getting on. They weren't there. They'd turned right two streets before. Taking a deep breath, Pete plunged back amid the Tykes, who, eyeing him with the same mixture of reverence and fear Navaho Indians reserve for the saintly and the insane, parted and let him pass once more unscathed through their ranks.

No one in the Holgate End today was dressed outlandishly.

In fact they all looked quite trendy. Things had certainly changed since the early eighties, when Middlesboreans still regarded hooped socks, velvet pedal-pushers and calf-length leather trenchcoats as the proof of Coco Chanel's old adage, 'Fashion fades, only style remains.' Nowadays, the youth of Teesside seemed uniformly up to the minute clothing-wise. I mentioned this to a friend of mine a few days later. He said, 'No, they're not. It's just a sign of ageing. Policemen look younger and Middlesboreans look trendier. In a few years' time you'll start fancying women called Rita.'

By kick-off there were just over 12,000 in the ground. It was the best gate at Ayresome for some months, but it was still 2,000 below the club's break-even point. Animosity towards Lennie Lawrence had been increasing all season. Now the crowd seemed sharply divided between pro and anti factions. 'Stingy Cockney wanker,' one section would chant. And the reply would come: 'We hate boo boys and we hate boo boys.' Every time a chorus of 'Lennie Lawrence's red and white army' began it was drowned out by catcalls and whistles. When Lawrence had been appointed, two and a half years before, it had seemed like an ambitious move on the part of Middlesbrough's board. He was, after all, a well-known manager; a TV face. After his first season had seen Boro win promotion and reach the semi-finals of the Coca-Cola Cup, the appointment had come to look like an excellent one. A year later things had changed. Ambition had come to look more like expediency. At Charlton Lawrence had earned a reputation as a man who could work wonders on a budget, a manager who balanced the books. In the close season he had off-loaded a number of first team players and not replaced them. In mid-season club captain Alan Kernaghan had gone to Man City for £1.6 million. A third of that money had been spent on Steve Vickers, a useful looking centre-half, bought from Tranmere, born in Spennymoor. The remaining million had stayed in the bank. By this stage, with John Hendrie injured, it was plain that Boro needed to buy a forward to play up front with Wilkinson. Lawrence seemed more concerned with the effect falling attendances were having on the club accountant's health. Goals were not scored, points slipped away. While the cash remained in the bonus-builder account, the possibility of an immediate return to the Premiership was disappearing over the horizon. Increasingly Boro fans were finding alternative ways to pass their Saturday afternoons. Those who still came to Ayresome were fractious, their loyalties confused.

Lennie Lawrence was a pragmatist. Realism has never had much to do with being a football fan. Most Middlesbrough supporters were aware that their club didn't have the potential for expansion enjoyed by neighbours Newcastle and Sunderland. The crowds at Ayresome have never matched those at Roker and St James's and arguably never will. But their expectations were still high. After all, this was the home town of Brian Clough, a man who had taken a club, Nottingham Forest, of no greater size or history than Middlesbrough, to two European Cup finals and won them both. Middlesbrough's fans wanted at least a promise of such glory. Instead they got post-match homilies on financial reality. It was as if Henry V had jumped on his horse at Agincourt and delivered a speech on the values of investing in life insurance.

The only person who seemed capable of uniting the crowd in admiration was local boy Jamie Pollock. Back from a series of injuries, the England Schoolboy international from Stockton was a revered figure at Ayresome Park. 'Oggie! Oggie!' the crowd yelled whenever he got the ball or waded into a tackle. In the North Riding 'oggie' is the slang word for an apple, but there was nothing particularly fruity about Jamie Pollock. Fair-haired, with a mouth that hung permanently open, he stomped around the midfield with the clumping, stiff-legged tread of a farm yacker with cement in his wellies, launching into challenges with a ferocity that would have made a rhino flinch, shaking his fist, yelling and generally making a powerful bid for the coveted Boro Player Who Most Resembles an Escapee From a Dickensian House of Correction Award. This prestigious trophy had last been handed out in the sixties, to centre-forward Stan Webb, a lurching hulk who had made all too few appearances for the Boro before shambling off in the direction of Carlisle. At Brunton Park, Webb briefly teamed up in attack with Stan Bowles, a partnership whose incongruity could only ever have been matched by a marriage between Margot Fonteyn and Tommy Cooper. Webb later headed the forward line at Feethams, where he was occasionally captured by Tyne Tees TV cameras, churning through the mud, elbows and knees pumping discordantly, like some Method acting hopeful trying out for the title role in *The Jabberwocky*. Stan Webb. The man was a hero.

So, too, was Jamie Pollock. As well as the bristling barbarity of his tackling he also ran powerfully and decisively with the ball and his passing was often more thoughtful than his appearance might have led you to expect. The worrying thought was that these aspects of his game might gradually be subsumed by the tough-guy theatrics; that a talented midfielder could end up another run-of-the-mill, home-crowd-pleasing clogger.

One person who would not have been in the least concerned at this possibility was the man on our right. Carlos Saldanha, coach of Brazil in the seventies, was fond of pronouncing, 'The ball is like a beautiful woman. You must love and caress it.' ('Should I take my boots off first, boss?' Tostao is alleged to have replied.) If the ball was indeed a woman, then the man on our right was in severe need of a counselling session and a set of educational videos. 'Don't fanny about, pump it up!' he rumbled. He had the deepest voice on Teesside. Which is saying something, because everyone on Teesside has a deep voice. If Barry White ever visited Middlesbrough people would say: 'What's the matter with you, pet? Did you get your nuts caught in a drawer? You sound like Kate Bush.' Even by these standards the man on our right was exceptional. 'Get your tackle in first!' he boomed. The ground vibrated. By half-time everyone within ten yards of him found their fillings had worked loose. If he'd got excited there's no telling what damage he could have done. Thankfully, the two teams battled hard to prevent any catastrophe.

Middlesbrough, even with Hendrie restored to the team, looked inept. Moore, inspirational earlier in the season, now seemed bewildered; had Wilkinson showed any less movement the club would have had to get planning permission for him, and the normally wild and crazy Liburd took a blow on the head early on which stunned him sensible. But if Boro appeared directionless, they were Sir Ranulph Fiennes compared to Wolverhampton. Wolves were hesitant in defence, clueless in midfield and up front former Newcastle favourite David Kelly and Guy Whittingham were not so much an attack as a polite reproach.

The second half was even worse. 'This is the drizzling shits,' the deep-voiced man grumbled. The ball ping-ponged about randomly around the midfield. The crowd fell into a sullen, adolescent sort of rhubarbing discontent. As the ineptitude on the pitch increased, so did the noise from the Holgate End. The chants for and against Lawrence began. There were jeers. Fists were waved. Across the terrace the rival groups gestured and sneered at one another. 'I'm going to blow a fucking fuse in a minute, me, Lawrence,' Gravel Tones bellowed. 'I'll blow a fucking fuse, like.' He was looking at the dug out, arm outstretched in its direction, but his jabbing index finger was bent at right angles to it. He was pointing with his knuckles. 'Second-hand shite gets better treatment than this.'

The game went on. Nobody paid it much attention, until, with three minutes left, Wilkinson, having convinced the Wolves defence he was clinically dead, moved unmarked into the penalty area, chested down Tommy Wright's cross and volleyed into the net. 'Ee-aye-oh. Ee-aye-oh,' the Holgate End sang. Afterwards we walked back along the side of the cemetery towards the Garden City Social Club. We took the lucky A19 route back to Tyneside.

Willington v. Evenwood Town,
Federation Breweries Northern League
Division 2
Saturday 12 March 1994

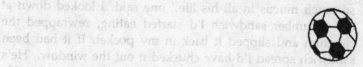

The bus from Durham trundled up the Wear Valley, past the Diana Ross Tap School in Langley Moor and a shop called Everything Tiny, which sadly proved to have nothing to do with Stan Cummins and Eric Gates, but sold furniture for dolls' houses. Beyond Brandon the countryside opened up and you could see for miles across fields of brightening grass. Spring had begun to make its first hesitant appearance. Snowdrops and aconites peeped nervously out from behind tussocks and tree roots as if preparing to nip back in at the first sign of trouble. It was a bright day, but there was still snow lying in the hollows and banked up on the north side of the drystone walls that criss-crossed the hillsides. Three weeks earlier I had come on this same journey to see Crook play Esh Winning and arrived at the Millfield Ground to find the gates padlocked and a snowman standing in the centre circle as lonely and idle as Malcolm Macdonald in the 1974 Cup final. Over the next ten days it had snowed heavily. On the Thursday night three inches had fallen and our new car had slid and slipped over the road with the unheralded spontaneity of a hyperactive child on a polished wood floor. That weekend only two games had been played in the North-East, on the coast at Blyth and Hartlepool. The thaw had come rapidly in low-lying districts. Willington, though, was high up in the foothills of the North Pennines. As the bus pulled westward up the steady incline the temperature plummeted faster than a bungee-jumping Ron Guthrie.

At Brancepeth, where the council had erected a bus shelter apparently with the express purpose of preventing anyone seeing the elaborately carved stone drinking fountain set in the wall behind it, a group of old ladies got on and began talking about operations. 'When the consultant, Mr Hurley, come in to see me the following day he said he'd never seen so much mucus in all his life,' one said. I looked down at the cucumber sandwich I'd started eating, rewrapped the clingfilm and slipped it back in my pocket. If it had been sandwich spread I'd have chucked it out the window. 'He's very good, that Mr Hurley,' another of the women said. 'He removed four feet of our Bobby's lower intestine.'

A freezing wind was blowing down the long main street at Willington. It was so cold the teenage girls were wearing tights. And it has to be very cold indeed to induce such weedy behaviour in the North-East, I can tell you. In all but the most extreme conditions a white mini-skirt and matching slingbacks are considered all the protection a girl's legs need against the elements. It's only when friends and relations have started stopping them in the street, pointing at their pins, and saying, 'Are those blue leggings new, pet?' that they opt for anything extra.

There was only a handful of people in the Hall Lane Ground. It was the first place I had been to all season where the players and officials outnumbered the crowd. It was a big ground, too, with cinder banking behind the goals and a large blue and white covered stand. Ten thousand people had come here to watch an Amateur Cup tie with Bromley in 1953; twenty years later 5,000 had turned up to see Willington draw with Blackburn Rovers in the FA Cup first round. I stood by the brick changing-room. A smell of frying chips was wafting from somewhere in the surrounding council houses. A Jack Russell pup ran past, danced up the steps of the changing-rooms and cocked his leg against one of the benches by the doors, spraying the seat with steaming liquid. A young bloke came round the corner with a leather lead in his hand. 'Ee, away man, Tinker,' he shouted at the dog. The Jack Russell looked up at him, appeared to chuckle, then bounded off in the opposite direction. The man smiled and shook his head. 'One word from me and he does as he likes,' he said, and chased off after the pup.

I walked across the rutted pitch to the main stand. The words 'One Win' had been chalked in a wobbly hand on the concrete steps as if by some Northern League equivalent of Ben Gunn. To the south you could see across the narrowing valley to a landfill site. Gulls plunged and tumbled above it, beyond were the outskirts of Bishop Auckland. It was a sad scene, the handful of spectators, the heavily vandalised clubhouse with the steel shutters across the windows, the rubbish and the motionless bulldozers on the opposite hillside. I flicked through the neatly produced programme, thinking about the smiles of the gatemen and the raffle-ticket seller. It only made me feel more melancholy. There was so much pride and history invested in this place. Yet time and circumstance had brought down the club, as it had the tough, proud men who had once served here, as it would all of us. Now, the best the future held was survival and the chance to relive old times.

For close on three decades Willington had been one of the top amateur sides in the country. The club had produced a string of players who later turned professional, among them Walter Holmes of Middlesbrough; Jimmy Banks, a member of Spurs' 1921 Cup-winning side; George Tweedy of Grimsby and Bill Ashurst of Notts County, both England internationals; Billy Hindmarsh of Portsmouth, and Ray Pointer, who played in the same Burnley side as Sunderland manager Mick Buxton. Willington had taken the Northern League title twice in the late 1920s. In 1939 they'd reached the Amateur Cup final, losing 3–0 in extra time to a Bishop Auckland side which included the young Bob Paisley. Eleven years later they got their revenge at Wembley in front of a crowd of 88,000, hammering Bishops 4–0. Old newsreel footage shows the two teams shuttling the ball from one end of the field to the other with alarming rapidity, while the commentator enunciates their names, his accent as crisp and glossy as fractured toffee, tagging on words like splendid, swift and superb, as if he'd got a job lot of sibilant adjectives on the cheap and was eager to get rid of them before they went soggy. Willington, the younger and quicker of the two teams, were three up within half an hour. Eddie Taylor, the club captain, headed the first. Taylor, a Sunderland shipyard worker, was one of eleven children. His youngest brother was 'Little' Ernie Taylor, the five-feet-four-inch inside-forward who, the following year on the same turf, would inspire Newcastle's victory in the FA Cup final. Stan Rutherford, a jug-eared architect from Cramlington, drove in the second after a passing movement involving all five forwards. Bill Larmouth added the third from Rutherford's cross. From then on Bishops, inspired by Bob Hardisty, dominated the game. But they couldn't find a way past Jack Snowdon, the willowy Jack Palance lookalike in the Willington goal. Fifteen minutes from time Matt Armstrong broke loose and thrashed home the fourth.

The standard of football played by the two teams that day was considered by many to be the best ever seen in an Amateur Cup final. After the match Sir Stanley Rous, then secretary of the Football Association, took Bob Hardisty aside and thanked him for putting on such a show. There had been many at Lancaster Gate who'd wondered if the quality of the amateur game was good enough to warrant a showcase at such a prestigious venue; Bishops and Willington, Rous said, had proved the doubters wrong.

An elderly man in a beige anorak and flat cap walked along the back of the stand, draped a tartan rug over one of the seats and sat down on it. The game kicked off. 'You're trying to play too much football, Willington,' the man on the rug shouted. It was hard to see what he was getting at. Willington had some good players, Brett Cummings, a fair-haired winger, and the red-headed centre-forward Simon Andrews among them, but Evenwood, in snazzy violet- and black-striped shirts, were easily the better team. They had a player sent off after twenty minutes, yet still cruised to a 3–1 lead. Their striker, Ivan Moxon, wreaked havoc all afternoon. He was a massive, bearded man who looked like he'd just leaped over the prow of a longship. Whenever he hurled his vast frame into a tackle everyone in the ground watched through spread fingers. And once he got the ball he was so difficult to dispossess you felt Willington would have to call the bailiffs in to get it back off him.

'Get someone out wide. Make the extra man count,' the rug man yelled. He was a lone voice crying in the wilderness.

By the end of the 1950s Willington had entered a steady period of decline. They revived briefly in the mid-seventies, winning the Northern League Cup and finishing second behind Blyth in the Championship. It was a temporary remission. In 1983 they were relegated into the Second Division. If anyone needed confirmation of the parlous state of the club it came shortly after the drop, when Malcolm Allison was appointed as manager. Allison was widely respected as a coach but by the mid-eighties his appearance at a ground was usually the harbinger of disaster. If you'd been casting round for a footballing fifth Horseman of the Apocalypse, Allison would have been right up there with Tommy Docherty at the head of your list.

With ten minutes to go a man walked round the banking behind the goal carrying two short ladders. He placed one against the high larchlap fence of a neighbouring garden, climbed up it, hauled the second one over the fence and lowered it down on the other side, then clambered across on to it and began lifting the first ladder over into the garden. 'Alert the committee,' one of a small group of Evenwood supporters shouted. 'Somebody's escaping!'

After the final whistle I walked up the road to a second-hand bookshop. I bought a copy of an illustrated history of Teesdale for my mum. When I came to write the cheque my hands were so numb I could barely hold the pen.

'Been out of doors?' the bookshop-owner asked.

I nodded, 'At football.'

'Whereabouts?'

'Here,' I said. 'At Willington.'

'Hell's teeth,' the bookshop-owner said, 'Are they still on the go?'

I had twenty minutes to kill before the bus came. I walked up the main street to keep warm. The sky was beginning to darken. There were council signs pointing the way to Binchester Roman Fort. There had been none for Hall Lane. No matter how many peoples' lives it touched, football was always denied a place in general history. Even in the North-East, where the game was so firmly imbedded in the culture you couldn't have removed it without a general anaesthetic, the guide books and the tourist maps turned a blind eye, as if to some marginal and slightly unsavoury ceremony partaken of only by the devout and the temporarily unhinged. In a volume on the villages of Durham in a short section on Cockfield you'll find a description of the geese once raised on the nearby fell and a brief biography of Jeremiah Dixon, the locally born surveyor, co-drawer of the Mason-Dixon line. But you'll find no mention of the team of unemployed miners from Cockfield who reached the 1927 Amateur Cup final, or of the twenty-two League players the village produced during a three-year spell in the same decade. Had they been writers or painters, ballet dancers or music hall comedians, their origins might have warranted some remembrance, a celebration even. But they were just footballers. Their skill, creativity and genius were destined to be recorded only on the memories of those who watched them. And when those memories faded, or the people who carried them died, everything of the hard brilliance of these men, save for the skeleton facts and figures of their careers, would die with them.

It was a sad and iniquitous business. And whatever way you looked at it, it was bollocks.

Benton is a leafy suburb. On a warm spring Sunday I walked along the empty streets. That morning it had rained and there was the musty smell of drying tarmac. In the smart gardens of the detached houses cherry trees were blossoming. The air was full of the buzzing of bees and the whine of motor mowers and dissatisfied teenagers. At Darsley Park, across an acre of green I could see some boys in striped football shirts and shiny tracksuit bottoms warming up for a game. Walking towards them I began to hear their coach, a middle-aged man with tinted glasses, barking, 'A hundred per cent. A hundred per cent. Come on, Gary. If it's not hurting, it's not working.' The boys were sprinting up and down, banging chests with one another. They were flushed and laughing and about twelve years old. 'Final effort, now,' yelled the coach, who'd evidently memorised the Berlitz Football Management Phrasebook. 'Let's really go for it.'

After the last push the boys collapsed on the ground. The coach walked among them like George Kennedy giving a pep talk to a bunch of raw recruits. 'When this game gets underway, I don't want to see any of you hiding,' he snarled. 'I want eleven winners out there. I want commitment. I want . . .' I resisted the urge to shout out: 'My head examining.' '. . . perspiration and concentration.'

The boys sat wobbling their calf muscles and eyeing him calmly.

I was less sanguine. I had come to watch Wallsend Boys' Club play and I was desperately hoping this wasn't them.

Even within an area which has produced as many footballers as the North-East there are pockets of particular richness. Seaham, birthplace of Micky Hazard, Brian Marwood and Gary Rowell, among others, was one; Chester-le-Street and South Bank were others. Arguably the most fruitful of all, though, was the old ship-building and mining district in the East End of Newcastle. Wallsend was at its centre, wedged between the river and the site of the old Rising Sun Colliery. Over the years this section of the city had produced a steady stream of high-class players: Albert Stubbins, Denis Tueart, Peter Beardsley, Chris Waddle, Steve Bruce, Alan Shearer, Lee Clark and Steve Watson. The last half-dozen of these had all started their careers playing for Wallsend Boys' Club.

'Let's get stripped off, now, and keep loose before kick-off,' the coach said, essaying a quick jog that set his stomach wobbling like an adolescent's Adam's apple during hymn practice. The boys peeled away their tracksuits, revealing immaculate shorts and socks. Their boots looked box-fresh, their shirts glistered in the sunlight.

This was not what I had had in mind when I set out. You see, I was brought up reading football comics full of characters like Nipper, Raven of the Wing and Lefty Lampton. Backstreet boys with smudged faces, flapping shirt-tails and unruly hair, whose painful lack of decent equipment could not disguise the blistering genius they carried in their grubby legs. They were urchins who dropped their aitches, said 'Cor, lumme! What sort of a scrape 'ave I got meself into now?' to their faithful terrier, Scraps, and rose to the top of the soccer ladder, without the aid of scouts or schools of excellence, simply by half-volleying a tin of peach segments on to the head of a fleeing felon who, by happy circumstance, had just snatched the wallet of Bert Brown, manager of prestigious Burnton Wanderers. 'Say, kid, that's quite a right foot you've got there. What are you doing on Saturday afternoon?'

It was a ridiculous and romantic idea, I knew, but part of me found it impossible to relinquish it. At night as I drift off to sleep I still sometimes find myself cursing my misfortune at having two loving parents and a childhood lived out in a pleasant house. If only, my subconscious tells me, you'd been brought up by an alcoholic gypsy in a caravan overlooking the town dump, fed on nothing but pineapple fritters and fizzy pop and run about in bare feet all winter, you'd now be celebrating winning the European Cup for Bolcaster United, instead of lying here trying to remember what tautology is.

The referee appeared. The boys in the fancy shirts practised penalties. A few minutes before the game was due to kick off there was a piping cry from over by the changing-room. The other team was coming. They were wearing slightly faded green shirts, white shorts made from an assortment of materials. The high-pitched shout was coming from the kid bringing up the rear. He was half the size of the tallest of the group, his shirt so big on him he looked like the sorcerer's apprentice. He was wearing plimsolls. 'Carl, Carl!' he was yelling. His voice hadn't broken and every time he shouted the mongrel that was standing near me instinctively cocked its head. The small boy ran with a rolling pigeon-toed gait. Carl passed the ball to him, the small boy knocked it back with the outside of his left foot, nonchalantly turning away after he had done so, confident that he knew where it was going.

This was Wallsend Boys' Club. They were 3–0 up inside twenty minutes. Every so often life lives up to cliché. I walked back up to the Metro Station grinning idiotically.

Crook Town v. Easington Colliery, Federation Brewery Northern League Division 2
Saturday 19 March 1994

There are many fine things about living in the North-East, but the coffee isn't one of them. The owners of the region's cafés, plagued by nightmare visions of elderly customers clutching their chests and pitching face-forward into plates of toasted teacake, served the most insipid coffee to be found anywhere on earth. A visitor from the South might be forgiven for thinking rationing is still in place. Andy and I were sitting in a café in Durham drinking cappuccino that was about as strong as a Glenn Hoddle tackle. It wasn't cappuccino at all. It was very milky coffee. It did have froth on it, though. Which was a bit worrying, because the café didn't actually have a cappuccino machine. It may have been merely coincidental, but just after we ordered a waitress rushed out and came back a few minutes later clutching a bicycle pump.

We walked up to the bus station without the aid of artificial stimulants. The bus driver was wearing dark glasses, a white shirt and black tie. His fists were resting on the steering wheel like discarded weapons. He was chewing gum. All the bus drivers in the North-East look like this. They were the inspiration for *Reservoir Dogs*.

The bus chugged out through Neville's Cross, past a clinic that offered non-surgical facial alterations and a nightclub that looked as if its clients would provide much the same service at a fraction of the cost. A few days had made a lot of difference. The previous Wednesday I'd passed through here on the way to Bishop Auckland in driving sleet and hail; now the sun was bright, daffodils nodded their golden heads, lambs gambolled, cotton-wool clouds scudded across a cerulian sky and that.

Crook, though described as a town, is really not much more than a large village. There's a Prestos, a short street of shops, a market square that doubles as a car park and a massive four-storey brick pagoda that towers over the surrounding buildings and proclaims itself to be the headquarters of Weardale Council. I don't know who designed it, but I suspect he's not allowed to use metal cutlery.

Near the Millfield Ground there was a pub advertising a happy hour. By the look of it an hour would be pushing things. Crook had a bleak, bleached mien. High up on the edge of the West Durham Coalfield it had taken a rare battering over the years, and not just from the wind. Mass unemployment had been endemic in this part of Durham since before the First World War. What work there was, in the pits at Pease West and Hole-in-the-Wall, was hard, dangerous and likely to be terminated at a day's notice if demand for coal fell. When the mines closed in the sixties, Crook passed its days in quiet isolation. Then, in 1993, in a bid to stimulate the local economy, the government announced that the town's junior school was the worst in the country and for a few heady weeks the place was invaded by reporters and TV crews from all over England.

Inside the Millfield Ground there was the usual raffle-ticket seller. The prize was a boxful of groceries. There were tins of ham and marrowfat peas, jam, meatpaste and jars of coffee with labels proclaiming 'Special North-East "Not Enough Caffeine to Agitate a Gnat" Brand! With Unique Damp Flannel Flavour Formula!' It wasn't a particularly stunning selection; still, at least it wasn't a meat packet. I'm not a vegetarian, but I couldn't help feeling that a display of animal innards was hardly the most welcoming sight when you entered a football ground. The one at Durham had been particularly off-putting. It was practically a whole cow. All that was missing were the horns. Walking past the table that held it was like stumbling across an autopsy.

The Millfield Ground is one of the largest in the Northern League. In the 1950s it regularly held crowds of over 10,000. The ground record was 17,500 for an Amateur Cup tie. There was stepped cinder terracing behind the goals, a covered standing area and an impressive grandstand, now heavily reinforced with scaffolding. This two-tiered building had been officially opened by Sir Joseph Pease in 1925, just in time to bear mute witness to a scandal that almost destroyed non-league football in the North-East, the so-called Crook Affair.

The trouble was rooted in the English FA's strict stipulations about the nature of amateurism. Rule 29 of the FA's legislative code, formulated among the button-back leather armchairs and cigar smoke of that body's old headquarters at 42 Russell Square, allowed amateur players only to be reimbursed for actual travel and subsistence costs on match days. If a man received any remuneration over and above this, whether it was a £5 back-hander from the treasurer, or a farthing handed over for a cup of tea he had not in fact payed for, that player, the men from WC1 announced, was a professional. Flat-rate expenses (the paying of a standard fee to cover travel and food) were outlawed; compensation payments for time lost at work were barred. In the latter case the English FA found itself out of step with Europe. FIFA had officially sanctioned 'broken-time' payments in 1927, an act in which they had been joined by the International Olympic Committee. Rather than comply with this grubby measure, the Corinthians of the FA withdrew from FIFA, and from the Olympic football competition. Had they accepted the ruling the 'Crook Affair' would have been averted, and the full England team might have won several more World Cups.

It was against this background that in the summer of 1927 the FA received an anonymous letter suggesting that the books of the newly crowned Northern League champions, Crook Town, had not so much been cooked as flambéed in rum with added sweeteners. The tip-off alleged that gate receipts were not being fully recorded, the balance being used to make cash payments to the players. An inquiry by the Durham FA was ordered and, while no proof could be found that players had been paid, enough irregularities were discovered in Crook's accounting system for the FA to ban the club's secretary, E. F. Peart, from all football for life. Three other committeemen were suspended indefinitely, five more for a full season. That was not the end of it. Five months later, with the season already well underway and Crook heading the Northern League table, the DFA announced that it had uncovered new evidence concerning illegal payments at the Millfield Ground. Every player and committeeman at the club was permanently suspended; the club was expelled from the Northern League and the results of their matches that season expunged from the record. Like a discredited communist leader, Crook Town had been air brushed out of history.

Peart was not a man to let things lie. While he knew he couldn't prove Crook were innocent, he was damned near certain he could show that they were only as guilty as everybody else. Over the next few months he set about his task in a manner that suggested he was not only prepared to cut off his nose to spite his face but several other fleshy protuberances as well. Bishop Auckland in particular came under his scrutiny. In Crook it was widely suspected that the original anonymous letter had originated from Kingsway. Certainly Bishop Auckland had protested after their defeat by Crook in that season's Amateur Cup that the victors 'were not a properly constituted amateur club'. The Bishops' holier-than-thou attitude was an irritant and an inspiration to Peart. In February of 1928 he sent a dossier of wrong doings at twenty North-East clubs to the FA in London. The evidence he'd amassed included testimonies from numerous players, all of whom alleged they had received payments in contravention of Rule 29. Top of the list of offenders were Bishop Auckland. Things were so fishy at Kingsway that several Icelandic trawlers were spotted sailing up the Wear.

Peart may have believed that his findings would be so damaging to the English amateur game that the FA would decide to ignore the whole business, Crook's misdemeanours included, rather than make them public. If so, he had badly misjudged the mood at Lancaster Gate. Frederick Wall, secretary of the FA, who just twelve months before had signed the letter withdrawing his nation's amateur team from global competitions rather than have them tainted by contact with the mercenary foreigner, must have been stunned by Peart's information. Wall's letter to FIFA had been couched in the most pompous terms. It recalled the English FA's long-running battle to protect amateurism from the encroachment of the professional game, and its success in doing so: 'Rules were accordingly adopted to remedy the mischief and have proved to be satisfactory,' it concluded. Now this funny little man from the North was threatening to make Wall look a complete fool and embarrass the FA in front of the whole world. Something must be done!

An inquiry was organised. As a result of its findings 341 North-Eastern players and over 1,000 officials were suspended from football. Their offences ranged from the Willington player who claimed to have received a fee of £2 10s per match to a sixteen-year-old boy from Sunderland who'd turned out for West Stanley reserves and received half a crown in expenses, despite the fact that he had not produced receipts totalling that amount. The FA had shown the Continentals the proper way to deal with 'shamateurs'.

Only five teams out of the fourteen who made up the Northern League escaped censure. Bishop Auckland lost 46 players and virtually the entire administration; Ferryhill Athletic, too, had 46 players suspended; Cockfield, beaten finalists in that year's Amateur Cup final, 37; Stanley United 29 and Willington 16. It seemed impossible that the clubs could continue after such turmoil. For a while it appeared the days of amateur football in the North-East were over. Some of the clubs, Bishop Auckland and Crook among them, examined the possibility of turning professional and joining the North-Eastern League; others talked of disbanding altogether, while the Durham FA threatened to split from the English FA entirely.

The FA now found itself in a strange situation. Not long before the 'Crook Affair' began a group of what one might term 'Amateur fundamentalists' had withdrawn from the Football Association and formed their own ruling body, the Amateur Football Alliance. Paradoxically, their reason for doing so was that they felt the FA was too much involved in the professional game. The AFA included most of the public schools' old boys teams and many of the universities. Now the FA found itself in imminent danger of losing the Northern League too. With the Football League already run as an autonomous body, this would have left the mandarins of the FA with very little to administer. They took a step back from the brink. The investigating committee invited all those who had been suspended to appeal. Encouraged by the possibility of clemency, the Northern League reconstituted. Crook, unsurprisingly, were refused readmission, though their presumption in actually applying surely merited some reward. In October the Football Association announced the results of the appeals. Almost without exception the suspensions were repealed and the players allowed to return to the amateur ranks. A year later, after a season in the Durham Central, Crook Town were back in the Northern League.

To anyone born in the 1960s who doesn't have an interest in Rugby Union, the whole concept of amateur sport is vaguely ludicrous; the idea that the upholding of amateurism should justify the public humiliation of decent men who've accepted tuppence more than their due, draconian. The concept of amateurism and the almost saintly regard in which it was held was, like so many things, rooted in the British class system. Association Football had emerged from the public schools and in the early years of the game its national competition, the FA Cup, was dominated by old boys teams from the likes of Eton and Charterhouse, or groups of army officers from much the same social backgrounds. The introduction of professionalism at the turn of the century changed all that. It also split football. The schism was not as violent as that which sliced rugby in two, neither was it blurred like that in cricket by the intermingling of amateurs and professionals within the same top-flight teams. Instead, the two factions went their more or less separate ways. As everyone in England knows, play is a more noble pursuit for a man than work. From now on, if the gentlemen could no longer prove themselves physically better, they could at least uphold their moral superiority. The virulence with which they did so is startling, to say the least. In rugby the very appearance of a Union player in the company of League men could lead to his suspension; in cricket an idiotic system was instituted in which amateurs' names were printed on the scorecard prefixed by title and initials while the professionals warranted only a surname – or, later, after a wave of liberalism had swept through the administration, their initials placed *after* their name. The Football Association, meanwhile, set up an entirely separate cup competition for the amateur game, refused, as we have seen, to countenance broken-time payments and would ban a man for life from the sport he loved over the price of a jam tart. Strangely enough, many of the same people who once merrily endorsed this type of mad pettiness now fill up the newspapers and airwaves with ravings about the terrors of 'political correctness'.

Stranger still, perhaps, is the fact that amateurism should have taken such a strong hold in County Durham, an area which historically has always been one of the poorest in Britain. The same was not true, for example, across the Tyne in Northumberland. Here, all the top non-league sides, Ashington, Blyth, North Shields, Whitley Bay, Hexham Hearts, were what was then termed professional (nowadays these clubs would be what we refer to as semi-professional, or part-time professional. The players were paid to play football, but most had other jobs they did during the week). Indeed, throughout the rest of the North of England there were just a handful of amateur clubs of any note (Northern Nomads and Crosby Marine were the only two to have made any impact in national competitions), yet in little impoverished Durham there were a dozen or more. It could be that the strength of amateurism in the county was mere coincidence – as with the popularity of rugby in some areas, football in others –

or it may be that it was in some way linked to Durham University; certainly Bishop Auckland had been founded by students from the theological college there. Whatever the reason, like the Rugby Union players of South Wales, the Durham footballers' misfortune was to have found themselves serving an idealistic notion their pockets were unable fully to support.

Why, then, didn't they turn professional? The answer was financial expediency. County Durham, with a population of around half a million, was already heavily burdened with full- and part-time professional clubs. Sunderland, Gateshead, Hartlepool and Darlington played in the Football League; Spennymoor, Durham City, Chester-le-Street, Horden and Consett in the North-Eastern League. And Newcastle and Middlesbrough were each just a few hundred yards across the county borders. As the likes of Darlington and Hartlepool knew only too well, there were hardly enough supporters to sustain the professional clubs already present, without adding a further dozen. Top Northern League clubs such as Stockton, which did turn professional, soon found themselves returning to the amateur ranks.

Conversely, the county was also arguably incapable of sustaining a fully amateur league. The amateur game was reliant on players whose employment left them with week-ends free. In an era in which men who worked in industry invariably put in a five and a half day week which included Saturday mornings, this effectively meant those who were self-employed, who worked in one of the professions, or who were so financially secure that going without a half-day's pay didn't matter to them. There simply weren't enough such players in the North-East to furnish sufficent teams for a league, let alone one of any sort of quality.

Faced with a choice between foundering as professionals or sinking as mediocre amateurs, many of the Durham clubs opted to steer a slightly different course. They held on to amateur status, and while those players who wished or could afford to play without pay did so, those who couldn't were compensated, either through payment in kind via friendly shopkeepers, or by the practice known as 'boot' money. 'When you came out of the bath,' an ex-foundryman who'd turned out in the Northern League in the thirties told me, 'there'd be a few shillings tucked in the toe of your shoe.'

In 1934 the recently knighted Sir Frederick Wall, secretary of the Football Association since 1897, retired. As a reward for his long years of service this gentleman, who had worked so tirelessly to uphold the purity of the amateur game was awarded an annuity of £10,000 by his former employers.

Andy and I went and sat in the grandstand. There were about forty other people in the Millfield Ground. The game kicked off. Alan Shoulder, the former Blyth and Newcastle United forward who was Crook's player-manager, hobbled past on a damaged knee. The players ran up and down, the ball pinged about. It was one of those disjointed encounters in which the two teams seem to be employing the footballing equivalent of the cut-and-paste techniques of William Burroughs; as if they've simply taken a taken a whole match, sliced it into random fragments, tossed it up in the air and stuck it back together again wearing blindfolds. Even the most determined mathematician would have struggled to establish any pattern. At one point Easington strung three passes together, but it was probably just a coincidence. All through the season I had filled dull passages of play, or long waits for delayed trains, by speculating on the person best suited to describing that day's game. Crook Town versus Easington Colliery Welfare called for the mordant brevity of Calvin Coolidge.

Too bad.

Behind us some old men filled the time talking about Crook's glory years. 'We played at Spurs,' one of them said. 'There wasn't a blade of grass on the pitch except over by the corner flags. It was like rolled clarts.'

In the ten-year period between 1954 and 1964 Crook had won the Amateur Cup four times. The first of those victories, over Bishop Auckland, had gone to replays at St James's and Ayresome and had been watched by a combined crowd of over 200,000. Crook, then managed by Joe Harvey, took the tie 1–0. In 1959 they defeated Barnet, currently in the Football League, 3–2 in front of 60,000 spectators at Wembley. Three years later, twenty-six coaches and two special trains were needed to transport Crook's fans to London for another final encounter, this time with Hounslow. The game ended 1–1. But a Crook team featuring Frank 'The Schoolboy Full-back' Clark beat the Middlesex men 4–0 in a replay at Ayresome Park. Later that year, Clark signed for Newcastle. He famously went for years and years before scoring his first goal for United; then, when he might have expected to be entering the twilight of his career, Brian Clough took him to Nottingham Forest where he went on to win Championship and European Cup-winners' medals. As managerial successor to Clough at the City Ground he was to take Forest to promotion in the 1993–94 season. In 1964, Town beat Enfield in the final, ensuring a unique record of four winners' medals for veteran winger Jimmy McMillan. Along with Bishop Auckland and Willington, Crook ensured that North-Eastern clubs remained the dominant force in the amateur game for over two decades.

By this time, Sir Stanley Rous had taken over as secretary of the FA and football's ruling body had begun to shift, unofficially at least, to a slightly more realistic interpretation of what constituted amateurism. However, the damage had been done. The earlier FA decision on the broken-time issue, far from stamping out illegal payments, had if anything had the opposite effect – just as prohibition in the USA had led to an increase in the consumption of alcohol. By denying the players any form of legal compensation for time lost at work, the FA had created a situation in which men were forced to break the rules to get what they honestly felt should have been an entitlement. After all, a man who lost wages in order to play football wasn't only playing for nothing, but effectively paying to play. In such circumstances subterfuge flourished and it was almost inevitable that payments would gradually increase out of all proportion to their original intention. By the early fifties a sergeant instructor at Catterick Camp would be able to answer my father's inquiry as to why he travelled all the way up into County Durham to play football rather than turning out for a local team by saying: 'Because they give me five quid a week, and that's only ten shillings less than I get off the Army.'

My mother's cousin, working as an apprentice draughtsman at Southbank Steelworks, doubled his wages by playing for a junior side.

An ex-player said sternly, 'I never received a penny,' then smiled and said, 'but I tell you what, I never paid for a new suit, a Sunday roast or a gallon of petrol for about ten years.'

Another said, 'The money was there if you wanted it. Some of the lads were well-to-do and they weren't bothered with it. Others worked down the pit or had big families and they needed every penny they could get.'

This practice was not solely confined to the North-East, of course. It was so widespread throughout the English amateur game that the suggestion was often made that Law 29 on the illegality of making payments be amended to include the clause: 'But if you do, don't get caught.' However, the involvement of so many of the region's top clubs in the Crook scandal undoubtedly led to a suspicion among the London-based administrators that North-Eastern players were 'less amateur' than their Southern counterparts – an attitude which might explain the marked regional bias, particularly in the 1930s, in favour of Home Counties players when it came to selecting the national team.

The fact that some of the players in the best Northern League teams were paid should not in anyway detract from their achievements. Many of their opponents were similarly remunerated and besides, there was no advantage gained from it. It is a strange irony that one of the greatest English sportsmen of all time, the cricketer W. G. Grace, undertook no occupation that anyone ever saw other than cricket yet was considered an amateur, while a man from County Durham who worked five and a half days a week down a mine, played football on Saturday afternoon and received a shilling for doing so was classed as a professional.

The second half wasn't much better than the first. Easington scored twice in quick succession from corners. They were the better team of the two, but that's a bit like saying that I'm harder than Charles Hawtrey. They had a pair of brothers playing for them called Ptohopolous. Thankfully, the referee didn't have to book either of them. Easington had come into the Northern League in 1985, given the chance by the League's expansion into two divisions in 1982. It wasn't the first time the Northern League had had a Second Division. There'd also been one in the 1890s. In those days it was populated by teams with bizarre names such as Stockton Vulcan, a team whose coldly unemotional football was so out of step with the passion and turmoil around them that they disbanded in 1902. Vulcan are believed to be the only team ever to have a man sent off for raising an eyebrow quizzically at a refereeing decision. Darlington Rise Carr Rangers were one of the Stockton club's chief rivals. The Rangers fan who started the 'Give me a D' chant was once the most unpopular man in the Northern League. In the 1930s he was superseded by his counterpart at General Chemicals (Imperial Chemical Industries) Billingham FC. As might be expected, Thornaby Utopian's brand of dreamy idealism was ill-suited to the brutal pragmatism of Victorian football. They folded in 1901. The application of the softies of Stockton Malleable to join the League was, unsurprisingly, turned down.

Easington scored from a corner again. One of the men behind us was compiling the club records.

'Didn't they used to keep them, then?' someone asked him.

'Oh aye,' the compiler said, 'but the bloke that did it fell out with the club, so he had a bonfire in his back garden and burned the lot of them.'

Sixty years had passed but the spirit of E. F. Peart obviously lived on in Crook.

West Auckland v. Hebburn, Federation Brewery Northern League Division 1
Saturday 26 March 1994

The bus dropped me outside West Auckland Working Men's Club. On the pavement a blonde girl of about twelve was running up and down leading a little white pony by a rope, getting it used to the noise of traffic. By the chip shop a group of teenage boys stood slouched across the handlebars of their mountain bikes, smoking and watching the passing cars. They seemed to have an inexhaustible supply of spit. In the windows of the houses around the village green there were posters up offering a reward for information leading to the recovery of the Sir Thomas Lipton Trophy, the 'first World Cup'. The trophy had been stolen from the Working Men's Club, where it was on permanent display, on 19 January. 'It's everything to the people here,' the club steward, John Turnbull, told reporters. 'The insurance money isn't important; the World Cup is irreplaceable.'

I went into a shop with a blackboard outside advertising fresh-cut sandwiches. The window was full of hot-water bottles. I bought a cheese roll, then walked over to the football ground. In the fields around it, farmers were muck-spreading. Tractors churned up and down, the cylindrical trucks behind them hurling hunks of dung in all directions. The sharp, rank smell of rotting cowshit filled the air. It was an unlikely setting for World Cup winners.

Around 1908 millionaire philanthropist Sir Thomas Lipton decided to fund the first pan-European football competition.

Because he had extensive business interests in Italy Turin was chosen as the venue. Invitations were sent out to the various national football associations. Germany, Switzerland and the host nation all agreed to send a leading club side to compete. The English FA, reluctant as ever to countenance anything new-fangled, demurred. Nearly half a century later they would still be taking the same attitude to the European Cup. Undeterred by this rebuff, the organisers in Turin decided to approach a top English club directly. Someone suggested a famous First Division team he had heard of. Unfortunately he couldn't remember the full name, only the initials W. A. Taking a look down a list of registered English sides, a colleague quickly identified the mystery team, West Auckland of the prestigious Northern League. An invitation was despatched and promptly accepted. Woolwich Arsenal's first appearance in Continental competition would just have to wait.

If this story appears to stretch credulity, what followed sets it straining like the waistband of Barry Siddall's shorts. Having pawned their furniture to raise the fare, the team, which only the season before had been playing in the Mid-Durham League, set off for Turin. Here they beat Stuttgart 2–0, then defeated the Swiss club FC Winterhour by the same score to win the competition and bring the silver trophy back to County Durham.

A photo shows the tour party sitting on the steps of West Auckland's stand. The trophy – the first World Cup – two feet tall, silver, apparently depicting Lord Asquith taking a throw-in – is mounted on a plinth in the centre of the group. In front of it sits Bob Jones, the captain, a handsome, fierce-looking man with a set to his jaw that suggests if you stare at him a second longer he'll leap off the page and land you one. His team-mates, miners mainly, face the camera with pale solemnity. One is a dead ringer for Steve Coppell; another has had his image retouched by the photographer, so that his head has the sharply defined flatness of Lord Snooty; a couple are beginning to smirk. Flanking them, the committeemen, in their moustaches, bowler hats and overcoats, wear looks of stern satisfaction, like Pinkerton agents who've just rounded up a gang of notorious desperados.

Two years later, as defending champions, West Auckland were invited back to Italy. Bob Jones and his men reached the final again and lined up in the Turin Stadium against the home team, Juventus. They hammered the Italians 6–1. In honour of them having won the trophy twice in succession, West Auckland were allowed to keep it. Sadly, they were not able to hang on to it for long. The cost of the trip to Italy had proved near ruinous to the club. Back in West Auckland they used the trophy as security on a £40 loan from the landlady of a local pub. Even this didn't prove sufficent to save the club. They reformed again two years later, but were not readmitted to the Northern League until 1934. They had to wait even longer to retrieve the Sir Thomas Lipton Trophy, eventually buying it back for £100 in 1960.

Now it had gone again, and this time the likelihood of retrieving it seemed much slimmer. The police suspected a collector – perhaps even the same man who'd masterminded the theft of the Northern League Championship Trophy from Whitby Town's clubhouse a month or so later. Local people said they couldn't imagine the sort of person who'd do such a thing. Personally, I'd start by visualising a total twat and work downwards from there.

West Auckland were currently struggling near the bottom of the Northern League First Division. So were their opponents, Hebburn. The game was vital for both sides, but Hebburn probably had the most to fear. They'd conceded fourteen goals in their last three games, including a 7–2 hammering from Consett the previous Saturday. You could tell Hebburn was on Tyneside just by looking at the players. Season-ticket holders at the local solarium, they were sporting enough hair gel to spruce up a herd of yak. Their shirts were day-glo yellow and black. West Auckland were altogether more rustic.

The crowd was small in number, but made up for it in quality. Two blokes from Hebburn, one a tiny man of about eighty with a bright smile, and the other a sprightly and combative sixty-five-year-old, soon became embroiled in what was to become the key contest of the afternoon. Their opponent was a vast, silver-haired pensioner from West Auckland. The conflict began after about five minutes when West's full-back put in a crunching tackle on a Hebburn player whose pageboy hairstyle, plump face and habit of pulling his shorts high up on his waist gave him the appearance of one of the Tweedle twins from *Alice in Wonderland*. Unsurprisingly, he collapsed to the ground clutching his shin.

'Ah, give him a jelly!' the West Auckland supporter boomed.

The Hebburn duo looked round at him – he was sitting up in the stand – then back at the pitch. 'Get him booked, ref,' the younger of the two yelled. 'He could have broke his leg.'

'Shirley Temple,' the West man replied.

The octogenarian turned. 'He's went in with his studs up!' he shouted.

The West man stood up. He was built to last. He had obviously once had a barrel chest but now the barrel had slipped somewhat and was resting on the waistband of his trousers. 'He's soft as shite,' he bellowed. He sat down again with a kind of swaggering deliberation, his hands resting on his hips, like a champion sumo wrestler after a particularly easy victory.

The blokes from Hebburn ignored him this time. Sort of. The younger one said, 'Stupid Mackem,' in a stage whisper and his mate said, 'Is he a Mackem, then, is he?' with a startled note in his voice.

'Bound to be, Tommy, bound to be,' the other said, shaking his head resignedly at a world that could produce such horrors.

On the pitch, too, things were not going well for Hebburn. A loose ball fell to the West Auckland midfielder Neil Teesdale on the edge of the visitors' area and he essayed one of those first-time volleys that normally dent the guidance equipment on passing Sputniks, only on this occasion it hurtled into the top corner of the net instead. The ball cannoned off the stanchion with a clunk like a tolling bell. A lad with a rave crop, coat-hanger shoulders and ten-to-two feet standing by the Hebburn dugout spat vehemently. 'Sod off,' he said.

Hebburn, prompted by their captain, a skilful dark-haired midfielder of the crisply competitive kind the Northern League seemed to specialise in, strove for an equaliser. They hit the post, they hit the bar. They attacked again and a forward went sprawling on the edge of the West Auckland box. He got up, then squatted down, staring at the ground, recovering his breath.

'What's up, pet? Have you dropped a false eyelash?' the big man inquired.

It should be said that these remarks were not made from the safe anonymity of a packed terrace, but from a stand holding a dozen or so people. Furthermore, whenever he delivered himself of anything particularly choice, the big man stood up the better to identify himself. Every time he yelled anything you could see the Hebburn players turning to stare at him. The big man stared back. Only when play recommenced and he felt honour had been satisfied did he sit down again.

At the start of the second half West Auckland went further ahead after the Hebburn goalkeeper fumbled a header from Gary Lowes, knocking it up in the air twice, then falling over backwards and scooping the ball into the net.

'A big round of applause for the juggler,' a voice boomed from the stand.

Hebburn, desperate for points, brought on a substitute. He had long, dark hair worn in a ponytail. As the linesman was checking his studs the big man got to his feet. He pointed at the sub. He didn't shout this time, he sang. He had a great, gravelly social-club-talent-night baritone: 'Take the ribbon from your hair,' he crooned, 'shake it loose and let it fall.' Everything stopped. The linesman stood with the sub's boot in his hand; the referee with his whistle in his mouth; the players froze in mid-movement like children during a game of Musical Statues. The big man reached his finale, 'Hyeeelp meeee make it through the niiiiiight,' he belted with the vibrato of a minor earth tremor. As the last note echoed out across the surrounding countryside, he raised his arms as if to milk imaginary applause, then sat down.

There was no way back for Hebburn after that.

It was Good Friday, April Fool's Day and the start of the annual Northern League Groundhoppers' Weekend. The conjunction seemed rather fitting; there was an air of jocular penitence about the groundhoppers, especially in the driving sleet of a cold Easter afternoon in the North-East. Good humour and discomfort seemed intrinsic elements of their singular hobby. 'Stop here and suffer with the rest of us,' one of them shouted as a group of home supporters sneaked out of Shildon's Dean Street ground as their side trailed 5–1 to Durham.

It was the groundhoppers' second game of the day. That morning they'd seen Norton and Stockton Ancients play Washington, in an 11 a.m. kick-off. The Northern League staggered the starting times to suit the visitors. An hour or so after they left Dean Street they'd be settling down at Stones End to watch Evenwood take on Esh Winning. The Saturday would see them at Tow Law, Ferryhill and Seaham; the Sunday at Horden and Darlington Cleveland Social. Groundhoppers, like train-spotters and twitchers, are volume men. They are tickers-off, collectors of football grounds. They are the antithesis of most football fans – boastful Casanovas in a monogamous world, bedpost, or rather goalpost, notchers. To them neither faithfulness nor passion within the context of a stable relationship meant anything. It was only the chase that thrilled them.

In the packed main stand at Dean Street you could hear them locked in salivating discussion; comparing conquests, contrasting techniques – who've you had, how often, how long did it take, have you done any French? They were a strange set of men to set such store by rampant promiscuity. Middle-aged usually, clad in cagoules and speaking with the nasal, reedy accents of the Home Counties suburbs. They spoke in ornately oblique sentences, tinged with watery sarcasm and full of euphemisms and well-worn comedic metaphors – Sheridan rewritten by John Major. They were solo in the main, though some were accompanied by women ('My better half', 'The Memsahib') or teenage boys ('Number one son'). They had travelled by car ('I pointed the trusty Ford Orion in a north-easterly direction') or train ('I threw myself upon the vagaries of British Rail') from all over the country. But mainly from Middlesex. They had come by a variety of routes, all of them quicker and more economical than the one chosen by whoever they were talking to. They were the people for whom the Traffic Cone Hotlines were instigated.

For some ageing roués amongst the groundhoppers mere football philandering was no longer enough to satisfy jaded appetites. They had turned kinky. One could only feel he had truly 'possessed' a ground if he had touched the cross-bars. Another had a fetish for corner flags, photographing a flapping pennant at every ground he went to and keeping an album of his favourites with him at all times.

It was the third such weekend the Northern League had put on. It was easy to see why they did it. The crowd at Shildon was 500 per cent higher than normal. Gate receipts must have been up by around £700; programme sales, given the groundhoppers' propensity for buying two of every issue so as to keep one in pristine condition while writing notes on the other, the same as for ten normal matches. And then there was the refreshment stall and the bar in the clubhouse. At this end of the League pyramid the groundhoppers' weekend was a goldmine. For a club like Shildon, the only other chance of landing such a bonanza was to progress to the first round of the FA Cup, a feat they hadn't achieved since 1962, or pray that oil was discovered beneath the centre circle. The Northern League had been the first league in the country to exploit the commercial potential of groundhopping. As far as I know it's still the only one that does so on such a scale. The only worry was that after three such visits the groundhoppers had already seen twenty-four of the League's grounds. That left just sixteen to go, or two more weekends. It was no wonder the management committee was starting to countenance promotions from the Northern Alliance and Vaux Wearside League.

As Durham added a sixth and Shildon's captain, a short man with the jaw-jutting, toe-springing, fist-clenching look of Dennis the Menace's dad after a particularly appalling prank, hopped about yelling, the blood rushing to his head at such a speed it threatened to send it rocketing into orbit, the man behind me said: 'Of course, if you'd switched to the A173 at that point you'd have avoided the contra-flow at Kirklevington.'

Ashington v. Whickham,
Federation Brewery Northern League
Division 2
Saturday 7 May 1994

You could tell summer was coming. The trees were in leaf, the air smelled of new-mown grass and the Easter Egg display in the supermarket had been replaced with a mountainous pile of charcoal briquettes, hickory sticks and lighter fuel that winked seductively at passing pyromaniacs and whispered the words, 'Come on baby, light my fire,' in a saucy purr. More tellingly, when I went to get a haircut the barber said: 'Going anywhere nice this year?'

I smiled sweetly. 'Well,' I said, 'I was thinking about it, but after due consideration I've decided to go somewhere crap instead.' And the barber cut my ear off.

Only joking.

As usual the football season wasn't so much ending as fizzling out. It was like one of those long car journeys of childhood when you shout, 'Are we nearly there, Dad?' excitedly every two minutes so that by the time you finally do arrive you've lost all enthusiasm and just want to buy a Cornish Mivvi and go home. There was little left that hadn't been resolved. Billingham Synthonia's defeat in the FA Trophy had ended the last chance a North-Eastern club had of winning any national competition. Newcastle's third place in the Premiership was secure unless Arsenal confounded a century of tradition, threw caution to the wind and won 12–0 at St James's. In many ways it would have been a result worth enduring just to see George Graham's post-match press conference:

'You must be delighted with that performance, George.'

'Aye, well, I'm always pleased when we keep a clean sheet.'

Middlesbrough, meanwhile, had achieved something they had not managed for nearly a decade – mid-table mediocrity. There wasn't exactly dancing in the streets of Teesside at this performance, but several people shrugged and went 'Puh!' Sunderland were three places below them. Manager Mick Buxton told the press he wanted to rebuild the club from the bottom. He'd obviously been paying attention to events in the Northern League a few years before when the manager of a Second Division side had said 'This club needs rebuilding from the top' and been sacked three days later.

Hartlepool were certain to be relegated to Division 3; Darlington, who had always seemed likely to stay in the Football League if only because the ground of GM Vauxhall champions Kidderminster didn't meet safety standards, scraped away from the bottom place on the final day with a win over Bury. Bernie Slaven, a player who spent most of the game trying to establish a sitting tenancy in the opposition penalty area, scored from three yards.

In non-league football Gateshead surprised no one by once again finishing round the middle of the GM Vauxhall Conference. Sponsorship by a leading belt manufacturer is surely long overdue. Bishop Auckland were fourth in the Northern Premier League Premier Division – their best-ever finish. Whitley Bay were seven places below them. In the First Division, Spennymoor were the only North-Eastern club whose fate genuinely hinged on the final match of the season. Moors needed to beat Ashton United at the Brewery Field to overhaul them and take the second promotion place. They were trailing 1–0 after eighty minutes, but came back with three goals in the last ten. As well as gaining promotion, Spennymoor had also lifted the Northern Premier League Cup and the Durham Challenge Cup. On the evidence of what I'd seen it was well deserved. Spennymoor were my North-East team of the season. Not that any one was asking, mind.

Despite their runaway start to the season, Blyth appeared not to have won anything. In the Northern League Durham City overhauled them in February and went on to take their first-ever title by seven points. Blyth lost in the final of the Northern League Cup to Northallerton as well. However, though the games were all over, the game was not up for Spartans. In yet another of the 'ground standard' fiascos that seem to be endemic in the non-league pyramid, the NPL refused Durham promotion because their new stadium at Belmont would not be ready in time for the start of 1994–95 season. Durham protested that they had a ground-share arrangement with Spennymoor for the Brewery Field but to no avail. Blyth Spartans were promoted to the Northern Premier League. Durham stayed put. The days when such matters were sorted out on the pitch seem long gone. It's only a matter of time before a newspaper starts running a Fantasy Football League management committee.

By dint of Blyth's promotion, West Auckland, who had finished third from bottom of Division 1, were not relegated. Neither were Hebburn. Esh Winning Albion finished bottom of the Vaux Wearside Division 2. They won only once all season.

In Newcastle there was so much black and white you felt like you were stepping into a 1930s film. The pubs were packed. There were uniformed men on the doors. They looked like bouncers but in fact they were just the opposite. They were the Geordie equivalent of those blokes who work on the Tokyo subway during rush-hour. They weren't keeping people out, they were wedging more in. You had to be careful not to get too close to the doors or they'd grab your arms and fling you in too. The next thing you knew you'd be waking up in Heaton with a terrible hangover and a wife and three kids.

In Eldon Square bus station they were playing 'Ride of the Valkyries' over the muzak system. The bus pulled out before the Wagner had finished so I don't know what followed it.

My money's on 'Dead Man's Curve' by Jan and Dean. You'd think there'd be some kind of sticker on the tapes warning that they are not suitable for certain areas. You wouldn't want to hear Barry Manilow singing 'Bermuda Triangle' when you were cruising round the Bahamas. Come to think of it, you wouldn't want to hear it anywhere.

The bus roared up through Gosforth, past the town moor and the racetrack, weddings and cricket matches and endless golf courses. One day someone will write a short story like John Cheever's 'The Swimmer' in which in a fit of existential angst a young businessman plays golf continuously from Lands End to John o'Groats. 'The Swinger', it'll be called.

On we went, past the turn off for Hazlerigg Colliery where Len Shackleton had worked alongside Jackie Milburn at the end of the war, through Plessey Woods 'nuclear free zone' and Bedlington, home of the team which had won the Northern League Second Division Championship, and a breed of terrier that looks like a sheep.

We arrived at Ashington at 2.20, so I went for a walk. I wandered down Third Avenue past Poplar and Chestnut Street. Midway along the theme of the street names changed. Aerial Street came up, then Juliet, Portia and Katherine. Women from Shakespeare. The next one was Beatrice. This was the street where Bobby and Jack Charlton were born. Two long terraces faced each other across tiny front gardens and a narrow pavement. I walked along it, dodging round dogshit and smiling maniacally at the pensioners tending their tulips. I knew the house was on the left as you headed south, but I didn't know which number it was. In the photo in *This Game of Soccer* the door was open and you couldn't see it. So I walked right along the street looking at each house on the left-hand side in turn until I reached the top. Ashington Hirst middle school was there. It was where Bobby Charlton had gone to school when he was the same age I was when I first conceived the desire to see where he was born.

Bobby Charlton was the finest English footballer of his generation. Pelé said he was the greatest player he ever saw. A friend of mine remembers Charlton in a match at

Molyneux in the early sixties completely controlling the game without once leaving the centre circle – like the man at Langley Park's hero Alfredo Di Stefano. He was a great playmaker; a creative force. As a boy such subtleties passed me by. The thing I loved about Bobby Charlton was that he had the most powerful shot in League football. When you watched him strike a ball on television it hurtled off towards the goal at such velocity you could almost see the vapour trail. A Bobby Charlton shot never seemed to rise much off the ground, but if it did it crept upwards unnaturally slowly as if G-forces were acting against it. On the black and white TV screen the ball blurred in such a way that for years I believed it was actually changing shape in mid-air; flattened by speed into an elongated party balloon. After seeing such a shot on *Sam Leitch's Football Preview* I'd rush out into the garden and practise, hammering my plastic football against the garage door and imitating Kenneth Wolstenholme's authoritative croak – 'Charlton!' Bang! 'Charlton!' Crash! 'Charlton!' Smash! 'Charlton!' Wallop! – until a neighbour leaned out of a window and yelled: 'Will you stop your racket! Our Ken's on nights.'

I turned and looked down the street at the row of houses, each one identical to the next. I had seen the homes of many other famous people and Bobby Charlton's was not as spectacular as any of them. It wasn't as beautiful as the boathouse at Laugharne, as architecturally significant as Strawberry Hill, or a work of art in itself like Charleston Farmhouse. Then again, when they hear you speak, Roman taxi drivers and Catalan barmen and street urchins in Brazil don't smile, stick their thumbs up and say 'Virginia Woolf!'

It had taken a long time, but finally . . .

And then I thought, hang on a minute. What if the photo in *This Game of Soccer* was inverted? I'd have been looking at the wrong houses altogether. I walked back down the street again, looking at the other side this time. When I got to the bottom I didn't glance back. I just kept on walking. It was a highly emotional moment. People in the North-East are kind in the extreme but I wasn't sure how they'd react to the sight of a six-foot-five-inch thirty-three year old stranger standing at the bottom of their road blubbing his eyes out.

By the time I got to Portland Park I had recovered my equilibrium. I walked round the ground to the newish grandstand studying my raffle tickets. I threw them into an oil drum. I hadn't won a raffle all year. Which, given the prizes, was quite a relief.

Portland Park was in a dilapidated state. There were abandoned buildings and bits of buildings everywhere. Around the outside of the pitch the greyhound track was overgrown with weeds. The rail was still in place, but racing was clearly no longer possible. The electric hare would have hidden in the thistles. Despite the ravaged surroundings there was an air of optimism at Portland Park. Ashington Football Club had almost folded completely at the start of the season, but supporters had got together to stop it from happening. Now there was a new committee and a new team and the people of Ashington had started to come and watch them again. Well, some of them had, anyway. There was a crowd of seventy or so, which for an end-of-season game wasn't bad.

Whickham were the visitors. I was delighted to see Monkey again. His blond bubble-perm had now frizzed up even more wildly into a sort of exploding Afro. There must have been a severe danger when he was in the dressing-room of a myopic cleaner mistaking him for a feather duster and locking him in the broom cupboard. Monkey was playing in a more withdrawn role than against Bamber Bridge, so he had more time to promenade about, Rivelino-like, dispatching the ball hither and thither with the disdainful authority of a monarch shooing away a particularly odious petitioner. Every once in a while he'd get possession and set off on a stroll, wandering through defenders with the ball hopping from one foot to the other, like a performing terrier. I had paid £1.20 to watch him play. It was the biggest bargain since the Dutch bought Manhattan.

I sat and watched the game. A few yards away a small boy in one of those anoraks which have had random English words plastered across them by factory workers in Taiwan

– 'South Baseball', 'Potato Boy', 'Brando Jelly Fish!' – and a
Walkman suddenly jumped up and shouted, 'Get in, Andy
Cole!' then shimmied across the aisle in a manner that
suggested someone had given him a couple of dead legs.
Moments later Ashington took the lead themselves when
their centre-forward got clean through on goal. He executed
a swanky little soft-shoe shuffle, rounded the 'keeper and
tucked the ball in the net.

At half-time I bought tea and wandered round the ground,
past a rotting Nissen hut and the debris of the starter's box.
Ashington had never been a great club. They'd spent five
years of their 110-year history in the Football League before
failing to gain re-election in 1929; most of the rest in the
North-Eastern League. They had never won anything of
note, but Jackie Milburn had started his career at Portland
Park; two other great North-Eastern players, Colin Todd and
Ray Kennedy, had finished theirs here and it was the place
where Bobby Charlton had first watched football.

In the second half Whickham's player-manager bellowed
bewildering instructions to his team-mates – 'Tuck in! Work
the line! Put your name on it!' – the comprehension of which,
in the freemasonry of football, must be the equivalent of
recognising a funny handshake. His team equalised after a
goalmouth scramble, the little boy in the Walkman squeaked
'Peeee-tor!' and pointed at the sky, then, with a few minutes
to go, Monkey, like the season, limped off.

Back in Newcastle the fans were on the pavements outside
the pubs laughing and singing. They'd beaten Arsenal 2–0.
'Tell your mam, your mam,' they sang, 'you won't be home
for tea. We're going to Italy. Tell your mam, your mam.'

United had qualified for Europe and they were happy; and
I was happy too, because it was a sunny evening in a place
I loved, I had seen Bobby Charlton's house and now I was
going home.

Epilogue

At the beginning of May Lennie Lawrence, the Middlesbrough manager, was sacked. A week later Bryan Robson was officially named as his successor. When I heard the news on the sports bulletin I instinctively began to dance – I use the word in its loosest possible sense – around the kitchen waving my arms in the air and making a noise which, if it were possible to render it in print would look something like 'Weeeywarhahahaha'. After thirty seconds I stopped. This wasn't through any sort of embarrassment – although the dog was looking at me in a vaguely scornful manner – but because it suddenly struck me that the reason I was celebrating was because I was thinking of Robson the player. Robson the human stock car who had hurtled around the football grounds of the world upending opponents and crashing into advertising hoardings with such disregard for his physical wellbeing you began to suspect he was joy-riding in a stolen body. A man whose groin muscles and toes had been the cause of national agonising during the finals of practically every international competition of my adult life. The player who had provoked his national team boss and fellow Durhamite, Bobby Robson, to burble the memorable lines: 'I need Bryan Robson to be Bryan Robson because that's the only Bryan Robson I want.'

But this wasn't the Bryan Robson we were talking about, now. This wasn't Captain Marvel any more, but some speculative figure in a suit. No one, least of all me, knew if Robson would make a good manager. Now the board of the club I supported had decided to gamble close to £1 million to find out. 'I'll sum up Bryan Robson for you in one word,' an ageing Boro fan told local news reporters. 'He's a winner.'

In the far corner one season had no sooner finished than the anticipation of the next had begun. Expectation on Teesside was enormous. Season ticket and merchandising sales rocketed. Excitement mounted to such levels that spontaneous combustion of the most explosive sort seemed inevitable. If you are thinking of visiting Middlesbrough in the near future I'd advise you to wear protective clothing and a helmet.

In fact, helmets are a sound idea at any time.

Index